THE DIARY OF LADY FREDE CAVENI

EDITED BY JOHN Ь

WITH ILLUSTRATIONS

VOL. I

NEW YORK
FREDERICK A. STOKES COMPANY
PUBLISHERS

First Edition .   . 1927

Printed in Great Britain by
Hazell, Watson & Viney, Ld., London and Aylesbury.

LADY FREDERICK CAVENDISH.
From a portrait by George Richmond, R.A., painted about the time of her marriage.

PREFACE

A PREFACE, commonly the first word of a book to be read, is as a rule, and indeed should be, the last to be written. I have already, in the Introduction which follows, explained the circumstances in which the Diary of Lady Frederick Cavendish came into my possession, and the reasons which induced me to offer some extracts from it to the public. I need therefore add very little here. Those who read what I have printed of it will, I think, see that Lady Frederick was a woman of very rare beauty of character as well as of an unusual energy and activity of mind. Whether in the great world or outside it, among the rich or among the poor, in her private affections or in her public activities, she lived to the full every hour of her life. She will never be forgotten by those who knew her : and most of them will, I think, agree with me in wishing that others should be given such opportunity as her Diary can afford of sharing their knowledge.

But if this had been all, if the interest of the Diary had seemed to me to be confined to the merely personal and biographical, I am not sure that I should have had the courage to print anything from it. Anyone, however, who reads beyond the first few years will see that the Diarist herself is very far from occupying the whole of its picture. She gives us not only herself, but also her world ; and her world includes a good deal of what was most prominent in English life during the twenty-eight years covered by the Diary, which ends in 1882 with the murder of her husband. The niece of Mr. Gladstone was born into the world of high politics, and the wife, sister, sister-in-law, aunt, and cousin of prominent statesmen remained in it, almost necessarily, all her life and especially during the lifetime of her husband. The Diary is a picture of the political world,

▼

seen from behind the Whig and Liberal curtains, between 1865 and 1882. So, again, the daughter of Lord Lyttelton, the niece of Gladstone, the sister and sister-in-law of Bishops, the ardent Churchwoman, inevitably gives the life of the Church a large place in her Diary. Both the political and the ecclesiastical world of those days seem in some respects curiously far off now. They begin to take their place in the history of the past. Still more is that true of the social world of that generation, especially the world of the great town and country houses, and of the big political parties, or " drums," which were then such a feature of the London season. The Diary furnishes one more picture of life as it was then lived among the great Whig families in their last phase, when they were reluctantly submitting to the dangerous and ultimately destructive leadership of Gladstone.

In all these ways I hope the Diary may offer itself as one of those minor and modest contributions to history to which the historian does not always disdain to give a passing glance.

Nothing remains for me to add except thanks. And my first thanks must be given to Lady Stephenson for help of many kinds, but especially for allowing me to persuade her to write the vivid and interesting account of her aunt which concludes the Introduction. I have also to thank the Hon. Mrs. Edward Talbot, now the only survivor of the four daughters of Lord Lyttelton's first marriage, for her kindness in sending me a note on her early memories of Lady Frederick, which reached me too late to appear in the earlier part of the book, and is printed as an Appendix. I am very grateful to Miss Egerton, who has allowed me to see and use the letters of Lady Frederick to her mother, Lady Louisa Egerton, and has generously given me much help in preparing notes and identifying persons mentioned in the Diary; to the Hon. Mr. Justice Talbot for allowing me to reproduce the portrait in his possession of his mother, Mrs. Talbot, and for placing at my disposition both the letters she received from Lady Frederick and her account of what took place on the night of May 6th, 1882; to the Hon. Mrs. Hugh Wyndham for permission to use a fragmentary early Diary of Lady Frederick's and for

other help ; to Lord Richard Cavendish for allowing me
to reproduce the portraits of Lord and Lady Frederick
Cavendish in his possession at Holker ; to Mr. Charles
Aitken, Director of the National Gallery, Millbank, for
his kindness in showing me the sketches of Bolton by
Turner in the collection under his charge and for
getting one of them reproduced for me ; to Mr. C. T.
Hagberg Wright, Secretary and Librarian of the London
Library, for allowing a photograph to be taken from
the engraved portrait of Lord Lyttelton which hangs
in the entrance-hall of the Library ; to my publishers,
Sir John Murray, K.C.V.O., and Colonel John Murray,
D.S.O., for many useful suggestions ; to my niece, Miss
Elizabeth Alington, who kindly typed a large part of the
Diary for me ; and finally to my daughter Jane, who
compiled for me the four genealogical tables which will
be found in an appendix and without whose accurate
help in reading the proofs the book would have been
disfigured by many misprints which had escaped my
notice.

JOHN BAILEY.

April 9, 1927.

CONTENTS

VOL. I

CONTENTS

BOOK VI
DECEMBER 1860—JUNE 1862

BOOK VII
JUNE 1862—AUGUST 1863

BOOK VIII
AUGUST 1863—SEPTEMBER 1864

BOOK IX
SEPTEMBER 1864—MAY 1866

LIST OF ILLUSTRATIONS

VOL. I

INTRODUCTION

SOME years ago my sister-in-law Lady Frederick Cavendish told me that it was her intention to leave me her Diaries after her death. When she died in April 1925 it was found that she had done so, and had confirmed in writing, what she had already said to me, that she wished my discretion as to the disposal or destruction of the Diaries to be absolute. On their coming into my hands I read them, of course, with great interest. But that could not be in itself conclusive in favour of offering any part of them to the public. What interested a relation who had known and loved the Diarist for five-and-twenty years, and who also knew, either personally or by personal report, many or most of the people who appear most often in her pages, would not necessarily interest the public. There are twelve volumes of the Dairy, and it was at once obvious that it could not all be published. Much of it as of most diaries is devoted to records of purely private doings and happenings in no way remarkable or even interesting. Such records too, with Lady Frederick as with most of us, inevitably recur again and again. What is done on one Sunday is apt to be done on the next also ; the spring or autumn of each year repeats the experiences of its predecessor. Each entry may by itself be interesting as a picture of the individual or the manners of the time. But too many of them are obviously tedious reading. Yet a Diary is a private and personal record, and to print only its accounts of the writer's contact with great people or great events is really to destroy its character. The question I had to consider was whether I could make such a selection as would exhibit Lady Frederick's life and personality

as they were, both on her ordinary and, so to speak, on her extraordinary days ; and whether, if I could, the book would have a chance of interesting a wider public than that of her own friends. I decided to try, and these volumes are the result.

The Diaries extend over nearly twenty-eight years, from the time the writer was thirteen years old till the murder of her husband in 1882. After that she gave it up almost entirely, and I have not thought it desirable to make any extracts from the little she wrote between 1882 and her death. Her life was divided into three periods ; twenty-three years of girlhood, eighteen of marriage, and forty-three of widowhood. Of the first forty-one years I shall give some account in the short introductions which precede each section of the Diary. But it may be advisable to give here a few biographical details of their principal events, before going on to say something about her later life which the Diary does not touch.

Lucy Caroline Lyttelton, afterwards Lady Frederick Cavendish, born in 1841, was the second daughter and second child of George William, fourth Lord Lyttelton, by his first wife, Mary, daughter of Sir Stephen Glynn. Lady Lyttelton's elder sister, Catharine, was the wife of Mr. Gladstone. A list of the children of each of these marriages, most or all of whom make frequent appearances in the Diary, is given in an Appendix. There were twelve of the Lytteltons, eight sons and four daughters, and Lord Lyttelton had three more daughters by his second wife. His mother, the " Granny " of the Diary, had been Lady Sarah Spencer, and through her Lord Spencer the statesman and Lord-Lieutenant of Ireland, with his brother and successor in the title (the " Bobby " of the Diary), and his sisters Lady Sarah Spencer (" Tallee ") and Lady Sandhurst (" Va "), were cousins of the Lytteltons. Most of them appear often in the Diary, especially Lady Sarah and Lord Spencer (" Althorp "), who was Viceroy of Ireland at the time of the murder of Lord Frederick Cavendish.

Through her grandmother, also, Lady Frederick was already, even before her marriage, distantly connected with the Cavendishes. She and Lord Frederick were in fact third cousins, her father, Lord Lyttelton, being second cousin to Lord Frederick's mother, Lady Burlington. But I am not aware that the future husband and wife ever met till within a year or so of the marriage.

Lady Frederick's childhood and youth were chiefly passed at Hagley, her father's house in Worcestershire. She loved Hagley all her life with devoted affection, but it was at all times the memories connected with it that stirred her affection, not the beauty of the rooms, decorations, furniture, and pictures, nor the historical associations of the place; to all of which her father and most of his children, at any rate till the latter part of their lives, were almost indifferent. Later on, however, her brother Lord Cobham took such proud and loving care of its treasures, especially its books and pictures, as only a few owners of such possessions have the intelligence to take; and all who knew him were thankful that, if the disastrous fire which destroyed a good many of them in December 1925 had to come, it did not come till after his death, for in his old age it would have simply broken his heart. It was happy, too, for Lady Frederick that she died before it. But in her case the sorrow would rather have been for broken associations than for ruined works of art. The whole attitude of the generation she grew up in, which reacted so crudely against the literature and art of the eighteenth century, as well as her own personal convictions, especially in matters ecclesiastical, put her outside the possibility of caring much either for the art or for the literary or political associations of the house, nearly all of which came from its builder, the first Lord Lyttelton, the ally, and afterwards by his marriage the cousin, of Chatham, the friend of Pope, Thomson, and other poets and men of letters of that day.

There were not a great many events in Lady Frederick's childhood. The only differences between the

early years of the Lyttelton children and those of others
in similar circumstances were that there was more
cricket, more Church, and more unity and affection in
them than in most families. There was a great alliance
between the Hall and the Rectory, of which Lord
Lyttelton's brother, the beloved "Uncle Billy" of
the Diary, was the occupant. The extracts which
follow will give a sufficient picture of the way the
years passed. The first event of importance in them
was a great sorrow, the death of Lady Lyttelton
after the birth of her youngest child, Alfred, in 1857.
The loss of a mother during the sensitive years of
childhood often makes a permanent impression of the
seriousness of life upon those who experience it : and
it was so with the Lytteltons, and especially perhaps
with Lady Frederick, who never forgot that terrible
time. Her elder sister Meriel, afterwards Mrs. Talbot,
though only just seventeen, took her mother's place, and
the two sisters shared from that time the care of the
younger children. But Meriel's marriage followed
in 1860, and for the next four years Lucy was the
mistress of Hagley and, so far as could be, the mother
of the motherless children.

In 1863 she became a Maid of Honour to Queen
Victoria : an appointment which she, no doubt, partly
owed to the high regard which her grandmother had
gained from the Queen and the Prince Consort while
acting in the capacity which made her son often speak
of her as the " Governess of England." Lady Lyttelton
had in fact lived at Court between 1842 and 1850, and
had had the supervision of the Royal schoolrooms and
nurseries, to whose occupants she was affectionately
known as " Laddle." She was all her life a capital
letter-writer, as may be seen in " Correspondence of
Sarah Spencer Lady Lyttelton, 1787–1870," edited by
her great-granddaughter the Hon. Mrs. Hugh Wyndham (Murray, 1912). The Royal Family from the
Queen downwards were therefore prepared to give Lucy
Lyttelton a warm welcome for her grandmother's

sake ; and it was to Lady Lyttelton that the Queen's offer first came. A letter of hers survives in which she describes both Lucy's excitement at the prospect— " she shrieked and kicked and jumped about, between delight and fright "—and the graver approval of the family conclave : " We all agree that, for Lucy herself, it is likely to be most beneficial. She will be taught *order* and *obedience* and a certain liberality of mind from contact with heaps of different people and places which are all sure to improve her." And if Lucy Lyttelton was to gain from her Maidship, her grandmother rightly thought that she brought with her one quality at least which Maids of Honour specially need and do not always possess. " Lucy is so entirely free from any disposition to gossip, which is the usual temptation in that profession, and so ready to occupy her time harmlessly, that she will do well in her place." Altogether the prospect was a pleasant one and, as the young Maid came to Court full of exuberant loyalty, her brief period of service was a very happy one. Large extracts will be found from her interesting accounts of what she saw and heard and did at Windsor and Osborne.

But she had hardly been six months a Maid of Honour when she became engaged to Lord Frederick Cavendish, second son of the seventh Duke of Devonshire. Her marriage followed in June 1864, and was from the first day to the last one of perfect happiness. We shall see her again and again reckoning a chance of a few days alone with her husband as a kind of heaven on earth. Not that she and her husband were much alike : in fact they were in many respects the very opposite of each other. She was one of a family who talked from morning till night, all at once and on all sorts of subjects grave and gay, especially perhaps on matters ecclesiastical and religious. He was one of a family who seldom talked at all and never on Church topics. The change from the enthusiasm and the noisy gaiety of Hagley to the ducal silence of the meals

at Chatsworth was, at any rate at first, very trying to
Lady Frederick. And as will be seen, she always stood
in some awe of the Duke and of her even more alarming
brother-in-law Lord Hartington, the " Cavendish " of
the Diary. Nor did the reserved and dignified atmosphere of Chatsworth assimilate very easily her exuberant
unconventionalities. There is a story of her being
asked by her sister-in-law, on one occasion when there
was a large party in the house, to find out what the
guests would like to do ; which she did by calling out
at luncheon, " Hands up those who would like to drive ! "
One would like to have seen the faces of some of the
lunchers. In these ways there was a gulf to be crossed
between her and her husband's family. But the
sisterly affection which grew up almost at once between
her and the Duke's only daughter, Lady Louisa, as
well as her easy and affectionate relations with her
husband's younger brother, Lord Edward, helped to
make her happy in her new world. Not that she
needed any help. Her happiness was complete in her
love of her husband and his of her.

The eighteen years of her marriage, as will be seen
in the Diary, were spent in a regular progression from
her own house in London to the three Devonshire
country houses, Chatsworth and Holker and Bolton
Abbey, with occasional stays at Hardwick. There
were also of course frequent visits to relations and
friends. The picture is one of a sort of social life which
has now largely passed away. Lady Frederick's London
life was crowded with dinner-parties and " drums,"
as they were then called, both of which were often more
or less a political duty in those days when the world
of politics was still also the world of society. But we
shall see that she made a great deal of time for good
works and going to church, even in her fullest seasons.
And though Chatsworth and Bolton were often filled
with large, and occasionally even with Royal, parties,
there were many quiet days too when there was no
party, and Lord Frederick was free both of business

and politics and she and he were able to enjoy delicious
" honeymoon " days, as she called them, riding or
walking or reading together. Or, if he was away, at
Barrow or in London, she and Lady Louisa and Lady
Edward (wife of Lord Frederick's younger brother)
had their neighbours and cottagers to visit and the
Duke to take care of.

Meanwhile politics were occupying an even larger
part of her life. She who had been a Tory, or at least
a Conservative, soon became a strong Liberal. What
she would have done if her adored " Uncle William "
had finally refused to join Palmerston's Ministry and
turned definitely to the Conservatives one cannot say.
But before her marriage took place he had become
the Whig Chancellor of the Exchequer, with the visible
and not very distant prospect of leading the party,
and leading it a good deal farther than Palmerston
would ever let it go. And probably in any case she
would have gone with her husband, though his
Radicalism rather shocked her at first. He was a far
more advanced Liberal than his more famous brother ;
indeed he advocated household suffrage when most
Liberals and all Whigs thought any such proposal
dangerous and even revolutionary. And though his
wife could get him to come with her continually to
church, often even on weekdays, she could not prevent
him, when he entered Parliament, from voting for
measures so abhorrent to her Anglicanism as the Burials
Bill and the Bill for allowing Marriage with a Deceased
Wife's Sister.

His Parliamentary career began in July 1865, when
he was returned unopposed for a division of the West
Riding of Yorkshire, which he continued to represent
for the rest of his life. He soon became a much
respected and trusted member of his party and of the
House of Commons. But he was a poor speaker, and
never overcame physical difficulties which prevented
his pronouncing certain words correctly. However,
Gladstone, with whom he was at once through his wife

I—2

brought into the closest relations, soon formed a high opinion not only of the nobility of his character, as to which everyone who knew him agreed, but of his brains and capacity, as to which there was less agreement. But Gladstone's judgment, of course, soon became, in the Liberal Party, the all-important one : nor could it be any disadvantage to Lord Frederick, in those days, that he was the son of a great Whig magnate, or, in that or any day, that he had a brother in the Cabinet. If he had been, oratorically and otherwise, a quicker man, his promotion would no doubt have been more rapid. If he had not been a Cavendish, he might have been overlooked altogether. As it was, he became a Junior Lord of the Treasury in 1873, went out, of course, with his party in 1874, became Financial Secretary to the Treasury in 1880 and Chief Secretary for Ireland for a few tragic days in 1882. His appointment had been received with surprise, to say the least, by the House and the country. But Gladstone was by no means alone in the high opinion he had formed of his abilities. The permanent officials who with Gladstone had seen his work at the Treasury wrote of it with the greatest admiration. More than one had looked forward to his becoming Chancellor of the Exchequer. As to the beauty of his character there was only one feeling. One proof of it is enough. Half the House of Commons went down to Derbyshire to attend his funeral.

The latter part of Lady Frederick's Diary is increasingly full of her husband's political career and of the political controversies in which he had his minor part, as her uncle Mr. Gladstone had the chief part, to play. They can be followed in the extracts here printed. But they by no means occupy the whole. Life in the country and life in London, shooting-parties and dinner-parties, days in the village and days at the London Hospital, Court balls and Church services, private friends and political allies, all crowd in upon the pages and unite to make a varied picture of the world of

those days. And above all, of course, of the little
world of the Diarist herself. Every event that varied
the fortunes of the families of her own intimate affection,
the births and deaths and marriages, the illnesses and
disappointments and successes, of Lytteltons and
Talbots and Cavendishes and Gladstones, to say nothing
of Lawleys and Wortleys and Clives and others who
stood a little farther off—all receive their record
and their comment. Some of these will be found
in their place. Here it will be enough to mention
the two or three of them that are of exceptional
importance.

In 1869 Lord Lyttelton married again, his second
wife being Sybella Harriet, widow of Humphrey Mildmay, M.P., and daughter of George Clive, M.P. By
his second wife he had three more daughters, the
" little sisters " of the Diary. In his later years he
suffered greatly from temporary fits of melancholia,
during one of which he unhappily committed suicide.
I have heard that after the catastrophe Gladstone
used to lament that he had not persuaded his brother-
in-law, who was a very brilliant scholar and had printed
translations of " Comus " and " Samson Agonistes "
into Greek, to undertake an English verse rendering
of Homer. He believed that the daily portion of more
or less mechanical but intellectual and congenial labour
might have kept the mind from brooding on itself
and averted the disaster. Lady Frederick and her
father's second wife were most affectionate friends,
both before and after his death ; and the connection
was drawn still closer in 1880 by the marriage of Arthur
Lyttelton, afterwards Bishop of Southampton, with
Lady Lyttelton's sister Kathleen Clive.

There are one or two other marriages which may
perhaps be mentioned here, as the persons concerned
in them appear very frequently in the Diary. First
there is that of the third Lyttelton daughter Lavinia
to Edward Stuart Talbot, first Warden of Keble and
afterwards Bishop of Winchester. This was also a

double marriage like the two marriages with the Clives : for Edward Talbot was the younger brother of the John Talbot who had married Meriel Lyttelton. Then there is the marriage in 1878 of Lady Frederick's eldest brother Charles, afterwards Viscount Cobham, with the Hon. Mary Cavendish, daughter of the second Lord Chesham. And there are the marriages of Lady Frederick's brother-in-law Lord Edward, who in 1865 married his cousin Miss Emma Lascelles, and of her sister-in-law Lady Louisa, who married in the same year Admiral the Hon. Francis Egerton, son of the first Earl of Ellesmere.

This is perhaps all that is necessary to say here by way of general Introduction to the passages which follow from the Diary. That ends, as I have said, with the murder of Lord Frederick in 1882. His widow lived on till 1925, and it may be well to add here a few words about her later life. When she lost her husband she had still forty-three years to live ; so that in one sense her life was not half over. In another it was over already. In all those years she never for a moment forgot that she was a widow ; and there were many things in her old life which she never cared to take up again. The social life which she had lived so fully between 1858 and 1882 she never resumed ; or, if she did, it was only to a small extent and for a short time, for the sake of a niece or a ward. In the main she now kept to her own circle of relations and intimate friends.

But that did not mean either a solitary or an inactive life. She was, for instance, very far from giving up her interest in politics. And so long as Mr. Gladstone lived she remained very near the centre of the political world. During her widowhood, as throughout her married life, he was a constant guest in her house and she in his ; and she entered enthusiastically into all or nearly all the crusades he embraced, especially into his Home Rule policy and his support of the Christian subjects of the Sultan. She was for many years, and

up to her death, President of the society called " The
Friends of Armenia." In that capacity she was indefatigable in urging upon the Prime Ministers and
Foreign Secretaries of her later life the duty and necessity
of protecting that unfortunate people for whom she
never ceased to feel a passionate sympathy. Here, as
in pleading other causes in which she was interested,
she was helped by her personal friendship with many
of the leading statesmen not only of her own party in
politics but of the other. On her own side there were,
besides the Gladstones, Lord Spencer, a cousin whom
she had known from her childhood ; Lord Granville,
her husband's cousin and perhaps the closest of Gladstone's political followers ; Sir George Trevelyan, a
devoted friend of her husband ; Lord Bryce, and several
others. On the Unionist side was her own brother Alfred,
whose work at the Colonial Office was particularly
concerned with South Africa, the one part of the British
Empire in which for various reasons she took an ardent
interest ; and there was her brother-in-law the Duke of
Devonshire, who was for some years the Minister
responsible for Education, a subject on which she
always entertained the strongest views, of which she
frequently made him the patient and polite but by no
means always convinced recipient. I have seen long
letters of his dealing with the educational policy of
that Ministry. But I expect he was himself happier
when replying to a letter she must have written to
thank him for grouse which for some reason or another
she does not seem to have expected to receive ; her
letter evidently went on to discuss the Education Bill
(it was in 1902) and to ask for a donation to one of
her charities. His reply handles all these topics with
characteristic dryness and brevity. He must have
enjoyed telling his serious sister-in-law, who was
much interested in morals and not at all in racing,
the company in which she would find herself on
the grouse-list.

CHATSWORTH,
CHESTERFIELD.
Nov. 8, '02.

MY DEAR LUCY,

The grouse were sent by Martin, not me. He was told to look over the old lists with care and discrimination, and it may diminish your gratitude to know that they were also sent to a jockey who has been warned off.

I am sorry you think that this Govt. wants its back stiffening and that only Non-Con. lies can do it. You may, however, be beginning to perceive that an Education Bill giving rates to Voluntary Schools is not quite so simple as you imagined. I send the cheque for £30.

Yours afftly,
DEVONSHIRE.

No two human beings were ever less alike than the cautious, common-sensical, most unexpansive Duke and his very exuberant and enthusiastic sister-in-law. But the common memory of Lord Frederick and the closely affectionate intimacy which always existed between Lady Frederick and the Duke's only and much-loved sister, Lady Louisa Egerton, kept the differences between his and her standards, tastes, and moral and political creeds from separating them so entirely as might have been expected. He remained to the end one of her links with the governing and Cabinet world. Another leading statesman on the Conservative side to whom she had easy personal access was Lord Balfour, from early years an intimate friend of her brothers Spencer and Alfred. Through all these and many other political friends she was pertinacious and indefatigable, till within a few years of her death, in pressing the claims of all the causes she had at heart, especially religious education, the maintenance of the Marriage Law, the protection of the persecuted Armenians, the union of races in South Africa, and above all, that peace and justice in Ireland for which in the very first hours of her agony she lifted up her eyes to pray as the possible outcome, by God's mercy, of her husband's martyrdom.

For most of these causes too, though not, I think, ever
for Ireland, on which she felt unable to say anything
in public, she often made appeals in the columns of
The Times and other newspapers. The position she
occupied was recognised by her appointment in 1894
as a member of a Royal Commission on Secondary
Education and by the degree of LL.D. conferred on her
by the University of Leeds in 1904.

But for all her public activities she was not primarily
a politician. It would be much nearer the truth to
say she was primarily a Churchwoman. The Church
of England had no more devoted son than Lord Lyttelton, and both he and Gladstone, who married sisters,
brought up their children to be what they all remained,
good Christians and strong Churchmen. Churchgoing,
the reading of sermons, and other religious exercises
were then practised, as Lady Frederick's Diaries show,
to an extent almost incredible to our laxer generation.
A visitor to Hagley is said to have reported that the
Lyttelton boys divided their time between cricket
and going to church; and in Lady Frederick's later
years a witty woman who loved her said of her:
" Church is Lucy's public-house, and unfortunately
there's no keeping her out of it." Nothing but physical
impossibility would prevent her going to church two
or three times on Sunday and whenever there was an
opportunity on weekdays. She was the despair of
Sunday hostesses, who found that two attendances,
perhaps, at church in the morning would not prevent
her insisting on walking off in the late afternoon a
couple of miles or more for an evening service. She
kept and loved all the times and seasons of the Church,
in public when she could, in private when there was
no church available. All this was no mere habit or
formality. It was the breath of her life; for her
religion, unlike that of some very good people, was
sincerely and almost passionately " institutional." She
was miserable, as we shall see in the Diaries, whenever
she was deprived of her Church services. It was a

great trial to her to have so often to spend Holy Week and Easter at Lismore with no better spiritual food than a very meagre supply of what was to her the very dry biscuit of Irish Protestantism.

Of course so devoted a daughter of the Church could not be content to receive without giving. The Diary shows her, as I have already said, from childhood onwards, and even during the most crowded years of her married life, giving herself freely to every good work for which she found opportunity. School teaching, hospital visiting, workhouse visiting, services of all sorts, direct and indirect, rendered to the poor or the sick or the sad or the sinful, occupied a large part of her life at all times. The Diary is full of them, much fuller than the extracts here given tell. But enough, I hope, has been given to show how full even her happiest days were of these things, and how far she was from being one of those who, so long as they are happy themselves, never find time to think of others who are not.

While her husband lived she felt it to be her duty as well as her happiness to be with him whenever he wanted her ; and she never allowed any other call to interfere with that. After she lost him and went little into ordinary society, she had of course more time to give and gave more. But of all that and of the spiritual beauty of her widowed life I shall say very little, for the reason that, as will presently be seen, what can be said has been said for me by one who knew her longer and better than I. I will only touch briefly on a more public matter. Few women, I suppose, were more consulted than Lady Frederick by those, whether clergymen or laymen, who played the chief part in the counsels of the Church. With several of them she was connected by relationship or close friendship. Whether on her own initiative or at their bidding, she was always ready to do battle for the Church either with her tongue or with her pen. Readers of this book will see that she wrote easily and well, and could state a case on paper with vigour and effect. Those who ever heard her speak will remember that she did it delightfully, with humour and lightness of touch as well as with earnest eloquence. Naturally she was in frequent request in both capacities, especially as a speaker. And, equally of course, the parochial, diocesan, and other societies with which she was connected used her as a means of getting hold of speakers more famous than herself. She would press her distinguished friends and relations to address meetings on behalf of her favourite charities. Among others the Duke was often called upon and, though his Churchmanship was not among his most conspicuous characteristics, he often responded. I have before me a letter, dated July 1906, in which he alludes to previous appearances, and declines on characteristic grounds to make another :

" I think you must let me off the Bishop of London's Fund Meeting. I have certainly once taken the chair at a meeting at Grosvenor House for the present Bishop, and, I am almost sure, at a former one for the late Bishop.

" My speeches on these occasions have been among my dullest, which is saying a great deal, and you had much better get some enthusiastic young man."

In all these ways, by what she did herself and what she got others to do, she never ceased to work for her beloved Church till her final illness came upon her.

I said that it would be truer to call her primarily a Churchwoman than primarily a politician. But to say that she was either in any narrow or exclusive sense would be to misrepresent her. She was no Mrs. Jellyby, either political or ecclesiastical. The first thing in her was the woman ; and there never was a woman who more visibly overflowed with the natural womanly affections, as wife and daughter and sister and friend. Not as mother ; that was the one sorrow which occasionally darkened the long honeymoon of her marriage : she had no children. But the love which she could not give to her children never ceased to be the strongest thing in her, never ceased to be human and personal, never for a moment dried up into that interest in a public cause or a party or a Church which makes such a very poor substitute for the love of men and women and children. She was the most devoted of aunts to her own and her husband's nephews and nieces. It was not in her, with them any more than with their elders, to be very perceptive of differences of character or temperament. But with them as with their elders she was always intensely alive, amusing, full of jokes and stories; so that she was the most popular of visitors in a schoolroom or nursery. The Diary shows her continually teaching the Cavendish and Egerton children who all loved her then and to the end of her life and were loved by her. Even after she had left London and become a complete invalid, it gave her great pleasure to see them, and with them sometimes their children and even their grandchildren. She gave to them and to the children of her own brothers and sisters and of her Gladstone cousins the affection she could not give to her own; and in each case took a most eager interest in the doings of the whole clan.

Family affection was, in fact, as appears on every page of the Diary, the root and essence of her being. From her earliest years she loved her own with a love to the intensity of which in her childhood it may be possible to find many parallels, but few for its continuance, as in her, throughout the whole of a long life. In her not altogether impartial eyes her brothers and sisters remained always, not only the most lovable people she had ever known, but also the most interesting and delightful, and even not immensely far away from the wisest and best! Naturally therefore she rejoiced with more than ordinary sisterly rejoicing in their youthful triumphs in the cricket-field, and later on in the honours and successes which several of them achieved in various spheres of public life. And as she got much more pleasure than ordinary people get out of happy family events, so she suffered much more from losses and sorrows. Every detailed happening of every hour in the last illnesses of her mother and her sister May is recorded in the Diary in the language of an agony of anxiety and love. Nor did she ever forget. Every year on the day of her mother's death she re-read a " record " of her which had been written that all her children might remember, or, if they were too young to remember, might learn, what a mother they had had. Nor was it only her mother whose memory she kept so wonderfully fresh. Nor only the memory of sorrows. So far as she could she carried all the past on into the present. Anniversaries of all kinds played an extraordinarily large part in her life. The returning days of family births, marriages, deaths, and other important events seldom fail of note and comment in the Diary. Her husband is reported to have once replied—on her informing him at breakfast that it was the anniversary of some wedding or funeral or perhaps even some Confirmation, " I do believe nobody ever did have the ' dayums '[1] like you, Lucy ! " And well he might, as readers of the Diaries, even as here abbreviated, will readily allow. She did not go out of her way to make herself remember these things. It was all spontaneous in her ; the natural outcome of her strong affections, retentive memory, and love of all such observances and commemorations, private and public, as bind the years of our lives together.

Only those who knew her personally can understand the difficulty of my task in writing these Introductory pages. She had been seventeen years a widow when I first saw her. I had not then any reason to believe that I should ever have more than an acquaintance with her. But no one could meet the heroine of such a tragedy as hers without interest and more than interest ; no one could meet the woman she was without being attracted by her rare combination of mobility, vivacity, and humour with high enthusiasms and strong

[1] See Appendix A.

convictions. In repose her face sometimes had an expression as of one who had been through an awful and unforgettable experience. And that was, I think, a true revelation of what was underneath. I do not believe she was ever long unconscious of the aching void in her heart which could never be filled. She wrote late in 1884 to her sister Meriel, who all her life, except of course during her marriage, was nearer to her than any other human being : " You can't think how heavy life is to bear, not from unbearableness, but from the utter vanishing of all my old mainspring of joy and delight." And when she was asked to allow her name to be put forward for the Headship of Girton College she declined in a letter which shows, what strangers would hardly have guessed, how utterly broken she felt. It was her cousin Mrs. Drew who had sounded her on the subject, and it was to her that she replied that she could not feel bound to take up work of that kind " unless God emptied my life of its natural calls and duties which rather increase upon me than diminish (the little Clives,[1] for instance : poor people in St. Martin's, etc.[2]). I cannot see why because my sorrow came upon me in that tremendous way I should conclude that I am called to be dragged up into prominent mountain-tops. Dear Freddy would wish me rather to be useful in quiet natural ways. And *nothing* (to speak selfishly) that I can work at, or live for, can be otherwise than deeply sad and drifting-like to me or to anyone the whole half of whose life is gone from her."

Both these letters, it is true, were written within three years of her husband's death ; but though she naturally spoke less of her sorrow as time went on, I do not think the secret load was ever lifted, though often borne so lightly that strangers would perceive very

---

[1] Children of her great friend Lady Kitty Clive. She was one of their guardians. One of them was afterwards Captain Percy Clive, M.P., killed in the Great War.

[2] Her house, 21 Carlton House Terrace, was in the parish of St. Martin's in the Fields.

little of it. Certainly I myself, as a stranger, was much
more struck by her eager talk and varied interests
than by any suggestion of the hidden sorrow. I remember that the thing she was full of at the moment
was the question of the erection of Lord Rosebery's
Cromwell statue which now stands by Westminster
Hall. Everything in her, her loyalty to the Crown,
her devotion to the Church, her dislike of militarism,
her Liberal faith in Parliamentary Government, her
Irish sympathies, combined to make the name of
Cromwell odious to her; and the proposal to set up
his statue at Westminster of all places, was, to her,
as offensive as it certainly was inappropriate. She was
getting up a petition against the project, and wanted
me to sign it, which, however, I evaded, on grounds
with which the reader, who is concerned with her
opinions and not with mine, need not be troubled.
But I shall never forget how ingeniously, persuasively,
and humorously she urged her case as we sat in the
garden of the house in which we were staying; and
how she at once won of me an admiring allegiance
which was to have more opportunities of renewal than
I was then aware of.

The last act of that allegiance, or rather of the affection into which it was soon afterwards transformed,
is the editing of these Diaries and the writing of this
and the other Introductions. It was a privilege to
know such a woman. But unhappily such a privilege,
even if it had been enjoyed longer and more intimately
than I enjoyed it, could not confer the power of so
describing her as to make her known to others. That
I have scarcely attempted, and happily I have had the
less need, as I have been able to secure the help of
one in whose earliest memories and affections Lady
Frederick played a large and much-loved part. Lady
Stephenson is one of the daughters of Mrs. John Talbot,
and from her birth till Lady Frederick's death I suppose
she was very rarely many weeks without seeing her
aunt. I am very grateful to her for doing for me

what I could not do, and giving the readers of this book, both those who knew and those who did not know Lady Frederick, a true and, I think, vivid picture of that beautiful character, those ardent and passionate affections, that restless energy of love and service, that quick, eager, humorous mind. Lady Stephenson's knowledge of Lady Frederick hardly began till after these diaries end; and she speaks of her chiefly as she was in the forty and more years of her widowhood. But I do not think that those who have read the Diaries will have any difficulty in recognising in the picture she draws the same woman, aged and saddened no doubt, but still very unmistakably the same, whom they had got to know by her own account of her earlier years. She makes plain for us what we can read between the lines of the Diary, though the Diarist neither wrote it nor meant us to read it. She makes us see in Lady Frederick what Lady Frederick could not see in herself, what she would have thought it almost wrong to see. But all who knew her saw it, and would wish that readers of the Diary should be helped to see it too. They scarcely need the help, no doubt; but still, I cannot think that any of them will find it, given as Lady Stephenson gives it, either superfluous or unwelcome. Indeed I am sure that they will read it with the same gratitude with which I received it.

LADY FREDERICK CAVENDISH: a note by her niece Lady Stephenson

After 1882, Lady Frederick would have said of the rest of her life that the mainspring was broken. For two years she never slept without desolate tears; no day in the long years of her widowhood passed without a definite thought of her husband; the expression of her face in repose reflected the tragedy that underlay all her being. Yet glowing energy, spirit, life, are the qualities which stand out in one's memory of her; sloth, fear, hesitation, were all foreign to her nature. One pictures her hurrying across from Carlton House Terrace to the ten-o'clock service at Westminster Abbey, always a little late; or sitting writing far into the night, shaking her fountain-pen with a characteristic movement of impatience; or setting forth, after a day of ceaseless activity, by omnibus or train to some far church for a special service, sometimes even to hear one hymn that she loved.

The whole of life glowed with purpose for her; there was nothing that did not matter. Her one preoccupation was to be allowed to help to the utmost in the forwarding of that purpose. Of the two great obstacles to a life of service—worldliness and self-consciousness —Lady Frederick knew nothing. She did not resist the standards of the world, because they simply did not exist for her. She valued every person and every thing in so far as they advanced or hindered the cause of righteousness. And if she was wholly unworldly, it is also impossible to exaggerate her unself-consciousness. She never considered anything in relation to her own comfort or her own popularity; she never thought of the effect she was making; or of the price in nerve-strain that her innumerable activities and her entire disregard of all laws of health would entail.

I recall a visit with her to a great doctor when the alarming symptoms of the illness that was to make a martyrdom of the last years of her life first showed themselves. As we sat in the waiting-room she was only concerned lest she should be summoned too soon. "They *never* give one time for these lovely picture-papers," she said. And when the doctor had examined her, she asked no questions as to the course of the illness or the future she might expect, but wished to engage him in conversation on quite other subjects. No personal anxiety ever disturbed her night's rest; but the fear that England might be committed to some injustice or that the Church might be missing some great opportunity would give her a sleepless night. And in the last months of her life, when speech was

difficult, she never spoke to us of herself or of her own
sufferings, but with all the old eager longing asked
for news of the Armenians or of Ireland or of some
one of the many she loved.

She had the defects of this great quality of unself-
consciousness. She was so filled with zeal and interest
herself that she could not realise that there were many
whom the causes dear to her bewildered or bored ; and
that even for those in sympathy with them, there were
times when their discussion was not appropriate. She
was too much possessed by the subject uppermost in
her mind at the moment or by her own vivid memories
of the past to be a good listener. And when she did
give her full attention, she was inclined to sympathise
too emphatically, even too tragically. She could not
understand pettinesses, meannesses ; they were so
wholly outside her nature. " So many of my mis-
takes," she said pathetically, " come from keeping the
Golden Rule." She could not understand why people
were annoyed by things she did or failed to do which,
coming from others, would not have annoyed her at
all. She was constitutionally incapable of grievances
and hurt feelings : " things," as she once said, " so
small I can't keep my eye on them." So she sometimes blundered in her dealings with others ; though
her splendid generosity of apology and her loving-
kindness usually righted the trouble in the end. She
too often had preconceived theories of the characters
of those about her, especially of the young, and she
had a passion for discovering hereditary traits from
babyhood onwards, so that her judgments of character
were sometimes wide of the mark. The same qualities
and defects characterised the public activities with which
she overcrowded her days. She found it very difficult
to say " no " to any appeal for help in a cause which
interested her. And her interests were many-sided :
the " Old Vic." in the early struggles of its pioneer
days, the Yorkshire Ladies' Council for Education,
the Girls' Public Day School Trust, Parochial Mission

Women, the Armenians, the cause of temperance—
for all these she worked and cared whole-heartedly.
She enjoyed public speaking and felt no nervousness
at all, whatever her audience ; she had a touch of
genius in expression, and, on the subjects which she
really mastered, remarkable clearness of thought.   But
she was liable to be led astray by her love of analogies,
and to go off at a tangent ; and she trusted too much
to her intuitions and to the inspiration of the moment
when a considered judgment was needed in committee
work.

It was her personal inspiration and her undaunted
faith in the ultimate issue that made her so delightful
to work with.

Miss Powell, lately Principal of St. Mary's College,
Paddington, writes of her work for the College : " In
spite of my assurances that she needn't feel responsible,
she felt herself in honour bound to help to pull the
College out of the ditch, and made Herculean efforts,
writing round to everyone who had an available shilling
long personal letters, using to the full her gift of per-
suasiveness.   It must have cost her hours of labour. . . .
Of the £11,000 we collected I am sure Lady Frederick
was responsible directly for more than half.   But that
is the least part of what she did.   Her sympathy and
faith and courage infected us all.   She never missed
a Council meeting, and her delightful humour carried
us lightly over the rocky paths."

I think she herself was happiest when any opportunity
for direct evangelisation came her way : in Confirmation classes for the girls in the Kent Penitentiary, a
share in a mission in Leeds, or even a Sunday lesson
to the children of three successive generations, for
which she had an inimitable gift.

One is anxious not to paint her picture in too heavy
colours ; but words inevitably fail to give that other
side of her that made her " such fun."   She had a
child's gay enjoyment of the simplest pleasures : the
most amateur effort at entertainment, the mild humours

of a seaside lodging, puppies at play. She had a real
love of animals, and the company of children never
failed to refresh and delight her. I can see her literally
running into the room in an ecstasy over one of the
family engagements ; and she was liable to be overcome by helpless amusement, however solemn the
occasion. Her humour had a flavour all its own, partly
because of the tragic gravity of her face and voice.
" Oh, Green," to the imperturbable butler, when one
of her awkward movements had upset the whole coffee-
pot, " *oughtn't* I to be in a lunatic asylum ? " " Yes,
m'Lady." Or " Green," piteously, " I could ride to
York on this knife." I recall the astonishment of the
clerk in the shipping office when appealed to for an
assurance that her return ticket to South Africa would
" do for my coffin " ; or of the captain of a liner after
a rough night at sea when she accosted him with :
" Break my heart, Captain, or tell me we have had a
gale." Her epithets had a delightful unexpectedness,
as when she writes of one of her brothers : " It will
be a comfort if we can picture him eating something
more sedative and uplifting than a slab of cold mutton
at supper-time." A scullery-maid of unusual perfection
is always alluded to as " the Aloe," and a landlord
whose business methods were elusive is " the Pim-
pernel." But it is useless to try to recapture for those
who did not know her the humour that was such an
unfailing source of delight to all who came into contact
with her.

To anyone who reads Lady Frederick's Diaries it
will be abundantly plain that her religion was the preoccupation of her whole mind, the motive of her every
activity, the standard by which every event was judged.
Her passionate loyalty to the Church of England was
part of the tradition of that home which, through all
her life, never lost its hold on her love and obedience.
Unquestioning obedience to, glad co-operation with,
the Will of God, made her life impressively whole.
Motive and action became one. There could never

be any doubt as to how she would act. When the awful blow of her husband's murder fell, it was inevitable that she should make a great gesture of forgiveness, and be satisfied with nothing short of complete resignation; but that was not enough. There must be obedience to the law of love in each detail. On his tomb was engraved " died," so that there might be no memorial of the cruel crime in stone; and every day of the long years of her widowhood she prayed specially for Ireland.

Nothing was outside the sphere of dutiful obedience. Money was wanted for some good cause; then her hard-worked carriage and horses must be given up and she must go by omnibus and train to her ever-increasing activities; and no unnecessary luxuries, however trivial, could be tolerated. Evil, in every form, hurt her, gave her personal pain. To her, wrongdoing could never be a subject of interest, of gossip, still less of amusement; she hated to hear of it, and suffered with and for the wrong-doer, though hers was essentially the love that " hopeth all things."

All the traditional framework of her faith appealed to her glowing loyalty. She loved the services of the Church: " they take and do for me," she said; it uplifted her to feel one of a great multitude; the romance of the long history and the world-wide challenge of the Church inspired her imagination; and corporate prayer and praise consecrated her untiring life of service. With unusual wide-mindedness and sincerity she welcomed any fresh developments in worship, or, more remarkable still, in criticism, as long as she could believe them compatible with the " faith once delivered to the Saints."

It would be true, then, to say that in the outer things of her faith she found most of the joy of her life; but in that inmost recess of her soul, where one would have thought to find peace and joy, there was, for the most part, only a burdened sense of sin, a longing, deep but unfulfilled, for an immediate sense of God. It is

tempting to compare her experience with that " dark
night of the soul " familiar to the Mystics ; but the
hunger of her soul was never appeased by the Mystics'
moments of ecstasy whose memory persists through
the " dark night " ; and she was always inexpressibly
saddened and humiliated by reading or hearing of
mystical experiences, because she had no share in
them. Her spiritual life was overshadowed, almost
submerged, by her sense of sin. This might have been
partly due to the austere teaching of her youth, to
which her sincerity and her amazing humility made
perhaps too complete a submission. But I think too
that she was temperamentally incapable of that indescribable spiritual experience which transcends time
and space. Up to the day of her death she was always
seeking for this vision, wistfully appealing to any
who might have the key to it, agonising over the sinful-
ness which, she thought, darkened her eyes to it.

In 1913 Lady Frederick was summoned to the death-
bed of her brother Alfred. From that shock dated the
beginning of her long illness. From that date, slowly
but relentlessly, her magnificent health gave way,
her powers of body failed, and she had to suffer the
peculiar distress of great exhaustion combined with
inability to rest. " If I had known what was coming,
I do not think I could have borne it," she once said.
But it was only once ; for her own sufferings were
apparently the least interesting thing in the world to
her. As I have said above, she still passionately
desired to hear of the causes for which she had always
cared or of the many whom she loved. Through the
long months of increasing distress, she, who had always
had the impatience of those who think more quickly,
and act more energetically, and care more vitally, than
others, was divinely patient. She grew graver, but
sometimes the old humour flickered out again ; and
there was a wonderful dignity about her demeanour.
" Isn't Aunt Lucy beautiful ? " said a little great-
nephew in those last days. There was indeed an

atmosphere of great spiritual beauty about her, so that her room seemed filled with light ; and never in the days of her tireless energy had she given more illuminating witness of the faith which upheld her. She died only two hours after the elder sister who had been the close companion of over eighty years. May this not have been the first of the rewards with which Love has surprised her in that other world ?

BOOKS I AND II

SEPTEMBER 1841—JULY 1856

INTRODUCTION TO BOOKS I AND II

LUCY CAROLINE LYTTELTON, afterwards Lady Frederick Cavendish, was born in London on September 5th, 1841. The Diary does not begin till she was on the point of being thirteen. Its first volume was lost. The earliest book that was bequeathed to me is headed "Vol. II" and its first entry is made on August 7th, 1854. But Lady Frederick's niece, the Hon. Mrs. Hugh Wyndham, possesses, and has kindly allowed me to use, a little account of her earliest years written when she was still very young. There is no date on it, but it was certainly written before August 1857, when her mother died, for it always speaks of her in the present tense. It was intended to "finish for the present with my Confirmation," which took place on June 4th of the same year. But it does not get so far, and may possibly have been written before with the intention of continuing up to that point. In any case it is certain that it cannot have been written much later, not only because of the allusions to Lady Lyttelton as still living, but because in it Lady Frederick always speaks of her fourth brother as George. His full name was George William Spencer, and he was called George as a child. But in July 1856 his great-uncle and godfather Lord Spencer gave him an estate in New Zealand and asked that he should be called Spencer; and for the rest of his life George and William disappeared, and he was always known as Spencer Lyttelton. The account of this is one of the last entries in Vol. II of the Diary. It is therefore possible that the unfinished sketch of Lady Frederick's earlier life was written a little before this volume was ended as a substitute for the lost Vol. I. But its less childish and more mature

3

style suggests some time in the first part of 1857 as a more likely date. In any case she was not sixteen when she wrote it.

Some people are dull on paper and dull in conversation. Others, while witty or brilliant on paper, never say anything worth hearing. Others again are delightful to listen to and dull to read. Lady Frederick, without any claim to be a wit, was almost as quick with her pen as she was, all her life, with her tongue. But the humorous topsy-turvydoms and incongruities which flowed so freely, even in her later years, from her tongue, and would send a roomful of intimates into a burst of laughter, were not the sort of thing that anybody writes down. And, as everybody knows, such things, when coldly recorded on paper and read apart from the occasion out of which they grew, are as unlike the original and genuine article as strawberries out of a bottle are to strawberries fresh from the bed. If I did not think her diary often amusing as well as interesting, I doubt if I should have tried to put such a book as this together. But most people, from Pepys downwards, no doubt, are graver in the solitude of their diaries than they are in the society of their friends. And Lady Frederick, especially in her earlier years, put more gravity into her records than I have cared to take out of them. That note is at once struck in this curious account of her childhood. Its very first words show how serious her character was, almost from her nursery days ; as later pages show with what force, ease, and abundance she could write before she was out of the schoolroom. I quote the greater part of it. Its very first pages show where she got her seriousness. Her account is one more proof of the unhealthily " sinful " atmosphere which Victorian parents, even very kind and affectionate parents like Lord and Lady Lyttelton, allowed to grow up in their nurseries.

I suppose that if I live even to middle age some sorrows will have thrown their shadow over the sunlight of my life. Therefore I would remember as distinctly as may be what my early years have been, that in future times, when perchance their brightness has passed forever from me, I may think of them, with much sadness no doubt, but I trust with greater fondness, and thank God for the exceeding happiness wherewith my life opened. For this purpose I mean to write an account of my life, to finish for the present with my Confirmation.

I was born in London on the 5th Sept. 1841, being the second child of my parents; my sister was fourteen months older than myself. I was baptized at a month old by the name of Lucy Caroline: the first name after a family ancestress of great goodness; the second after my godmothers, both of whom had the same name. I believe I was a pretty baby, but must have given more trouble than I was worth by convulsions, etc., which gave some anxiety and left me a very whining, fretful child, even when I was put into short frocks and able to toddle. I had hardly reached this stage of existence when my eldest brother was born in October 1842, and we were three babies together in the dear dear big nursery on the third floor of the house. This room faced the S. and W. It may have been different quite at first to what it is now, but my earliest remembrances of it show it to me almost exactly as I see it at present. Two windows; the work-table, much battered, dirty red, with a curious round hole in it that I was always poking my finger through, standing in one; a high white cupboard where the toys were kept, in the other, with flower-pots standing on the top. A massive, towering, white wardrobe, with deep drawer forming its lower part, stood in one corner, filled with frocks, linen, etc.; and where the ornamental pin-cushion little basket, Xning cap, powder-box, etc., were always kept before an expected Baby required them. A dark wood cupboard, also of great height and based by drawers, [stood] against one wall, wherein the breakfast, dinner, and tea things were kept, with cold plumpudding wont to be preserved from the servants' supper. The fireplace on your left as you go in, with a heavy carved old-fashioned mantel-shelf; half-way up the wall two large rows of bookshelves hung up, whereon grotesque china ornaments, superior toys only played with on grand occasions, and a very few books stood, the latter consisted of a portentous family medicine-book and suchlike drab-coloured volumes. A large map, always my great delight, representing all the birds, beasts, and fish imaginable, and many old prints of foreign men and women, the principal picture being one of the Queen and Duchess of Kent, standing as if they were about to set off on a polka, completed the decorations of the walls. In early times a swing hung from the ceiling ; the hooks used for that purpose remain there now. By the fireplace stood the little low rocking-chair wherein I fancy we have all been sent to sleep. The middle table was round, the carpet and paper bright.

That is the dear old nursery. I have spoken of it in the past tense because I am writing of byegone times, but it is essentially the same now.

I have not one of those wonderfully good memories in books which can recall their second birthdays and their feelings on that occasion. Of my first years I have no distinct ideas. I remember a very cross nursery-maid, Betsy ; a very good-natured one, Teresa ; a period of invalidums doses and going to bed ; one awful administration of a tumbler of castor oil, which was forced down my throat with the greatest difficulty ; and perpetual sparring with my sister Meriel, whom I called Missy, in common with herself and everyone else ; a triumphant victory over my propensity of thumb-sucking ; then later, some feeble French lessons with Mme Rollande, then a daily governess, during which I was very conscious of my great stupidity, and strangely enough wondered at her patience as we ploughed through a scrap of poetry, of which I only remember the first line ; " Si quelqu'un m'appelait un petit ange " ; I very clearly remember the vagueness of my ideas as to the meaning of this ; a nursery-maid, Old Sarah, sharp with us, feared, but I fancy liked, and a sin I committed in stealing an apple out of her drawer—well I remember that ; how I hid behind the bed, but inconsiderately munched at the apple when she was in the room, and was immediately detected! dear me! beginnings of naughtiness : pilferings of the above-mentioned cold plum-pudding ; cutting off a front lock of my hair and saying Charles did it ; I am not sure, but I have a dim fancy that he said he did at last ; the punishment Mamma used to inflict upon us when we had been very naughty, taking us into Papa's room and putting our small tender hands under a thing for pressing letters together ; a bronze hand it was, which pinched us slightly, leaving the dents of the fingers on the back of one's hand. This was done very solemnly, Mamma shaking her head slowly at us all the time. I used to think that I should never lose the marks ; oh, the disgrace ! . . .

I have not the dimmest recollection of learning to read, which I was hopelessly stupid over, but I do remember my contempt of it before I began it, and one single lesson out of " Rosamond," when I read the unfortunate chapter over and over during I believe the whole morning, because of a mistake I either could not or would not avoid. At last I did it right without knowing it. It began with the words, " Are you busy, Mamma ? " I was always doing things like this. I was not happy in Miss Nicholson's time. I was horribly naughty ; sly, obstinate, passionate, and very stupid. Then she managed me ill ; over-severe and apt to whip me for obstinacy when I was only dense, letting me see her partiality for the other two, and punishing too often. So I was always labouring under a sense of injustice, and felt myself injured innocence instead of trying properly to get the better of my faults.

A very naughty little French girl called Léonie, of ten years old, came at this time to teach us French, which she did very satisfactorily, but it was certainly the only good thing she did teach us. She was impudent, dreadfully false, nasty in her ways and tricks, without the faintest idea of principle or religion. I perfectly remember her arrival ; the quick little shuffling French steps on the stairs, our shyness, and how when she came in Charles would only say a gruff " How d'ye do ? " instead of the " Bon jour " that had been instilled into him. He and I took refuge in the window, while Léonie, without a scrap of shyness in her, rattled out some long unintelligible story to Meriel.

She would steal Newmany's pomatum and smear it over her head, then cut up her ribbons and dizen herself out with them. The first English she learnt was " Cross Nurse " ; she made me teach it her, and went and said it repeatedly to Newmany. She used to stick her multiplication table on her nose, make me laugh, and when I was scolded and said that it was her fault, would put on a shocked look and exclaim innocently, " Lucie !   Comment pouvez-vous dire un tel mensonge ? "   Then I was put between the doors. However, at length her naughtiness caused her to be put always to learn her lessons with her back to us all ; but this was certainly not favourable to her studies, for she gazed out of window the whole time.   It was impossible to get anything serious into her head, though she had daily lessons from the Bible with Papa.   Her levity and giddiness were dreadful.   She was once sent to bed in the daytime for some misdeed, and went with the greatest effrontery to wish Mamma good night : " Bon soir, Madame ;   je vais me coucher."   She could learn fast enough when she chose, but choosing was a rare thing.   After everything possible had been done to reform her she was sent away in despair, but Granny still looked after her, got her into a nice school, and gave her every advantage ; but no good was ever effected, and she had at last to return to her father. We have now lost sight of her.

To return to myself, things went on very much the same with me as well as I can remember.   I was very unhappy, very ill-managed, and very naughty.   At Brighton I used to be taken out walking on the parade with my hands tied behind me, terrified out of my wits by Miss Nicholson's declaring it was ten to one we should meet a policeman.   At home my usual punishment was being put for a time into a large, deep, old-fashioned bath that was in one corner of the schoolroom, before which hung curtains, so that I was partially in the dark.   I was continually put between the doors and often whipped.   Still, I had a sort of affection for Miss N., for when I heard she was going I spoke with dismay of a " nasty new governess." I suppose I was afraid of falling out of the frying-pan into the fire. I remember blurting out before Miss Nicholson at dinner, appealing to Mamma : " Miss Nicholson's going to be married, isn't she ? " I was instantly squashed, and can only hope she didn't hear, for such was the cause of her departure. It blew up, however, and she went to Australia to be governess in the family of the Bishop of Tasmania. Léonie was succeeded by Amélie Jacquard, a very nice Swiss girl, who remained some time with us. . . .

Miss Nicholson was succeeded by a pretty, gentle, little lady with the unfortunate name of Miss Crump, who came to Hagley in October 1848. By that time there were six of us, Georgie being the youngest. I well remember her arrival. We were sitting on our high chairs sewing, and in an agony of shyness, when she walked into the room, with a pleasant smile. I remember how very short I thought her arm was at tea, after tall Miss Nicholson's, which could reach everything on the table.

Palmy days now dawned upon me in the way of indulgence at lessons, etc. The next morning Miss Crump completely won my heart by her leniency over the first lesson I repeated to her. But Miss N.'s rod of iron was better than Miss Crump's broken reed of government. We had quite our own way with her, for she soon grew passionately fond of us and let us get the upper hand. The only punishment she ever dreamt of inflicting was setting us lines of poetry to learn by heart, and these we never thought of doing unless she kept us up to it, really never thinking of the deceit of such conduct. We " shirked " duties, and became untruthful, disobedient, and self-conceited. Nevertheless we were very fond of her, and I believe sinned more from thoughtlessness than from deliberate intention, for I know I was by no means devoid of serious thoughts of religion and being *very* good, and I find in an old letter of Meriel's that we had talks with Miss Crump about our faults. But we were not much the better practically for all that, and I must say, as I think of my conduct then, I feel inclined to hate

myself. For many things there was no excuse, for
Mamma had taught us our Bible when we were very
little, and Papa as we grew older ; and we had them
always to help us by their example as well as training.
I remember complacently setting myself down as
unselfish because I let Mamma take some little trifle
of mine to give as a present, without being cross, and
I was certainly happy in the conviction. I did not
think of my greediness and deceit, my nasty temper
with the others, and all the other faults which spring
from selfishness.

I had a severe conscience prick once, however, in
spite of my general self-satisfaction. For a long time
I had been in the habit of going from my lessons on
some pretext, for the mere purpose of dawdling about
on the stairs. This I one day confessed with deep
repentance, and I rather think I became more scrupu-
lous. . . .

In 1851 Miss Crump left us. She was quite incon-
solable, and cried abundantly. We were very sorry,
for we were fond of the gentle, affectionate little woman,
though we used to wrangle and argue with her ; but
it was high time that we should have a sterner hand
over us. And this we certainly got in Miss Pearson.
She was a woman of stern and upright mind, with a
high and stern standard of duty, and little pity for
those who did not reach it. Truth and openness were
the first of human virtues with her. She had no mercy
upon the equivocating habits that had grown upon
us, and punished them relentlessly. She quickly won
our affection, though it was ever greatly mixed with fear,
and her influence over me was such that, though I knew
her hatred of what was sly, I confessed many things
to her, choosing rather to face her bitter indignation
—for she would not allow that confession palliated the
fault—than to have anything on my mind in the presence
of her clear and unshrinking openness. Her character
was indeed a noble one, though too stern ; and it
was well for me to have my faults exposed to me with
an unsparing hand, though it cost me many times of
almost despairing tears, and a good deal of bitter
repentance.

If we had not had Mamma, perhaps Miss Pearson's management would not have answered as it did ; but there was no fear of our getting cowed and spirit-broken while we had that gentle and loving care always over us, though she interfered little directly between us and our governess. It was not long before Miss Pearson clung to Mamma with the whole affection of her earnest mind, and there is no one who so appreciates the exceeding beauty and perfection of Mamma's character as she does. Thus we were indeed blest, and gradually we learnt to aim at a higher standard, and to strive more earnestly against our faults. As I grew older, I trust I overcame the habit of untruthfulness, which, in fact, never came natural to me.

As to lessons, we did them in a peculiar way. Miss Pearson had wretched health and was often laid up ; moreover she was no advocate for great regularity, so we became very independent ; often heard each other our lessons, and wrote exercises and worked sums a good deal alone, and pretty much when we liked. But there was no more " shirking " now. Holidays were very rare, and it was seldom we were let off a lesson. I have often worked till bedtime, and always after tea, finishing what had been left undone. We learnt a good deal, for all we did was useful. I have mentioned my love of poetry ; it was very great. When I was quite little Mamma taught me several of the Hymns for little Children, and it used to be a great delight to me. The last of all, " So be it, Lord ; the prayers are prayed," I used to think nothing could come up to ; and to this day the beautiful little hymn has a particular charm to me. With Miss Pearson I learnt a good deal of poetry ; the " Christian Year," bits of Shakespeare and Milton, and long things out of a book of collections. . . .

We got daily fonder of Miss Pearson, and I believe improved in all essentials under her sway. We were both inclined to argue and answer again, but she squashed us at once, and it was gradually left off. At twelve years old I was a heedless tomboy of a child, the worry of the servants, and the ruthless destroyer of frocks. Nevertheless I had a curious mixture of

I—4

religious feeling and poetical fancies. I wrote verses, and was fond of quotations in my letters, had plenty of warm-heartedness, and was quickly roused or touched. I'm afraid I was a sad handful to Miss Pearson, what with my carelessness and forgetfulness, and the underhand ways that cost me many tears, and her so many headaches, but which at length were, I trust, quite got rid of.

We were at Hawarden in the autumn of 1854 when I was thirteen, and here my conscience, which had been growing daily more tender under Miss Pearson's care, would not let me alone till I had confessed one or two little slynesses that I had long time ago been guilty of. One I remember. I had been sent on a message to Elly, and on my way bounced into the dining-room, where the remains of the luncheon were standing, and crammed my mouth with cherries. On my return, Miss Pearson's sharp eye found out some red juice on my lips, and she questioned me. " I've had some cherries," said I, relieved at speaking out the truth. But Miss Pearson supposed Elly had given them me ; and as she scolded me for that, I had not courage to say I had purloined them. At the end of this confession I paused in mortal terror, but to my infinite relief was spoken to leniently, and was thus encouraged to tell of something else, which, strange to say, I have forgotten, but for which I caught it so dreadfully that I was utterly miserable for some days.

Altogether this time at Hawarden has left a grim impression on my mind. I was working a stool for Miss Pearson very lazily indeed, so much so that she at last declared she would not accept it ! Great was my anguish ; I began to slave at it so hard that she was mollified at last, and it now stands in her drawing-room at Clent. Moreover I was not well for some time ; but for one circumstance that happened at this time I shall be earnestly thankful to the end of my life—perhaps for all eternity.

I have said that I had always been thoughtful about sacred things ; very far back I remember doing right from a sort of *principle*, not merely to save punishment, and this made me wretched over my perpetual falls.

I used to pray for help with much faith, and make many resolutions ; but hitherto I had done so almost mechanically, following what I had been taught from babyhood, with no strong personal realisation of what was meant by God, Heaven, Death, Eternity. I had not brought these things before me as realities so vivid that they may almost be called tangible. I was indeed but a child. But in church one Sunday at Hawarden, whether some words suggested it to me, whether the distress of mind I had been going through had made me peculiarly susceptible of strong impression, or whether an angel spoke to me suddenly, I cannot tell ; but there flashed upon me, like blinding light, a great thought of Eternity as bearing upon myself—as an unchangeable certainty—as something that was irresistibly advancing—in short, in some awful and present manner, to such an extent that I was aghast and overwhelmed with the tremendousness of my thought. For a moment I thought I should have fainted. I was a young and foolish child ; a very small thing among God's Infinite Mysteries ; can I wonder that —awaking to the realisation of things into which the Angels cannot look—my immortal soul struggled in a sort of agony within its narrow prison ?

I shall never now lose that impression, and for this I thank God.

It is unwillingly that I leave the record of my earlier years : I mean my life before entering my teens ; so certain I feel that I must have left out many of the little incidents that gave it its own calm and happy colouring ; for indeed my childhood was a bright, unruffled river, and I would not lose any of its memories. Our Christmases ! How they shone out at the end of each year with an indescribable joy of their own ; made up of the " bright leaves and red berries " with which the old house was lit up, the joyous home-gathering, the circle of our dear home-faces without one missing from arriving. Then the wonderful excitement of the whole number of us going in the early morning to sing " Hark the herald," at all the doors, beginning with Papa and Mamma, scrambling on to their bed for the kisses and " Merry Christmases." Oh, what a delight

it was !—ending with the nurseries, where we all assembled to drink coffee and eat tea-cake, surrounded
by the admiring maids, with the holly all round the
room shining in the firelight.   And all going to the
church down to the youngest but one, to hear the dear
old hymns and Uncle Billy's beautiful Christmas
sermons.   The ecstasy of dining late, the mince-pies,
the snapdragon, the holiday, the listening to evening
carols ; and perhaps the dawning of true joy because
Christ was born in Bethlehem, and it was to His tender
love that we owed all our happiness.   Strong and
loving, and shining with ever-increasing brightness,
is my memory of the Christmases of my childhood.
The return of the holidays, seeing the dear boys' faces
again, and rejoicing over the prizes, their begging a
holiday for us, and the wild scampers over the place
with them.   The gathering of aunts and cousins from
time to time, when the old house echoed with children,
and it was our especial aunt's (Papa's maiden sister,
Aunt Coque) delight to range our goodly and unbroken
numbers in files according to age.   The astonishing
excitement of packing and journey days, when even
sober Meriel could hardly sleep from delight, and when
my imagination woke into song !

> Packing-day !   Sweet packing-day !
>   The subject of my lay.
> Come, come !   Thy pleasures bring,
>   Thou sweet dear darling thing.
>
> Packing is my delight.
>   I'll pack from morn till night ;
> Next day is journey-day !
>   Hurrah !   Hurrah !   Hurrah !

Even when nothing was going on the dear home-life
was as happy as anything in its way ; the schoolroom,
where day after day we went through the well-known
routine, the time there enlivened by Papa's visits to
Mamma and hers to him ; our room being the passage
between them.   We were never interrupted by this,
for one got so thoroughly accustomed to it, and it
was seldom that either took any notice of us, beyond
a smile from Mamma and " You little pigs," or " Absurd
monkies," from Papa.   But it always gave me a happy

feeling when I heard Mamma's little cough outside
the door, or saw her tall and graceful figure passing
through the room, and it was nice to feel that they
were so close to us. The glorious summers! After
lessons there was the walking out into the beautiful
country; the hills, park with its stately trees, the
bright village and green lanes; or a ride, or a drive
with Mamma in the pony-carriage; both great delights;
sitting under the trees with the song of birds and hum
of bees all round one, or on the lawn, mossy and velvety
with age, from whence we looked over the grassy hills
rising gently one over the other, crowned with the
beautiful trees, and where we loved to bring our reading
or have tea on summer holidays. Then in the evenings,
coming to dessert in the high cool dining-room, and
sitting on the perron out of doors till the first stars came
out, while everything slept in still beauty, and Malvern
and Aberleigh rose deeply blue against the sky.

The winters, when the house felt so snug with its
wide grates and roaring fires, and snow and frost were
the greatest pleasures of life; when we slid with the
boys, enjoying it full as much as they, or played at
" Earth, Air, Fire, and Water," round the fire in the
library. And as I grew older and understood more
and more what our happiness was, thought of our
unclouded home, of the exceeding blessing to us of
such parents as ours, of all the dear brothers and sisters,
uncles and aunts, of the little pleasures with which
God filled our cup, and the many deep and lasting joys
with which He crowned our life—I trust I grew year
by year more grateful, while at times there would
mingle with the happiness, a feeling ever increasing
that it could not last for ever, and how should we prize
it and turn it to good account! So might God grant
that those bright years should lead us to him from
Whom all good things do come. . . .

Besides little Katie Glynne (her first cousin), there
was another death in the spring of '54; I mean Grandmamma's. We have never known grandfathers. Our
grandfather Lyttelton died a year or two before Papa's
marriage; our grandfather Glynne when Mamma was a
little child! And I may say we have never known

more than one grandmother, for the impression that remains on my mind of Mamma's mother is a very confused one. She came to live at Hagley before my birth and became gradually a confirmed invalid. I just remember her driving out in her own carriage with her companion Miss Browne, the hood up, and a large umbrella held over her. Meriel remembers when she was able to dine with Papa and Mamma, but for the last years of her life she lived quite secluded in her own rooms. From time to time one of us might be sent with a message, but this was rare, and when I did see her, her tall bent figure and, to me, stern expression [here follow some lines partly scratched out : they evidently described how Lady Glynne used to wear a black patch on her nose] awed me very much. We were not allowed as a rule to go up the staircase near her sitting-room, and were kept very quiet whenever we were on her side of the house. (She had the drawing-room as her sitting-room, and the little tapestry dining-room as her bedroom ; her maid had the little room next door.) Latterly we quite left off going to see her, and I remember my dismay when I bounced into the dining-room at an irregular hour, and saw her passing with her slow, careful step across it from her bedroom to her sitting-room. From all this it may be seen that we could know little personally of Grandmamma, and looked upon her more as a sort of awful mystery than anything else ; but I well remember the devotion of Mamma and Auntie Pussy to her ; how much time they spent with her, and how much talk with Miss Browne about her health ; also the instinct early taught us, and which I have hardly yet lost, of avoiding, or going softly by, the staircase and passages near her rooms.

And now having spoken about *Grandmamma*, I must describe *Granny*,[1] for so we always called her as a distinction, and the fond familiar name best suits her. My first recollections of her are as making us charming presents ; frocks, sashes, and so on ; and later, little " tips " of money, so that her arrival was always a great event. I suppose she cannot be called a pretty

[1] Her father's mother, Sarah, Lady Lyttelton.

old lady, as she has lost the sight of one eye from brow
ague ; but in spite of this defect, to me, and to most
I believe, she has always had a charm about her better
than beauty. Tall, with great dignity and grace of
manner, a sweet smile, a low melodious voice, and a
power of winning and attracting everyone who knows
her ; this is the best *superficial* idea I can give of her.
But I can't do justice on paper to all that is admirable
in her mind and character. Clever and brilliant in
conversation, with a somewhat satirical turn, and a
great gift of *humour*, the best letter writer I ever knew
—which may partly be accounted for by her complete
disbelief of the fact, and consequent ease and simplicity ; she is full of information, a first-rate teller
of stories, or reader . . . [Here the account breaks off.]

The account breaks off abruptly in this way and was
never finished. No occurrence mentioned in it took
place later than the year 1854. In that year the
regular Diary begins. It is, as I have said, entitled
Vol. II, and covers the period between August 7th,
1854, when the first entry was made, and August 31st,
1856, when it ends. It is written in a childish hand
much less legible than Lady Frederick's later writing,
and is frequently illustrated by pen-and-ink sketches
of the scenes or persons mentioned. It is, of course,
mainly a record of the routine of schoolroom life at
Hagley. Enough is given, I hope, in the extracts
which follow to show what this was like. To omit it
would have been to leave out an essential part of
the picture. For Lady Frederick kept all her life the
mark of her early years. And the object aimed at
throughout all the selections has been, first, to give a
picture of the character and life of the writer herself,
and only after that, and second to it, to illustrate
generally the manners and customs, and the social,
political, and religious world, of Victorian times.

The extracts here printed are about one-fifth of the
whole book. They and its other four-fifths exhibit
the picture of a very good, very intelligent, and very

affectionate child and a very happy home. There is more about sins and prayers and sermons than is thought quite healthy by a later generation, even by that part of it which has no sympathy with the modern fashion of dismissing sin as a mere theological bogy. This gravity sometimes takes amusing forms. One admires the decision with which this youthful critic pronounces the sermons at St. Leonard's " good on the whole " ; and entirely sympathises with her when she finds a book on " The Influence of the Clergy of the First Centuries " " much dryer " than Macaulay. That was Macaulay's Essays : with Lucy Lyttelton, as with so many of us, in spite of youthful Royalist feelings " desperately exasperated " by Macaulay's Whiggery, the first or almost the first " grown-up " book to be appreciated. Among other books which the Lyttelton children are recorded as reading are, of course, Shakespeare (though Bowdler's), " Half-hours with the Best Authors," Scott's novels, Hume's History, and even something unspecified of Burke. Evidently it was not for nothing that they were the sons and daughters of a very fine scholar and the nephews and nieces of Gladstone. Even in these early years Lucy was beginning her life-long enthusiasm for her famous uncle. During a visit to Hawarden she records the delight of " long rides over a country new to us, with Agnes, and sometimes Uncles William or Henry, the former being able to answer any question you may ask him." Already too she shows more interest than most children in public affairs outside her own family and circle. Not only does she frequently allude to the cholera, then actually a scourge and terror to England, but she devotes many pages to the Crimean War, and even records the resignations of Ministers. The young politician, brought up in a political atmosphere, is also seen in a long declamation about the War and the Peace. I have spared the reader its semi-parliamentary rhetoric with a long series of passages each opening with " Look back, look back to the nobly fought and nobly sustained

battles, look back to the long long siege," etc., etc.
But perhaps the peroration may be quoted here :
" Shall we talk of having got no good by the war ?
Was it undertaken for ourselves ?   Let it be enough
that we took up arms in defence of the just rights of
a nation, that we accomplished our end and humbled
the pride of the oppressor ; and then let us thankfully
receive the honourable Peace and strive to make much
of it : for is it not the greatest of blessings ?   I say,
Amen, and thank God."

There is no mention of the reading of newspapers
in this volume of the Diary ; but one wonders whether
if the Crimean debates were searched one would find
some speech of Gladstone or another, of which this long
outburst by his youthful niece is an echo. If she
had been a boy, or if she had been born fifty years
later, she would certainly have been either a preacher
or a politician.   She came very young into the possession
of the mental and physical energy, the moral enthusiasm,
and the command of language, the combination of which
naturally leads to one or other of those careers.

But these high matters are, of course, only occasional
visitors in the diary of a girl of fourteen. We hear
more of family births, marriages, illnesses and deaths,
which, filling her heart, naturally filled her pages ; and
of the lessons and amusements, the walks and rides,
which occupied her girlish days. There was boating
(as well as scarlet fever) at St. Leonard's, and dancing
in London ; there were evenings of cards (commerce
and beggar-my-neighbour seem to have been the
games), and occasionally of acting ; now and then,
too, the children were taken to the real theatre or to
hear Fanny Kemble read " Lear " or " Othello."
Serious as the home was, it is evident that there was
no Puritanical or Evangelical ban on innocent amusements. And of course when they were in London
there were such glimpses as children can have of the
great world. The extracts which follow describe
several Royal functions at which the diarist was present,

including two Court balls for children. She records
that in preparation for one of them her younger
sister " Win," afterwards Mrs. Edward Talbot, had
" her hair curl-papered every night " for a week " to
make it look a little less Irish and wild." In fact the
Diary is like life, full of a lot of very little things, with
a few greater ones thrown in from time to time.

And now it is more than time that the Diary should
begin to speak for itself.

HAGLEY HALL.

DIARY, AUGUST 1854—JULY 1856

HAGLEY, *August 15th*, 1854.—Between twelve and one o'clock, we were doing some French with Dove ; and heard Mamma talking to Uncle Billy in the lobby. I offered to call Mamma, for Dove wished to speak to her, but she stopped me. " She's busy," quoth she. Presently they both went into Papa's room, from whence in a minute or two proceeded a roar of laughter and exclamations. Somewhat curious I remarked : " Oh, what's the joke ? " Meriel looked odd, Dove said, " Don't go in," and went on with the French. We had hardly done another sentence, when Mamma appeared at the door of Papa's room, beckoning to us. Up we jumped and went in. There was Papa, Mamma, Uncle Billy, Granny, and Aunt Coque. " Go and stand together," said Mamma. (I can't think why. Probably to see our different ways of taking it.) " What do you think's happened ? " roared Papa. " Guess. Eh, dears ? " quoth Mamma. Meriel guessed, she suspected before. I was entirely puzzled, hadn't the least idea what was what. " You've got another aunt ! " exclaimed Aunt Coque. " Uncle Billy is going to be married ! ! ! ! " says Mamma. " Oh," simply said I. And sat flat down on the floor. Indeed, who can wonder ? Mortal man was never so thunderstruck since the year 1, as I was at that moment. What is what ? What is one to do, laugh or cry, or both together ? Uncle Billy of all people in the known world ! By the bye, she is Miss Pepys, daughter of the Bishop of Worcester. A very worthy person I believe, charitable, young (21), amiable, humble, good-looking, not a " nice young lady," and above all, beloved by Uncle Billy. One's first feeling is bewildered amazement ; one's next, that it's somewhat of a blow ; one's third, great hope that it will be very good for Uncle Billy, and turn out well for everybody. At first I felt choking

21

weight, and egg in my throat ; then after wandering
about the room, talking to Dove, etc., I rushed upstairs, gave a hurried announcement to the nursery,
and then to my own room, where I prayed for both of
them.   Then I felt a little less odd.

HAGLEY, *August 26th*, 1854.—Lovely. We played
cricket with the boys in the morning, read on the
lawn, and walked with Aunt Coque in the afternoon.
The little pigs grow and prosper.   Uncle B. came home :
they had the moneyums [1] and the deadums [1] all the
evening.   Poor old Sultana is shot, and buried near
the iron gate leading to Ashmore's.

HAGLEY, *August 28th*, 1854.—Cholera in Stourbridge,
and the black flag hung over the worst places in London.
Lord Joscelin died of it a few days ago.

HAGLEY, *August 31st*, 1854.—The school feast came
off.   Dove's leg better.   The prizes were given between
1 and 2 : both the little Daphnes, 3 Wyatts and 3 Tandys
got prizes.   They dined very soon after, at the S.E.
side of the house ; and eat no less than six rice, and six
plum puddings, two legs of mutton, besides lots of beef,
bread, and beer.

HAGLEY, *September 1st*, 1854.—When we were on
our way to Mrs. Billin, we sat there some little time,
Aunt Coque spouting poetry, and we witnessed a curious
fight between two wasps on the ground.   The victor
cut off his enemy's head and tail and we left him with
the body in his arms.

By the bye, Granny reads the " Rivals " to us after
dinner ; it is capital.

HAGLEY, *September 6th*, 1854.—The cholera is fearful
in London ; more than 1,000—200 fatal cases.   Four
children in one family.   A poor clergyman caught
the typhus fever from one of his sons, and his wife
was confined with an eighth baby while he was so ill.
She recovered to find herself a widow with eight children,
and not a farthing to support herself or them ; his
living having been given away, and so no money from

---

[1] Appendix A.

thence, he hadn't insured his life, and had no fortune besides. They are collecting money. I gave a little, and Albert. They have already collected a great deal, and have taken three children off her hands.

HAGLEY, *September 12th*, 1854.—Had the most delightful ride of 9 or 10 miles with Papa ! and Charles ; round Clent Hill, up Walton, and Calton, by Fairleigh Coppice, through lanes, on heaths, by farmhouses, cornfields and grass-fields ; through villages, amongst donkies, cows, sheep, and horses, and—home. Raced with Charles. Most delightful. I learnt to-day that the reason of the holes in the barns is to let in air, that their contents may not catch fire.

HAGLEY, *September 17th*, 1854.—Mr. Pipps as usual came to Church. He has chosen for his pew the foot of

Thomas Lyttelton Bart.

where he sat most of the service. Uncle B. preached again in the afternoon.

Pippy's kennel was brought home on Saturday : it is very pretty, painted and varnished to look like oak, with " Mr. Pipps " in black letters over the entrance.

HAWARDEN, *November 2nd*, 1854.—We are leading a quiet life here, but have great [1] breaks in the way of rides. Meriel has taken wonderfully to that mode of exercise ; indeed who wouldn't enjoy long rides over a country new to us, with Agnes, and sometimes Uncles William [2] ! ! ! ! or Henry, the former being able to answer any question you may ask him ? and then tolerably pretty scenery, and beautiful cantering ground, 'twouldn't be human nature to dislike such.

HAWARDEN, *November 12th*, 1854.—On the 12, Uncle Billy and Aunt Emmie went home after their honeymoon at Althorp, and met with a grand reception, that oh, I could scratch out my eyes for not having witnessed. I know the details, however, by heart. The schoolchildren with banners, the members of the Working Men's Club ditto, and the spectators in processional

[1] Appendix A.　　　　[2] Mr. Gladstone.

order, marched down a little way past the Nabbian gate, where they formed on either side of the road. In a few minutes up drove Uncle Billy and Aunt Emmie, who hadn't expected anything. The postboy was much astonished at having his horses taken out of the carriage, which was done by the members of the Working Men's Club, who then placed themselves in their place and drew them through two triumphal arches, to the door of the Rectory, where, standing on the steps with his bride, Uncle Billy heard an address read to him by Mr. Marsh, and answered it. The procession then marched off, and stopped before the house, gave three cheers for Papa and Mamma, one for the family, and the band played " The Good Old English Gentleman." They then went away ; it being a lovely day the children had tea out of doors, games, etc., and there was also a feast at the Arms. Everything was most satisfactory.

HAWARDEN, *November 11th, 12th, 13th, 14th*, 1854.... The heavy cavalry was hereupon ordered to charge a much superior force of Russians, which it did grandly, and entirely broke and dispersed them. All would have been well, and unmixedly satisfactory, if nothing further had been done. But through some mistake of orders, partly from Lord Lucan's, more from an officer of the name of Nolan's, fault, a light cavalry [1] brigade consisting of 609 men was soon charging the Russian army, entirely unsupported, and crossing a plain of half a mile for the purpose of re-taking the guns. The slaughter was prodigious. The number of men who returned was 200 and something. The glorious fellows ! On they rushed to certain, or almost certain, death, and flinched no more than if they were exercising in Hyde Park ! They never paused in that fearful charge, that sent so many into Eternity. " God forgive me," said one of the Scots Greys afterwards, " but I felt like a devil during that charge."

HAGLEY, *December 15th*, 1854.—When we arrived, the little boys had come, so jolly for their holidays, talking of carn't, harf, and clarss [2] like anything.

[1] The famous charge of the Light Brigade in the Crimean War.
[2] The older pronunciation, at any rate in those parts, was " can't," not " carn't," etc., and Lady Frederick used it, more or less, all her life.

HAGLEY, *January 26th*, 1855.—Lord J. Russell has resigned, and they expect the rest of the ministry will soon be picked out.

By the bye, Aunt Wenlock was here the other day, gave me a delightful book : " Half-hours with the Best Authors."

LONDON, *May 1st*, 1855.—A memorable day indeed ! My head was washed by Strathearne, a hairdresser, and he says it ought to be a " very good 'ed of 'air." He did Agnes'[1] and my hair in the evening, at about 7. At $8\frac{1}{2}$ we were to be at the Palace for the Queen's ball. We were rigged, figged, and launched into two carriages in tolerable time, and our dresses were something magnificent. A beautiful muslin frock trimmed with ruches and daisies. White silk stockings, white satin shoes with white bows, white kid gloves trimmed with white daisies and a wreath of two rows of daisies on polls, was the dress of Agnes and me. On the way a bathingfeel[2] for nearly the first time assailed me. We went under the arch, and into Buckingham Palace Hall, from whence we proceeded to a grand room where we took off our wraps. We then went up the grand staircase into a beautiful gallery. Presently the glorious National Anthem struck up ; the numerous company divided on this side and that and a crowd of grandees appeared at the further end of the Gallery. Presently Prince Albert came forward alone, holding by the hand the loveliest little being I ever saw. It was Prince Arthur, in honour of whose birthday the ball took place. His Highness is four years old, and the smallest child of his age I should ever think was born. In a Highland dress, with a dear little curly head, large blue eyes, little chiselled nose, fair complexion, and oval face, he looked like a blessing sent to be beloved of everyone ; bless him !

Well, the Queen came up soon, everybody curtseying as Her Majesty passed, and soon she came up to where we were. Oh, ecstasy, she shook hands with me ! imagine my feelings and my curtsey ; I kept hold of her dear hand as long as I dared.

---

[1] Agnes Gladstone.   [2] See Appendix A.

With the Queen were the Prince of Wales, Prince Alfred, the Princess Royal, Princess Alice, Princess Helena, and Princess Louise, the two latter pretty and one of their Royal Highnesses very like the Queen. Besides these there were the Duchess of Kent, and a number more of fat duchesses. One of them shook hands with me : everybody curtseyed to them, and when they had all passed, we moved after them. Presently we arrived at the Throne Room, where the ball was to be. The Queen and the Royalties went to a sort of low platform at one end ; and a fat duchess stood on each side of the Queen and Prince. Then the dance began, the Royalties dancing with the rest. But the whole was a sort of romp, the little ones not knowing exactly what to do, and an unfortunate dancing master in vain endeavouring to establish order. There were valses, quadrilles, galops, and two reels, the last of which we did not witness, being having some refreshments. But the first we saw, and very pretty it was. The Prince of Wales asked me if I could dance it, but alas ! I couldn't. His Highness danced with Agnes, and so did Prince Alfred : happy girl ! in a quadrille and galop, I think. Little Prince Arthur danced a little after a fashion. I danced mostly with Willy, galops, and every time we went close up to the Queen and Prince ; so near that I verily believe Willy would twice have " punched " Prince Albert, if I hadn't drawn his arm back. There was one quadrille in which the Queen and grandees danced, but as the children were romping through another, we didn't see much of it. After a time Her Majesty descended from the platform, and led the way to the supper-room. Such a magnificent one ! with a table this shape.[1] Nobody eat much, though, I think ; everybody stood. Then back we went, and I had my most delicious of all galops with a little page, and Willy. Prince Arthur, precious little darling, went to bed after supper. Then the ball broke up, and passing through a door, we had another beautiful view of Her Majesty and the Prince, while the National Anthem crashed from the band. Oh-h, didn't it thrill one ! We then went thrilling home, which we reached

[1] Drawings frequently adorn the original.

at about 1 o'clock. So ended that memorable 1st of May.

LONDON, *May* 18th, 1855.—I, only think what a privilege ! went with Aunt Wenlock to see the medals given to the Crimean heroes by the Queen, bless her ! It was in the open part of the Mall, just before the Horse Guards. We went into a gallery placed here [1] where several were erected, one above the other. We arrived before Her Majesty came, so saw the troops arriving, manœuvring, passaging, and all the rest. Then, punctually at 11 a.m. through the Horse Guards swept a whole troop of Life Guards, who wheeling to the left joined another body, of Blues and Cuirassiers, stationed nearly just under our gallery. Then up came the Royal carriage, drew up at a sort of low platform placed here,[1] with two gilt chairs and a flag-staff ; out stepped the little Queen, while loudly echoed the reports of cannon, and the National Anthem crashed from cymbal and drum. Everyone stood up, and inexpressibly grand it seemed to me. Then it began. The long file of wounded passed before the Queen, and as each received the medal from her own gracious hands, he passed on, and joined the other soldiers. Thus.[1] There were the noble grenadiers who fought at Inkermann, and the glorious few remaining from the Balaclava Light Cavalry charge. There were three wounded officers drawn in Bath chairs and seven on crutches, both men and officers. There were several hundreds, and the giving away lasted two hours. There were present Lord Cardigan and the Duke of Cambridge, both of whom received medals. The Duke of C. has large white whiskers,[2] and Lord Cardigan large yellow ones. All the while the bands played different tunes, Scotch ones when the Highlanders passed, " Rule Britannia," " Hearts of Oak," etc., when the sailors came, and " The Grenadiers," etc., when the Bearskins and others passed. When all was over, the Grenadiers defiled before the Queen, to the tune of " The British Grenadier." There was but little cheering, people

---

[1] Illustration in original.
[2] The Duke was only thirty-six at this time ; so his white whiskers are even more inexplicable than Lord Cardigan's yellow ones.

I—5

felt it in a different manner to what would be expressed
by that.   The Royal carriage came up and Her beloved
Majesty drove away to the same crash as before, guns
firing, bands playing " God save the Queen."

LONDON, *July 22nd*, 1855.—The 22nd was my own,
own, precious Mamma's birthday, and on that day
moreover was Meriel confirmed by Forbes, Bishop of
Brechin, being of the age of fifteen, a month and five
days.   She went to Falconhurst, Mrs. Talbot's place,
on Friday, which day also Mamma went up to London
for her eleventh confinement.   God bring her safe
through it !

LONDON, *July 23rd*, 1855.—Thank God, oh ! thank
God ! to-day at 4 p.m. came into the world No. 11,[1]
a seventh son.   He came a fortnight or so before he
was expected, and is little and thin but prosperous, as
is his Mamma, thank God !   We *are* sorry he is not a
little girl, but after all, it doesn't very much matter,
and the blessing of his happy birth is too great to let
one feel really disappointed.

September 19*th*, 1855.—Oh, what a wretch I am !
If I haven't forgotten to put in the grand news ! !
SEBASTOPOL HAS FALLEN !   Yes, thank God, at
last He has sent this much-prayed-for blessing.

September 29*th*, 1855.—In the evening about 8¼ came
the new French woman, more hugely fat than imagination can picture, or tongue describe.   No, I cannot
express it in drawing, but she looked just as if an
immense pillow had been laid across her chest.   Below
was fragment [2] ; no legs, no arms, and about Nanny's
height.   Mamma looked a poplar beside her.   She was
merry as a grig, and chattered away about the Queen,
the French Emperor, William IV, George IV, Bona-
parte, Lord Palmerston, Uncle William, and what not,
all while she was still further enlarging herself with
some mutton and tea.   We then showed her up to her
room, and left the little fat tumbler to her reflections.

October 22*nd*, 1855.—Our lessons are now the very
essence of regularity, but nevertheless the squabble,

[1] Edward, afterwards Head Master of Eton.   [2] Appendix A.

the chatter, the clatter, the laughing, the scolding, the crossness, the " Do this, Don't do that, Go there, Come here " that goes on all the time is quite bewildering.

November 8th, 1855.—I have read some of Bowdler's Shakespeare ; like very much " Henry VIII," " Romeo and Juliet," and " Hamlet," but don't care for " All's Well that Ends Well," and " Midsummer-Night's Dream," particularly not the former ; uninteresting plot, rather coarse, no poetry, half prose. " King Lear " is beautiful, " As you Like It," great fun. I have begun " Love's Labour's Lost."

December 13th, 1855.—" Love's Labour's Lost " is trash. " Othello " very fine. And oh, " Henry the VIII ! "

HAGLEY, *December 20th*, 1855.—Then, in the evening of this too delightful day, we all went to Stourbridge to hear Papa's lecture on Shakespeare. There were Papa, of course, Mamma, Uncle Billy, Aunt Emmy, Charles, Albert, Nevy, Meriel, Johnny Talbot, Mr. and Mrs. Oxley, Mademoiselle, Mr. Johnstone, and me. Oh, it was so beautiful, and such quotations, and he read them so grandly too. I think I liked Constance's agony about her " pretty Arthur " best, and then parts of " King Lear " and Desdemona and Othello when he is going to kill her, and numbers more, oh, Catherine of Aragon's speech before Henry the VIII.

ST. LEONARD'S, *December 22nd*, 1855.—We have an enchanting house, into which we are packed delightfully tight, as follows. Little front room on the ground floor, choked up with table, sofa, and arm-chair, hardly room to turn : schoolroom (for the studies of M., Georgy,[1] Winny, and me, with Mademoiselle's more than portly person presiding). Opening from this (but the door between is blocked up), Mademoiselle's room, bigger than the first, but somewhat gloomy, looking into the high cliff. These two open into the hall about a man's stride wide, on the other side of which are, opposite the school-room, and very little bigger, the dining-room ; next to it Papa's study and dressing-room in

[1] Her fourth brother, afterwards always known as Spencer.

one, not *too* big either.　Up rather a narrow and steepish
staircase, you arrive at the second floor.　Here are the
two drawing-rooms, of moderate size, front and back,
opening into each other, folding doors.　The back room
is to be used by Johnnie for his reading.　Next to the
front rooms is a splendid apartment, probably destined
for a sort of boudoir, small of course, but devoted to
Meriel, Winny, and me, for bedroom.　Win on a sofa
against the wall, and M. and I in a bed together.　The
worst of this room is, that there is nothing where*in*,
and little where*on*, to put anything.　Next to this,
Mrs. Talbot's room.　On the third floor are Baby's
and Newmany's slip of a bedroom, next to that a small
apartment containing Amelia's bed, and answering
the purpose of sitting, washing, and day's noise nursery.
Next to it is Papa's and Mamma's room (who by the
bye came on the 20th following us), and next to them
a bedroom for two maids.　On the top floor is a room
where some three or four maids sleep, a sleeping-nursery,
containing Harriet and Bobby in one bed, May and
Arthur in another, a little hole of a room ; Mr. Hook's
sleeping-apartment, " sans " fireplace, and Johnnie's
bed-chamber.　The tight fit is great fun.　So are the
beds, which are perfectly unparalleled for hardness.

St. Leonard's, *February 26th*, 1856.—At 6 Johnnie
read to Mamma, Mrs. Talbot, M. and I some of
Macaulay's Essay on Hallam, very interesting and
well written, and fearfully enraging from its horrid
roundhead views.

St. Leonard's, *March 17th*, 1856.—Poor me was
debarred from church both times, as I was in bed with
this sore-throat epidemic.　I do so pity myself, feeling
quite well, and a whole Sunday without any church !
Last Sunday in Lent too !　Oh !

London, *April 21st*, 1856.—In the afternoon I had
the first ride I have ever had in London on our old
friend Niger that we used to ride at Hawarden : he is
rather rough and will do nothing but trot, but spirited
and good.　I went to Rotten Row, and all about there,
and home by Piccadilly and Pall Mall.

LONDON, *April 24th*, 1856.—A pleasant day. Such a busy one! Breakfast, prayers, Sunday reading, preparation for Mme Greco, music-lesson with Mad^elle, reading, dancing from 12 to ¼ past 2, dinner, Italian, Hume, drive, tea and cards all the evening.

LONDON, *April 25th*, 1856.—The Day of the Queen's Ball!! The second I have had, and both described in the same journal-book. This time the ball was at 9, instead of ½ past 8. Auntie Pussy,[1] Aggy, Lena, and Willy and Stephy who both came from Eton in the morning, dressed at Carlton Terrace, I was sent to George Street, to dress with Mamma and Winnie. Aggie, I, Lavinia, and Lena were all alike, in tarlatane frocks, trimmed the three skirts with white ruches, twined round with some pretty pink trimmings. Wreaths of pink roses, the little ones smaller than ours. White kid gloves, white satin shoes, and white silk stockings completed our attire. We set off in three different equipages ; Mamma, Win and I were in Mrs. Talbot's chariot : we went from George Street to Carlton Terrace, where we got out for a minute to show ourselves, and there standing in the hall, amongst the rest, was Aunt Coque. We had a hasty embrace, Win and I made a low curtsey to the admiring servants, and then rushed back into the carriage, for it was rather late. The others had just gone. My bathingfeel[2] fast increased as we drove up the Park, through the gates, into the court, and under the arch of Buckingham Palace. We got out, and were ushered up the well-remembered grand staircase, on either side of which were masses of flowers, and through a door which led into an ante-room ; when lo from a side door issued a " gallant train." First Her dear little gracious Majesty, my own Queen. Down went our curtseys, and we had her smile and bow all to ourselves. After the Queen came the Princes and Princesses. Down went our curtseys. Then came the fat Royal Duchesses. Down went our curtseys. Then the rest of the company. We fell in with them, and moved on to the Throne Room. How well I remembered it ! We were late, or else we should have

---

[1] Mrs. Gladstone.   [2] Appendix A.

gone into the long Gallery like last year. We soon
found Auntie Pussy and hers, and had a good look at
the Royalties. There was my own darling Prince
Arthur, grown much, and there was precious little
Prince Leopold, whom I have never seen before, a
lovely little fat darling, with the same large blue eyes
and curly head as his Highness's little brother. Princess
Alice, in honour of whose birthday the ball took place,
is very plain, poor child, and was further spoilt by her
hair which had been forced into stiff curls. Princess
Royal looked very nice indeed, quite pretty in fact ;
she is now quite out, and consequently only danced
with grown-ups, the Duke of Cambridge principally.
The two little Princesses looked beautiful and dear
as usual, in their Highland dresses, in which they look
so very well always. Little Prince Arthur was also
in Scotch dress, all except the plaid. There were the
fat duchesses like last time. Now a thing was done
that I don't remember was done last time : everyone
filed before the Queen, made a curtsey, and received
her gracious welcome. So we set off, I think, the first
of all, and when about half-way, I discovered that
Mamma had stayed behind. In woful distress I looked
all about amid the crowd, to see if I could catch a
glimpse of her, but I couldn't, so I thought I must
move on with Auntie Pussy, etc., as we were already
half-way. So we came up to the Queen : there was
her gracious smile, and down went my curtsey (a
beautiful one). Auntie P. said " Lucy Lyttelton,"
for the Queen looked at me, and said, " This is not one
of yours." Her Majesty shook hands with me !
and then turning to Auntie Pussy : " And your sister,
where is she ? " So Auntie Pussy looked round, and
said something about her soon coming and we had to
go forward, for there were more people coming up.
It was very vexatious, and Auntie Pussy was very
vexed, for of course I should have come up with my
own Mamma. However I daresay the Queen was not
angry, for when Mamma did come up with Winny, she
smiled at her, and said, " Is that another of your little
ones ? " Well, the dancing began, and I danced very
nearly every one thing. There was a reel, which I

couldn't dance, but the Prince of Wales danced just opposite to where I was standing ; so I saw his beautiful dancing famously. I danced once with Willy, with the son of the Belgian Minister, with one of the Farquharsons, and I forget the rest. Aggy again danced with Prince Alfred, and talked to Princess Alice, oh, happy girl ! There was supper like last time, and I had wine and seltzer water, and ices, which were delicious. Little Prince Leopold retired after the first quadrille, led by a grand lady. The ball was over at about half-past 12, when the Queen came down from the dais, and made a lovely curtsey to everyone. I managed to get with Winny near the side door at which she went out, and got a dear bow and smile to ourselves. Then came the National Anthem. Then we managed to find our belongings and went home. Oh, how delightful it was !

LONDON, *April* 26*th*, 1856.—We stayed in bed till I don't know what o'clock. I was not a bit tired, but oh, last night, how my feet did ache ! M. acknowledges that when she saw us set off, she and Edward agreed that they would have liked to go. She is such an odd old creature, this is the last chance she could have had, for next year she will be too old.

LONDON, *May* 14*th*, 1856.—Oh, on the 14th, we all went to Fanny Kemble's reading of " King Lear " : it fully has answered my highest expectation, has grown on me since. The most wonderful variation and power of expression, every single character with a different voice and look, the most astonishing change in the voices of each man, a different look of malice and wickedness, a different toned voice to the two atrocious sisters : oh, one positively hated her, as one saw her put on one of those demoniac faces, and the beauty of the change to Cordelia's quiet placidness, and touching sorrow, or to the broken-down, majestic, agonized old king. The worst was she missed so very much of Edgar, and a great deal of the scene on the heath, and all the scene with Gloucester on the top of the cliff, and more besides. But she could not have done all, I suppose ; *two* madnesses would have been all but impossible.

LONDON, *May 23rd*, 1856.—We went with Papa and
Ed. Talbot to the Princess's, to see " The Winter's
Tale "; I never imagined, much less saw, anything
so beautiful and perfect as the scenery : the palace
in the first scene with its splendid dresses, incense
vases, lovely women and children, statues, etc., was
lovely, also a splendid interlude bringing in the moon
and then a glorious sunrise. Apollo in his chariot.
Then the judgment scene was fine and the statue scene
perfectly wonderful. But the acting—there were Mr.
and Mrs. Kean, but it all seems to me so very vulgar,
accent, gesture and all. Nevertheless we were enchanted, and a Pyrrhic dance was exceedingly beautiful.

LONDON, *May 29th*, 1856.—Her Majesty's birthday,
God bless her with many more happy and prosperous
years on the throne of this realm ! The day, moreover,
of the illuminations in honour of the Peace, the which
we went to see in the following manner. We set off
at about 8 o'clock, fondly hoping to reach Spencer
House by nine, when " festivities were to commence."
All the day large crowds had been spreading over the
town, which seemed gradually to thicken and condense,
and some time before, and all during and after dinner,
one continuous unbroken stream poured past our
windows, till it almost made one dizzy to look at them.
We had the most knowing little illumination, large
night-lamps hung on wire in this shape. Well, we set
off, and got on famously for about a hundred yards,
when took place the first stoppage. From that time
we went on at the most wonderful pace, standing still
for twenty minutes or more together, and when one did
move, at the slowest possible crawl. For before, behind,
on either side, sometimes creeping under the horses'
necks, as far as one could see through the lit-up darkness,
was an unbroken black mass of swaying heads, flowing
on incessantly, and all round a hoarse murmur, intermingled with laughter, little shouts, and a few raised
voices. But the whole crowd was in the highest state
of good humour and docility, nearly every face had a
delighted smile on it, children, some such tinies, were
held up to look at the blaze of illuminations, jokes

passed between the occupants of the thronged vans,
omnibuses, carts, carriages, waggons, etc., and the
foot-passengers, and oh ! most amusing of all, were the
things addressed to our carriage, a subject of much
interest, Papa being in his uniform, cocked hat, etc.
" Whose your hatter ? "   " How many cocks did you
shoot in the Crimea ? "   (allusion to the feather).
" Ooray for the Duke of Wellington ! " (a little cheer
raised).   " Lord Ebrington ! "   " Lord Balmerino ! "
" Lord Lovat ! "   " Colonel Windham ! "   " You're
a beauty ! "   " Room for another there ? "   " Here's
a lot of pretty faces ! "   " Take your time, Miss Lucy ! "
" Now then ! "   " Whose your tailor ? " etc., etc., etc.
When we got to Trafalgar Square there was a delighted
sort of rushing cheer, several rockets from the Parks
sprung over the tops of the houses, scattering their
bright stars.   It was at this juncture that we did get
a little despairing as to ever reaching our destination ;
the fireworks had certainly begun, and we had been
nearly an hour coming the bit of a way from George
Street to Trafalgar Square.   We had once asked a
policeman if we could get on better.   His answer was :
" You will not get there these two hours."   But, just
here, Mrs. Talbot applied to a superintendent, on a
white horse, who went before us, cleared a way directly,
and to our amazement we drove off briskly, round a
way which proved much less crowded, where of course
we met with some stopping but in course of time arrived
safely at Spencer House, whither we went to get a good
view.   We were in very tidy time, and were ushered
on to the terrace, among a lot of old generals and officers.
It was very beautiful but rather same ; however I
enjoyed it immensely.   Some of the rockets were most
lovely, scattering bright showers of gold or silver that
looked like beautiful sheaves of corn.   Then after
these and others had gone on for a couple of hours, I
suppose, there was suddenly an enormous explosion,
a huge, dazzling blaze spread high upwards, so that,
looking down, we saw a vast sea of upturned faces,
packed thicker than I can describe, lit up in a weird-
like, glowing lustre ; it was too dark to see the bodies
they belonged to ; bright fantastical patterns were

cut in fire in the midst of the blaze, rockets hissed,
whizzed, exploded, cracked, popped, rushed, boomed, the
blaze increased, " God save the Queen " was traced in
letters of living flame in the midst, a rushing excited
sound of cheering rose from the gazing millions, an
immense quantity of dazzling rockets shot upwards—
and it was over.   I never saw anything more striking
than that last display.   Then we went in, and had some
supper, saw dear Tallee,[1] and little Harry Lyttelton,
much gone off in beauty, and set off again home, which
transit was accomplished like the former one, quite if
not more difficult.   I only heard one thing the least
like even a bad word, *that* was only " Confound you,"
from a man who had to rush under our horses' necks.
It was delightfully amusing, and so the people seemed
to think.   We reached home at past one.   There never
had been a more tractable and orderly crowd, only
once did I see anything like a dangerous squash, and
there were hardly any accidents.   The people had all
dispersed by next morning.   I was so delighted all
the time.

HAGLEY, *June 5th*, 1856.—On the 5th came our new
governess, a nice real comfortable English one, ladylike
and pleasant-looking, she has begun us so well : our
week divided into Monday and Thursday for Italian,
Tuesday and Friday for French, Wednesday and
Saturday for English, with a half-holiday on the latter
day.   Our studies are learning of Goldoni's plays,
Italian conversation, verb, translation and reading of
" Metastasio," writing translation of " Le notti Romane,"
hour's music a day, small hand copy, reading and
writing abstract of Arnold's " Rome," translation of
Bossuet's " Histoire Universelle " to English and back
again, translation of " Pigeon Pie " (Miss Yonge),
drawing, repetition of Racine's poetry, and Campan's
" Fr. Conversations," reading of Lamartine's " Gironde,"
Fr. dictation, writing of English composition,
arithmetic, repetition of Cornwall's geography, Longfellow's poetry, Mangnall's Fr. dates, reading of
Reed's " English History," and poetry, definition of

---

[1] Her cousin, Lady Sarah Spencer.

words, and mental arithmetic. We ought to get on,
I think.

HAGLEY, *July* 19*th*, 1856.—Baron Alderson, the judge,
his son-and-marshal, and Mr. (Matthew) Arnold, the
son of the great Arnold, came. The baron, very
amusing, his son very like a small yellow rabbit. I
don't like Mr. Arnold :

> I do not like you, Dr. Fell ;
> The reason why, I cannot tell ;
> But this I *do* know, very well,
> I do not like you, Dr. Fell.

Those are very much my feelings. But I can tell
partly : he seems light and vain, and does not talk
sense.

HAGLEY, *July* 20*th*, 1856.—Mr. Arnold did not kneel
in church, because he had no hassock ; rather horrid
for a strong man. Moreover, he recommended Mamma
to go to a dissenting chapel to hear some wonderful
" preacher " ; I don't like Mr. Arnold, but I do like the
old Baron.

HAGLEY, *July* 25*th*, 1856.—Oh, such a break [1] ! Be-
hold, Uncle Fritz makes a present to George, in honour
of his Godsonship, of an estate in New Zealand ! ! ! ! ! ! !
So my small fourth brother, aged nine, is the Honble.
George William Spencer Lyttelton, landed Proprietor !
It is really most delightful, and a whole son taken off
Papa's hands, and so nice his son to have land there.
It will be of real value when he is old enough to go out,
increases in the same every year.

[1] Appendix A.

BOOK III
SEPTEMBER 1856—APRIL 1858

.

INTRODUCTION TO BOOK III

THE third volume of the Diary covers about a year and a half, between September 1856 and April 1858. It is headed " Begun aged 15 and 12 days. Ended aged 16 and 8 months." It is still therefore the diary of a child, but a rather unusually mature child. And that maturity, or at least the seriousness in which it was partly exhibited, was increased by the principal event recorded in this volume : the death of Lady Lyttelton. Her twelfth and last child, a son, was born in February 1857 ; and it is curious to read that his sister, unconscious of the name by which she herself was to be known after a few more years, strongly objected to the suggestion that he should be called Frederic (presumably after Lord Spencer), even declaring that name to be " my abomination " ! He was in the end called Alfred, and was, from the first, as she writes a few months later, a " sunny and prosperous " baby with a look of " happy thoughtfulness," as his baptising uncle discovered, giving promise in both these ways of what he was to become, the adored Alfred Lyttelton of Eton and Cambridge, cricket and law and politics ; whose personal charm was so extraordinary that men who had only seen him for a few hours loved him for life ; whose voice and manner, as Lord Curzon wrote after his death, " seemed almost to partake of the nature of a caress " ; whose character was such that Lord Oxford, speaking as Prime Minister in the House of Commons, said of him that " he, perhaps, of all men of this generation, came nearest to the mould and ideal of manhood which every English father would like to see his son aspire to, and if possible attain." It is a great thing to give birth to twelve children, especially when the last is such a child as Alfred Lyttelton. But his poor mother paid for it with her life. The proud father, all unconscious of the near impending fate, might boast, as his daughter relates, that "it would be difficult to find a man who, a few weeks before his fortieth birthday, would have a twelfth child, and could look round upon his multitudinous family without a noticeable grey hair." He adored his wife, but seems to have been strangely blind to her increasing weakness. She had for some time not been in good health, and after Alfred's birth the references in the Diary to anxiety about her become more and more frequent till she died on August 17th, 1857. Her devoted sister Mrs. Gladstone was with her at Hagley for the last few weeks. The loss to her husband and her children was immeasurable. Her loving influence while she lived and her cherished memory after her death counted greatly in the making of all the older children. Gladstone wrote of her : "She seemed to be one of those rare spirits who do not need affliction to draw them to their Lord. . . . When she was told she was to die, her pulse did not change : the Last Communion appeared wholly to sever her from the world, but she smiled upon her husband within a minute of the time when the Spirit fled."

Outside this great event the Diary describes much the same life as its predecessor. There is the same continual riding and walking ; and the games include "battledore and shuttlecock" and croquet, "a nice Irish game," which makes the first of many appearances ; whist begins to replace commerce ; and a play is acted at Hagley with great excitement and success. In the last volume she had recorded her dislike of the young Matthew Arnold who came to stay at Hagley as a judge's marshal : in this he is replaced by an older poet, Monckton Milnes, afterwards Lord Houghton, who read aloud his own poetry, and is pronounced "odd, nice, rough, ugly, and good." The diarist is frequently seen taking classes and going to read to sick parishioners old and

young; is much occupied with the Christmas decora-
tion of the church, and writes at great length of its
testoration, which was almost a rebuilding, and ended
in a reopening with which the volume concludes.
There are entries which seem, happily, a long way off
to-day : references to typhus fever and to anxiety
about every railway journey as an alarming and dangerous experience. So to-day, happily, one can hardly
imagine a state of affairs like that described after the
burning of Hawarden church, when, in the belief that
it was the work of criminals, " all the clergy are sending
for six-barrelled revolvers "; and a rector coming to
dinner shows " his beautiful little pocket revolver."
And it is fortunately not now necessary, when people
visit their undergraduate sons at Christ Church, to
purchase chloride to purify their rooms from unwhole-
some smells, as Mrs. Talbot is here reported to have
done when she took Lucy Lyttelton to visit her son
John, afterwards Member for the University. And, less
happily, it is not now possible after going to Merton
Chapel to walk straight " into the fresh country fields
with the Cherwell running by them." Besides Oxford,
there are also visits to Canterbury and Tunbridge
Wells. These take place from the Talbots' house in
Kent, where the young Lucy stayed for her Confirmation,
and while preparing for it discovered the delights of
fishing and bird-nesting, as well as the risks of going
on an expedition with her father, who turned out to have
only half a crown in his pocket ! His little book, " The
Glynnese Glossary," is full of allusions to the family
impecuniosity : which in this volume is painfully seen
in the difficulty arising of providing the invalid Lady
Lyttelton with a proper carriage. In fact, Mrs. Gladstone has to bring hers, with coachman and horses, to
Hagley. After Lady Lyttelton's death, presumably
for reasons of economy, the family house in St. James's
Square is given up.

In this volume, as in the last, the books read are
frequently mentioned. Among the poets are Words-

I—6

worth, Byron, and Longfellow ; among the novelists
Scott and Jane Austen and Charles Reade and Miss
Yonge ; among other writers Prescott, Macaulay, and
Sir James Stephen. Other intellectual amusements
include hearing Mario and Grisi sing, visiting an exhibition of Turners at Marlborough House, and attending
a debate at the House of Commons. Meanwhile all
the old intimacy with the various cousins plays its full
part : the Gladstones and Glynnes, in particular, make
very frequent appearances ; and there is a curious
entry, written at Althorp after her great-uncle's death,
showing a doubt as to what she was in future to call
her cousin, the new Lord Spencer, afterwards the statesman. " We are put to it what to call Althorp, but
there's nothing to say beside that name ; so we avoid
naming him as much as possible. He isn't at all
altered, save that he has whiskers." In the end he
remained " Althorp " all his life.

GEORGE WILLIAM, 4TH LORD LYTTELTON.
From a drawing by George Richmond, R.A.

DIARY, SEPTEMBER 1856—APRIL 1858

September 1st, 1856.—Well! I wonder how many things will be in this book when I finish it, if I ever do so. I wonder what length of time will elapse ere I end it. I wonder whether when I end it I shall be able honestly to say that I have mounted Higher, come Nearer. Excelsior! My own motto. I like beginning this book on the first day of my birthday month, though no particular event characterized it, beyond a cricket match, which, after a long contest, we lost.

HAGLEY, *September 15th, 1856.*—On the night of the 15th Mr. Milnes read aloud some beautiful poetry of his own. He is such an odd, nice, rough, ugly, good (apparently) man.

HAGLEY, *September 20th, 1856.*—When we were back we had some games of croquet, a nice Irish game introduced here by Miss Smith. I only won once. In the evening I came up to dine at the Rectory, and Uncle B. read aloud. A very nice day altogether.

HAGLEY, *September 25th, 1856.*—A game of croquet in the morning, a nice drive into Clent in the afternoon to give some pudding to the boy Cowper : found him and his eyes nearly well.

HAGLEY, *December 17th, 18th, 19th, 1856.*—The most glorious plans for the church arrived. The church will be entirely re-seated, and lengthened considerably. The galleries pulled down and the whole new-roofed. All the windows new, except the old S.E. and the Turner one, the vestry and organ-room to adjoin the chancel, which is to be perfectly restored, with encaustic pavement, stained glass, seven steps, sedilia, and straight altar-rail. The obnoxious monuments to be stowed away in less glaring places. A bell-turret, as at present of course neither tower or steeple are feasible.

HAGLEY, *December 22nd*, 1856.—At it in earnest ! The evergreens are dragged head and shoulders into the billiard-room, and we began business by measuring off the lengths of cord, by pack-thread measurements taken yesterday in the church, with Mr. Johnstone, he, the invaluable ! We worked like Trojans and progressed rapidly.

HAGLEY, *January 1st*, 1857.—The whole tribe of Gladstones poured into the house to-day, and we make up the goodly number of eighteen children under 17. Willy and Stephy, at least, did not come to-day.

HAGLEY, *January 2nd, 3rd*, 1857.—Willy and Stephy turned up. The dear old house is choked, overflowing, echoing with children. The meals are the fun. Breakfasts are composed of two tables, a loaf and a half or two loaves, a plate of bread and butter, three or four good-sized pats of butter, two teapots, a dish of meat, a dish of bacon, and a toast-rack full. They are attended by Miss Smith presiding at the top of one of the tables, dispensing drinkables, me at the bottom, dispensing meat, bacon, and butter, and cutting hunches of bread like a machine ; at the top of the other table, Meriel presiding. Round the two tables are little Mademoiselle, Albert, Nevy, Spencer, Winny, May, Agnes, Stephy, Mary and Lena. The four little girls are at Meriel's table, the rest at ours. The noise pervading the room, as much from scolders as scolded, from bellowers as bellowed at, from children, boys, women, girls, may be imagined, mingled with clatter of crockery, pouring of tea, hewing of bread, and scrumping of jaws.

HAGLEY, *January 4th, 5th*, 1857.—Oh, the whirlpool of excitement we are fizzing in. The PLAY is to come off on the 7th. The actors are to be (I put them in ages) : William Henry Gladstone, aged 16. Lucy Caroline Lyttelton, aged 15. Agnes Gladstone, aged 14. Charles George Lyttelton, aged 14. Stephen Edward Gladstone, aged 12. Albert Victor Lyttelton, aged 12. Neville Gerald Lyttelton, aged 11. Mary Gladstone, aged 11. George William Spencer Lyttelton, aged 9. Helen Gladstone, aged 9. Lavinia Lyttelton, aged 8. Mary Catherine Lyttelton, aged 6. Arthur

Temple Lyttelton, aged 5. Henry Neville Gladstone,
aged 5. Robert Henry Lyttelton, aged 5. Herbert
John Gladstone, aged 3. All these are getting up their
parts in different ways ; rehearsals are ceaseless, lessons
droop, disorder prevails.

HAGLEY, *January 7th*, 1857.—Behold ! the excitement
becomes dangerous and boundless. A last grand rehearsal, and I feel secure of my part. An immense
amount of work is got through, and the dresses, which
arrived last night, tried on and applauded. At last
we go and get ready, soon after tea. The whole thing
is to be in the gallery, behind the pillars, between which
hangs the splendid dark red curtain, which draws not
vulgarly aside, but right up. . . . I first went to the
nurseries, where I saw the eight small fairies attired,
winged and star-crowned ; Mary Gladstone, the eldest,
being the Queen, distinguished by a larger coronet and
a star-tipped wand. They looked most aery in their
short standing-out transparent skirtlets and spangled
wings.

HAGLEY, *January 15th*, 1857.—In the evening the
great Monro (staying at the Rectory) lectured in the
school on Longfellow, chiefly his new poem " Hiawatha."
It was about twice too long but delighted me much,
from the surpassing beauty of his quotations, occasional
grand poetry of his language, and the way he appreciates, and has made others appreciate, " Hiawatha,"
which is throughout curious and interesting and very
beautiful in parts.

LONDON, *February 7th*, 1857.—When I was called
this morning, Amelia whispered to me that the Baby
might be expected soon, that Locock had been in the
house during the night (having returned), and Fergusson.
She frightened me dreadfully when she bent over me ;
oh, such a turn ! In fact one's anxiety was great after
the 'words had been said. I wrote out a short prayer
for the little ones, and made them say it with their
morning prayers. Little they knew of it all ! Then
I got up myself and when half-dressed, Miss Smith
came into the room. I said : " Oh dear, so it's coming
to an upshot at last ? " She said yes, but went out

directly. I said my prayers and had just ended them, feeling much comforted by them, when Auntie Pussy came eagerly into the room : " The Baby's born ! " I was stricken with astonishment, I never expected it was to happen at once : if to-day at all, did not think till much later, fancying Amelia's words only meant the illness had just begun, or was likely to begin. " Oh, Auntie Pussy !—boy or girl ? " " Oh, boy—never mind what it is." " Oh, how is she ? " " So quiet and well." Oh, the relief ! This dialogue was just outside my room door, and took about four seconds. We both dashed away, Auntie P. stole into the room, and I rushed to the stairs. I had to pass the little room destined for the baby, the door was ajar, and there I saw the broad back of Loftus the nurse, and a tiny red head, covered with brown down. A thrill shot through me. On the landing were Miss Smith and Meriel. A demand for ice, for water was heard ; Miss S. and M. shot noiselessly downstairs, and appeared with the requisite articles. I seized hold of the pail of ice, and put it down by Baby's door. Locock came out : we sat down on the window-seat and presently heard a tiny little wailing cry. I crept in to look at the Baby, and saw a small pink scrap, with quantities of brown hair, and large eyes. Oh, the *precious* ! I forgot to say that after Auntie P. had told me, I met Miss S. who asked eagerly, " Boy or girl ? " When I told her, she said something about Papa, and we had a sort of race downstairs. I reached his room, told him. He made a curious pucker with his mouth, opened his eyes wide, and said, " A boy ! Why, I was never told ! " and stamped upstairs with a terrible noise. I followed him ; on the top he said to Miss S. and me with a delighted chuckle, " Another boy ! What in the world shall we do with another boy ! " and went into the room. Well, we sat on the stairs for some time, and baby was taken in to see Mamma. I went on tiptoe to the room-door, which was ajar, peeped through the crack, and saw a bit of Mamma, heard her dear weak voice saying, " Oh, what a darling ! " —and fondling him. There was Locock and Loftus there, the former in a state of rapture over the baby, whom Papa took in his arms to the light, I suppose to see the colour of his eyes, which is always his mania. When at last we went downstairs (it was now about 9 o'clock) we found Auntie P. and Mrs. Talbot in Papa's room, and had a quiet cry together, with a gushing overpowering sense of thankfulness and relief that made the tears grateful. By and bye, Uncle William came to the house door. I let him in, and he and Auntie P. had a confabulation in a low voice. He had heard : how I don't quite know, for Locock had declared that no one must be told till more time had passed. He seemed hardly to imagine that she could be so well, with good reason as we heard afterwards. We went to the schoolroom (I had told the little ones, who were first utterly incredulous and then over the moon : had known nothing about it) ; and there Auntie P., Mrs. Talbot, Miss S., M., and the children knelt while I read, with such an egg in my throat ! some earnest thanksgivings which were the greatest comforts to us. Oh dear ! I think it was now that Auntie P. and the others told Meriel and me how much more awful the danger which was over had been than we knew.

LONDON, *February 26th*, 1857.—Meriel went to the debating in the House of Lords, I to that in the House of Commons with Miss S., on the China question. It was very interesting : we heard Labouchere, flatissimus,[1] especially coming as he did after Cobden, of whose speech we did not hear the beginning, but what we did was most interesting and excellent. He made the motion. We also heard Sir Bulwer Lytton, but lost his speech, which we hear was excellent, for he spoke so loud that we heard nothing but ringing echoes. There were one or two others ; then in the beginning of Lord John Russell we were sent for. So horrid ; we ought to have heard him out. It was one of the most delightful things to go to that I have ever been at ! I was enraged by the abominable grating we had to sit behind.

LONDON, *February 27th, 28th*, 1857.—Mamma lies

[1] Appendix A.

on a bed-couch during the day, and is getting on : such nice appetite. Such a debated point Baby's name : Duodecimus, or Octavius, though appropriate, have been rejected. Papa dares to think of Frederic. My abomination. Mamma talks of Grenville or Grey. I have been building on the hope of being his god-mother more than I can express, but I hear that Aunt Emmy is to be. I suppose I shall not be confirmed in time, but it is *such* a dreadful disappointment.

OXFORD, *March 8th*, 1857.—One of the happiest days I have ever spent. As soon as we were dressed, after Mrs. Talbot had read aloud the Xtian Year for the day, Johnny appeared, in his cap and gown to please me, for he says the men of Ch. Ch. are not wont to walk about in them, though every other college does, and he is an anxious martyr to manners and customs. Well, under his escort, we walked to Ch. Ch., which I am happy to say we found free from smell, and Johnny's rooms much the better for the chloride of zinc, and looking bright and comfortable. The breakfast one is much longer than broad, and had its whole length filled with the breakfast tables, covered with an elegant *spread*. The grate amused me : its bars were of the most collegiate and ecclesiastic appearance, of this shape.[1] Mr. Majendie soon turned up : in fact we had, I thought, rather too much of these gentlemen, one or other of whom, or all together, were with us nearly all day. The toast was cut in a collegiate way also, triangles of an impressive appearance. We had an excellent breakfast ; the coffee alone being rather inferior. Beautiful sort of hashed fish, which was obtained after some little difficulty, caused by some regulation against the importation of fish for breakfast. However we had it, and it was lucky we did, for Mr. Majendie had two or three helps of it. Indeed, one of my notes of Oxford was the large quantity everybody eat, myself included, for there was no help for it. . . .

We went to luncheon at Mr. Majendie's rooms in Peckwater Quad, adjoining Tom Quad (e.g. Johnny's quad), where we found an excellent *spread*. A young

---

[1] With a sketch.

Mr. Villars, son of the new Bishop (on which account Mrs. Talbot warned me not to speak disrespectfully of Lord Palmerston's bishops : as if I was likely to !), Mr. Henniker, and Mr. Palmer, all came in to luncheon : all being Johnny's friends. They made pleasant talk, and we had a very good luncheon. It was in fact a very complete dinner.

LONDON, *March 25th*, 1857.—M. and I had the lark of going to Eton, with Papa, Auntie P., and Agnes. We found Charles in the heat of a game of fives, which he lost by one I believe in our very eye. However it was an excellent game. All were flourishing. We dined at Seymour Neville's rooms, which he is making elegant to suit his Minor Canonship. It was great fun. Before luncheon we saw the boys' rooms, with characteristic differences between Charles' and Willy's, and Mr. Coleridge who received us most affably, and told us several mournful particulars about the health of his wife, whose brain is in some melancholy state of dilapidation : not softening like that of his friend Miss Hawtrey, but something analogous. We went in the afternoon to Eton Chapel, wherein the flood of boys looked very striking, especially when they all stood up, with a sort of rushing sound. But the unfortunate thing was that there were no proper responses, only a muttered whisper. We went to the Castle : most beautiful view.

LONDON, *March 31st*, 1857.—Baby was baptized. Uncle Billy came on purpose to do it ; the first of the whole twelve that he ever has. Such an addition to the brightness of to-day. I went to see the precious one dressed : he was perfectly good during the trying operation, though it was his crying time. He looked lovely in his robes, and Mamma's wedding-veil, with the tiny Christening cap surrounding his little placid face, which struck Uncle B. on first sight with its look of happy thoughtfulness. Mamma came to church, so nice. Mr. Selfe, Althorp, and Aunt Emmy were godparents ; Mr. Cavendish and Auntie P. representing the two latter. Oh, the beauty of the service and Uncle B's reading of it ! The little one was wide awake all the time, gazing round him with his beauteous eyes, and moving his little arms. He never made one cry, and only uttered a little low sound when Uncle Billy took him tenderly, becoming quite quiet again, and looking earnestly up at him. The Water touched the calm white forehead, and the Cross marked Alfred Lyttelton as Christ's soldier and servant, sealing him as God's child, purifying his immortal soul, and filling it with the Spirit that makes him an inheritor of glorious Eternity. God for ever bless the new Christian enrolled under His banner.

BRIGHTON, *April 21st*, 1857.—Nevy and Spencer went back to Geddington ; niobissimus,[1] poor, dear, old fellows.

BRIGHTON, *April 23rd*, 1857.—Mrs. Talbot came up again. A lovely apparition sent to be a moment's ornament, for—
April 24th, 1857—She went back again.

BRIGHTON, *April 27th, 28th, 29th*, 1857.—Such a number of little tobies up and down the parade. (So I call all wicker carriages, in fond remembrance of Toby and the little black one at St. Leonard's.) Had the most enchanting boating in a long boat, with four oars, Charles, Albert, and two sailors. Herewith we skimmed away briskly ; to the Pier in five minutes, a little coasting, straight out a mile and a half to sea, gaining upon, beating, and heading a boatful considerably in front of us, rowing up to a large coal brig, letting her pass us some hundred yards, with her sails all spread to the fair wind, beating her, under the pier, out to the end of Kemp Town, and home in an hour and a half.

FALCONHURST, *May 16th*, 1857.—Oh, such a beautiful house ! Built of yellow-grey stone, large, with one wing, and a long pretty range of offices. Bow windows, and all of them plate glass. A very pretty front door, with a cut iron hook for handle. Opens into a good-sized carpeted hall, with such pretty white and gold pillars, supporting the staircase landing and passage above. The staircase is of dark waxed wood with the

[1] Appendix A.

most beautiful banisters I have ever seen. Oak, and very massive and low, with some of the interstices filled up with T and one with C, I suppose for Mrs. Talbot, as her name is Caroline. The staircase leading into a long passage, out of which open four rooms, the first and last of which are Mamma's and ours, facing the stairs. Both with bow windows, and such delightful rooms. The passage turns down at the top leading to Cecil and Miss Harris' room, and the schoolroom. On the ground floor are the library and a little study opening out of it, which rooms we occupy. Then a large uninhabited drawing-room, with pillars at one end. These all open out of a passage corresponding with the one above. At the end of the passage, the nice large dining-room. A door on the opposite side of the passage, leading to the kitchen and other offices, all on the same floor : so nice. On the south of the house a terrace, and all round it a large garden. The approach on the north. The view a pretty cultivated wooded country, with a few rare cottages, and much rising and sinking ground. One or two woods close to the house. On rising ground within a quarter of an hour's walk, the little church, whose spire is seen from the house. The trees bushy and plentiful, but small and slender, without much variation, being chiefly dwarf oak. Witherby, the butler, showed us to-day a darling linnet's nest, with five birdlings in it, in a little box tree close to the house. We also saw a thrush's nest in a laurel in the garden, with five eggs. There is daily service, and we went through a lovely wood, by a little grassy path to the church, which is lovely. Of the same stone as the house, only one aisle, and a beautiful porch, with these words over the church-door : " This Church was founded and begun by the Honble. John Chetwynd Talbot, and completed in fulfilment of his instructions by his widow, to the glory of the Most Holy Trinity. The memory of the just is blessed." So beautiful ; surely what he would like to be there.

FALCONHURST, *May 19th*, 1857.—We have found two more nests : a chaffinch's, and a darling robin's among the roots of an oak, six eggs, one a cuckoo's, which I rejoiced to purloin.

FALCONHURST, *May 26th*, 1857.—Mr. Hunt saw me
again : went through some of the Commandments,
and spoke about Amelia, whom he saw, and advised
me to go on speaking to her. A very nice talk. We
have got in the garden seven nests, all eggs except the
linnet's. Besides those mentioned elsewhere, a cole-
tit's lying on its side on the ground wherein we found
first two, then three, then four, then five, and now six
lovely eggs, pure white, with red spots on the thick
end. And I found a perfect little chaffinch nest, in
a Portugal laurel, with three eggs, and there is another
with three eggs in a little cedar. There was a sparrow's
near this one, but alas ! four pretty eggs disappeared
mysteriously. We have taken the cuckoo's egg from
the robin, for it would only turn the little robins out.
Alack ! to-day an egg vanished from my nest, and
horror of horrors ! abominable Gip, Edward's dog,
caught and killed a darling linnet, now full-fledged and
able to flutter about. A most mysterious event has
happened with regard to the nest in the cedar. The
three eggs were hatched a few days ago, first two, and
then the third. Visiting it on Monday, I found but
two birdlings, the nest weighed down on one side, and
the third suspended by its poor little claw to a branch
below, quite cold and dead. Having fully ascertained
this tragical fact, and in vain tried to recall the little
thing to life, I buried it, and settled to my Prescott's
" Peru " in the library, when Behemoth and Cecil appeared frantically at the window. " Lucy ! Lucy ! it's
alive, and we've put it back in the nest." " Alive ! "
quoth I, " why I've buried it ! " They stuck to their
assertion, having found a little nestling under the little
cedar, in a weak state but alive, of exactly the appearance
of the other two, which after a little warming, they put
in the nest, where it recovered. Behemoth disinterred
my little bird, and produced it studded with bits of
mould, to prove the truth of my words. And the event
remains a mystery, making us believe that take 1 from
3, 3 remain, or else, that transmigration of souls—and
bodies too—exists among birds. . . .
(By the bye, I have had two rides with Edward, on
a little mouthless, perverse creature, whom I force

with some difficulty to follow my way, not her own.)
We had a delightful picnic tea in the wood. Our own
fire, boiling, etc.

FALCONHURST, *May 27th,* 1857.—We boiled two eggs
ourselves, to a nicety, and the elders came to look
at us. Agnes has actually been to the Opera !

FALCONHURST, *May 30th,* 1857.—I went to look at
the robin's nest, wherein all the eggs are hatched but
one. The chaffinch's in the P. laurel have vanished
like the others : it must be a weasel. We went in the
afternoon to a pond some way off, where we fished :
Witherby presiding. I had been in common with all
the others tantalized by perpetual bites, and had twice
I think brought a roach above water, which then
splashed away again, and had in some despair changed
my place, when behold ! two or three little bobs of
the float, a very great one, a dash of it towards the
middle of the pond, a stiff tightening of the line, a
frantic tug upwards on my part, a flight through the
air of a great flapping fish and a landing of a—carp ! ! ! ! !

With this overwhelming exploit, my afternoon deeds
ceased ; I caught no more. Two little roach had been
caught before, one by Cecil, and one by Edward, but
the capture of the carp seemed to exhaust the pool,
for even bobs of the float became rare. But it was all
great fun, especially the frequent excited appeals to
Oracle Witherby, on the occasion of deceptive Bobs,
or Roberts, as Meriel's wit denominated them. We
ordered the carp to be done for dinner, in spite of its
single blessedness, and had the two small fry for tea.
But alas ! the carp was let fall by the culpable cook
and rendered unfit for presentation.

FALCONHURST, *Thursday, June 4th,* 1857.—I was confirmed at Penshurst Church with many others by the
Archbishop of Canterbury, Sumner. We left Falconhurst
early ; I was so sorry Aggy didn't come and wasn't confirmed with me. She and Cecil had got me a little bunch
of daisies, which I loved taking with me. It was very
quiet and all fear and trembling seemed gone. The
long drive was nice and stilling, and the glorious bells
chimed as we came up to the church. I had Papa on

one side, Mamma on the other. We waited in the church for a long time before the Archbishop came, but it didn't seem so to me. And I seem to remember nothing very distinctly till I went up and knelt on the altar step, feeling the strangest thrill as I did so for the first time. And I know how I waited breathlessly for my turn, with the longing for it to be safe done, half feeling that something might yet prevent it. And I know that I felt when it was I that should come next at last, though my face was hid down in my hands. And I know that I shall never forget the touch of the hand on my head : " Defend, O Lord, this Thy servant with Thy heavenly Grace . . ." and the glorious rush of trembling calm that followed in indescribable feeling. And then I went back and knelt down. The crying came then, and the Thanksgiving and Prayers mingled and repeated in unutterable gratitude, while the " Defend, O Lord," blended with them in the gentle faltering words unceasingly. And the new Life has begun.

FALCONHURST, *June 5th*, 1857.—Mr. Hunt [1] saw me before the evening of yesterday, and again either to-day or Saturday Agnes and I went through the Communion Service with him. My two godparents, Aunt Coque and Uncle Stephen, were there. Aunt Coque gave me yesterday the medallion of a Head crowned with thorns : most beautiful. I have had two such letters : one from Uncle Billy and one from Dove.[2]

FALCONHURST, *June 8th*, 1857.—Our last day ! I went to the dear little church for the last service, and hovering about near it was caught by Mr. Hunt, who walked and talked home with me. A sort of recapitulation of what he has said before. I made Witherby show me at the last minute a cunning nightingale's and a nettle-creeper's nests, close to each other in some brushwood, and was only back in time for some good-byes. I saved a daisy from among my Confirmation ones which were all expanding in water, stuffed the beautiful little nest of the Portugal laurel chaffinch into my pocket, with the cuckoo's egg in it, and we

[1] The Vicar of the parish, a lifelong friend of the Talbot family.
[2] Her former governess, Mrs. Oxley.

all set off in the car, and two other conveyances : Papa and Mamma in the pony carriage. We have left a bright blessed time behind us.

HAGLEY, *June 19th*, 1857.—Mamma had a drive in the Robins' carriage : a most acceptable loan, view [1] our deficiency of vehicle, for she cannot bear the rough jolting of the pony carriage : she has had one or two drives in it ; me driving, to my extreme pride. Mamma seems quite to trust me, which she never used to with the ponies.

HAGLEY, *June 30th*, 1857.—Our coach-horses ! took Mamma out in the brichtzka for the first time, with good success ; Uncle William's Budget, spirited and a desperate puller, and a slow solemn creature whom Mamma has named Oenone, viewing [1] Papa's beautiful translation of that poem, just printed.

HAGLEY, *August 13th, 14th, 15th, 16th*, 1857.—It is of no use—God has set His seal. She speaks about it, and the soul-light on her face makes her wonderful to look at. On Sunday she kissed all her twelve poor children, and said good-bye, and then she took the Blessed Communion with many of us, and then she lay still, waiting. Her precious eyes were very blue and clear, shining strangely, and looking on, away, beyond us, except when she turned them on us with a depth of wistful tenderness. No more suffering all Sunday, and such precious words : remembering everyone ; no fear and distress.

HAGLEY, *August 17th*, 1857.—Suffering, and discomfort, and wearing, and sinking, only for a little while more. The Peace of God, which passeth all understanding, is hers now—it's all over, all left behind ; the Everlasting Morning has dawned on the short weary night. With Christ, which is far better, and all tears wiped away ; and the calm of Paradise, and the Arms of God.

HAWARDEN, *October 22nd*, 1857.—We read " Waverley " in the evening ; it seems to me heavy and prosy, but improves as it goes on.

[1] Appendix A.

HAWARDEN, *October 23rd*, 1857.—We read " Waverley " in the evening : it gets interesting.

HAWARDEN, *October 29th*, 1857.—The much-loved, time-honoured old mother church was set on fire between three and four in the morning, and before the afternoon was destroyed with the exception of the walls, tower, and chancel windows and stalls. The whole of the nave and aisle roofs fell in, and the chancel one will have to come down. The W. window, stone work and all, is destroyed ; the tracery of the others still stands ; all the glass shivered, except in the chancel. Miss S. awoke me at about ½ past 5 to tell me, news having been sent to the Castle of it. We scrambled on to the leads of the house, and from thence saw the red glow beating high into the sky above the trees. Before 7½ we went to see. The flames were then being subdued, but the whole floor of the body of the church was a mass of burning beams and red-hot ashes : the columns blackened and stripped of their plaster (a good thing, by the way), the last of the nave rafters burning away in its place across the top of the chancel, and the broken mullions of the W. window alone remaining, the font a shapeless ruin, the roof of the chancel, which still stood, smouldering and occasionally breaking out into flame, the fire-engine fizzing, roaring, rushing, spouting, drenching, a line of schoolboys passing buckets, rather enjoying the fun, an excited crowd all round ; the beautiful Memorial windows looking down upon the wreck serene and unmoved in the morning light, and the old clock melodiously chiming the quarters as if nothing had happened. While we stood on the tombstones bouche béante, the last rafter gave way, and fell amid showers of sparks. Uncle Henry and Mr. Troughton were busy on the top of the chancel wall hauling up buckets, in the hope of saving the roof. The S. chancel aisle roof is saved. Uncle Stephen was there, almost niobe,[1] as was Uncle H. ; Molly Glynne pink and green with dismay ; Miss Brown with her gown and shawl over her night-gown ; Mr. Brewster with his white hair in indescribable confusion,

[1] Appendix A.

looking like a wild foreigner ; old Bennett helplessly
wringing his hands. The engine was kept playing
incessantly about the chancel, and at last the fire
in the roof was put out, but not before the beams were
charred and wasted, and the intermediate spaces done for.
Then there was an alarm about the tower floor, the
principal beam of which seemed almost self-supported,
and true enough while they were spouting at it, crash
came part of it, and nearly smashed young Waldegrave
Brewster. We picked up particulars as we looked on,
and later. The Grammar School master was roused
a little after 4 by his dog barking, and saw flames breaking out of the W. window. He rapidly alarmed the
village, Mr. Br. among the rest, who instantly sent to
Chester for the fire brigade, which arrived promptly
in 20 minutes. Meanwhile he, Uncle Henry, and Uncle
William later, worked wonders at the church. Mr. B.
crept on all 4s through stifling smoke into the vestry,
and, with the aid of a maukin [1] and Uncle H. who got
in through the window, saved therefrom the parish
registers. They penetrated into the chancel, brought
out the seats of the choir, arrested the progress of the
fire with mere buckets of water, had the organ fetched
out, while the candelabras, altar-cloth, and a mass
of books were also saved, either by them or by others.
Now, the horrid part is that it is proved the church was
fired on purpose, probably about 8 o'clock. For the
organ was fired inside, and the W. end had also been
set fire to. Moreover the poor-box was broken into,
its staple was found on the ground, with the tool used.
It is an act of diabolical wickedness : destroying the
House of God, and a part of it too specially used for
His praise, the noble organ whose voice has ever pealed
through the church divine music, speaking to Him in
what may well be thought echoes from the " Seraph
choir," for there is something more than earthly and
human in the voice of music.

HAWARDEN, *November 5th,* 1857.—We feel like living
beset with dangers ; great fears for St. John's, for a
man keeps skulking about it. However they are on

[1] Appendix A.

the watch. All the clergy are sending for 6-barrelled revolvers; Uncle Henry has his gardener under his stairs, and Mr. Austin sows gunpowder on his window sills : he will probably blow up. The Rate gives 1000,[1] so there is over 3000. Such weather.

HAGLEY, *December 17th*, 1857.—Lord John Manners came.

HAGLEY, *December 18th*, 1857.—High soft wind. Papa rode with Lord John. He said there were *ripe natural* strawberries and raspberries a month ago. I walked with Miss Smith : began Thierry's " Norman Conquest." Lord John gave Charles (his godson) a perfect little leather case, containing Bible, Prayer Book, and Christian Year.

HAGLEY, *December 27th*, 1857.—A telegraph with most alarming accounts from Althorp summoning poor Granny.

HAGLEY, *December 29th*, 1857.—Alas ! Granny was too late. Uncle Fritz[2] died an hour after she left Hagley, for he had no strength of constitution to resist the illness. And the short brightness of Althorp is clouded —sorrow has come upon them at the height of their happiness. Tallee and Althorp are lonely orphans, and the two little children are fatherless. Poor Aunt Yaddy, only two months ago rejoicing in her little son, who came to gladden his father's eyes, so short a time before they were to close !

HAGLEY, *January 1st*, 1858.—Do we but cling on to the Chain of Thine Everlasting Mercy, we are sure of the Blessing—through life, in death ; for neither life nor death can separate us from that unutterable Love which is in Christ Jesus our Lord. A day exactly like yesterday in weather, most beautiful.

HAGLEY, *January 14th*, 1858.—We read Inglis' account of the siege of Lucknow, which will be a great historical name, therefore I need not give details. It is more like the siege of Londonderry than anything, and gives one sure and exulting confidence in the nobleness of English hearts and hands.

---

[1] I.e. £1,000 for restoration of the church.
[2] 4th Earl Spencer.

HAGLEY, *January 15th*, 1858.—Still more magnificent
Sir C. Campbell's Relief of Lucknow, the whole population of which, garrison, women, children, wounded, and
sick, he brought out, unhurt every one.

HAGLEY, *January 29th*, 1858.—Very good and interesting letter of Eddy Watson's ; only rather horrid
his saying he could almost like to see the sepoys tor-
tured : as Granny said, the logic of the day seems :
" Oh, how horrible the conduct of these sepoys ! What
diabolical cruelty ! what villainy ! Let's go and do
exactly the same ! "

HAGLEY, *February 2nd*, 1858.—We have got a '54
Peerage, wherein I diligently insert alterations gleaned
from *The Times*' births, deaths, and marriages, chiefly
in the sanguine hope of improving my knowledge of
people's families, titles, relations, and circumstances.
To-day there was the birth of a son to Honble. Mrs.
Brand, daughter-in-law of the house of Dacre, and the
marriage of a great-niece of that of Mar and Kellie to
a stick [1] in Siam. There ! I trust I shall remember
them.

ALTHORP, *March 3rd*, 1858.—We came to Althorp,
where we were last four years ago, just before Bobbie's [2]
birth ; the account is in the first volume of my journal,
which I have lost, alas ! We seem to have stood apart
during these four years and watched the rapid changes.
When we were here then, Aunt Yaddy was Tallee's
friend Miss Seymour, Uncle Fritz sat at the head of
the table, the house was full of company and amusement but at grave moments the shadows of the two first
great griefs one might still fancy hanging over the
place. Now, there is a young widow with two babies
beside her, and Tallee is an orphan. And we, children
then, grief never known to us, and feeling strange and
grown up in being away from Papa and Mamma. Now,
coming with Papa, alone, bringing our own heavy sorrow
into this changed and sorrowful house. God be thanked
we knew not what was coming !

Such dear little children. Victoria says next to

[1] What sort of gentleman a " stick in Siam " is I have no idea !
[2] 6th Earl Spencer.

nothing, but in a tiny bell-like voice, and compensates for her extreme ugliness by the most winning signs and movements, pointing and gesticulating with a pair of fairy hands, or with little rounded wrists. The baby fair and pretty, placid and happy with everyone.

HAGLEY, *March* 10*th*, 1858.—We played at battledore and shuttlecock, went to the church, and to see a new-born family of rabbits. I read Is. LIII to Nanny. Mg. and Evg. services : a good sermon at the latter.

HAGLEY, *March* 13*th*, 1858.—Delightful stirring S. wind ; rainy, with flying clouds : deep blue distance ; snow disappearing ; my cold at a climax.

HAGLEY, *April* 4*th*, *Easter Sunday*, 1858.—Tolerably fine, more chilly. Such a sermon of Uncle Billy's, sounding inspired in parts, going into great heights and depths. Church twice.

BOOK IV
MAY 1858—JULY 1859

INTRODUCTION TO BOOK IV

The fourth volume of the Diary begins in April 1858 and ends in August 1859. There is little in it which requires further introduction. Its great event is the " coming out " of the diarist. On May 26th she records that " there was a party " (at the Gladstones', where they were staying) " at which I appeared *en qualité* of child, not of grown-up young lady, in which capacity was Meriel." But in June we hear of her dining with her father " at the Bishop of Worcester's, where for the first time I was bowed at to leave the room, and taken in by the Bishop ! I didn't know if I was on my head or my heels." A little later, still aged sixteen, she orders dinner at Hagley " for the very first time in my life." But she did not leave the schoolroom till she was seventeen, on September 5th, a few days after which she began a series of visits to country houses, by going with her father and sister to Hams, not far from Hagley, the house of Sir Charles Adderley (afterwards Lord Norton). These visits occupy a great deal of this volume. At first they naturally alarmed her ; and on leaving Escrick, her cousin Lady Wenlock's place, she records with evident relief that she has " kept quite clear of all scrapes." After the round of visits came her first ball, which was at Stourbridge, close to Hagley. The chief excitement about it appears to have been that " we were not in bed till past 3 nor up next morning till 11½ ! "

·' But of course she scarcely felt really out till she was launched on her first London season. They went up for that in May 1859, having " a most smutty journey, for we travelled in the open britschka " : so that her father had " the complexion of a stoker " after facing

" wind and rain and dirt on the box " ; and Lucy
herself had to beg off dining with Lady Wenlock on
arrival, " being the colour of a blotchy turkey-cock from
having to wash my face with cold water." Such was
a journey to London from the Midlands in those days !
The next pages record the beginnings of grown-up
gaieties : the first dinner party, which was at Lady
Wenlock's ; the first evening party, which was at the
Admiralty ; and the first ball, the hostess at which
she forgets to name. It is soon followed by her presentation to the Queen and by a Royal ball, of which
there is a full account. She has a passionate devotion
to the Queen and her children which takes all opportunities of expressing itself : one of which in this
volume is the birth of Princess Royal's first child, whose
future career as German Emperor scarcely justified
this English welcome of his appearance. The diarist's
loyal enthusiasms extended beyond her own country,
especially to the members of the House of France, of
whom we get several glimpses, especially of the Comte
de Paris, with whom she dances and exchanges pretty
speeches. One of the occasions on which she met him
was at a great garden party, or " breakfast " as they
were then 'still called, given by Lady Marian Alford
at Ashridge.

Balls and dinners continue in the changed world of
to-day ; and even the evening parties, which they used
to call " drums," and which were in those days of
everyday occurrence and of social and even political
importance, have not become quite unknown. But the
" breakfast," as it was a hundred and more years ago,
and continued to be within the period of this Diary,
is now as obsolete as the bonnets with which young
girls adorned themselves for it. Lucy Lyttelton goes to
several of these " breakfasts " at Chiswick and Wimbledon as well as at Ashridge. They were a very lengthy
and elaborate form of entertainment. To the Ashridge
one the Lyttelton party went by train at four o'clock
to Tring, where Lady Marian's carriages met her guests,

But the scramble for them was so great that the Lytteltons did not get to Ashridge itself till seven o'clock.
They and the other eight hundred guests then had cold
dinner, walked and talked, and after dusk began to
dance.   Dancing and illuminations occupied the evening ; then came the drive to Tring and a long wait
at the station ; and finally arrival at home at two
o'clock in the morning, " feeling wicked " because it
was already Sunday.   On the whole it must have been
a very fatiguing business, and perhaps there is no need
to catalogue the giving of " breakfasts " among the
now lost virtues, or the attending them among the
now lost pleasures, of the Georgian and Victorian
" nobility and gentry " !

Another kind of " breakfast," which really was a
breakfast but is now equally extinct, finds frequent
mention here.   It seems strange to us, but it was then
the practice of statesmen and men of letters to sacrifice
on certain days a large part of the morning to break-
fasting together !   There was actually a Breakfast
Club—whose meetings are recorded in Sir Mountstuart
Grant Duff's Diaries ; and Mr. Gladstone, whom one
would have supposed likely to have his mornings fully
occupied, was not only a member but a frequent atten-
dant.   Whether the meetings recorded here are meetings
of this Club I am not sure ; perhaps not, as the ladies
of the host's family seem to have been allowed to be
present.

For the rest, the family life at Hagley and elsewhere
goes on here much as we have seen it in the earlier
volumes.   There is daily service at the Church at which
Lucy usually attends ;   there is frequent amateur
singing at all gatherings of friends, in their own and
other houses, a practice commoner then than now ;
Lucy draws a good deal ; they ride continually ; they
play cards in the evening ; and she records that she
first played for money during her visit to Escrick.   Lord
Lyttelton hunts, and gives lectures, and chooses High
Sheriffs, and works at " a wonderful new Dictionary

that is contemplated by the Philological Society," and is since accomplished as the great Oxford English Dictionary. The brothers are a frequent topic ; always arousing expressions of passionate affection which are sometimes tempered by candid criticisms of their boyish defects, as seen or reported from Eton. Their tutor was " Billy " Johnson, afterwards Cory, and author of " Ionica," the most famous, I suppose, of the Eton tutors of that day, among whose pupils were Lord Rosebery, Lord Roberts, and Lord Balfour. She records that he prophesied great things of her eldest brother Charles, but made certain complaints of Neville, the future General, including one, which she endorses, that he is " distinctly cheeky." But whatever she has to say of her brothers always ends with " Bless them all ! "—and the little Alfred is already " Alfred the King," and never mentioned without enthusiasm.

There is a good deal of reading recorded again : more Waverley Novels ; "The Rivals"; "Adam Bede," read aloud by their grandmother, and partly " Bowdlered for our young minds " ; Bourrienne's " Napoleon " ; Montalembert's " Avenir de l'Angleterre " ; Church's " Dante " ; and the " Promessi Sposi " of Manzoni. Among the public events mentioned are the joint war of France and Italy against Austria, and the building of the *Great Eastern*, then by far the largest ship in the world. Home politics do not yet receive any great amount of attention. The diarist, it is to be noted, is still a Conservative : she regrets a Liberal victory in a Worcestershire election, and calls Bright a " wretch." She twice sent up a contribution to *Punch* ; but no editorial notice of her efforts is recorded.

DIARY, MAY 1858—JULY 1859

LONDON, *May 6th*, 1858.—There was a breakfast.[1] Poor Papa had an attack of influenza ; he has never been poorly so long together I should think. Now for a good bit of news. Althorp is to marry Miss Charlotte Seymour ! who is good, lovely, darkish, not over tall, and everything delightful. Edward T. is going on well, his pulse improving, and his appetite better. Such a blessing. A delightful concert at St. James's Hall which is most magnificent.

LONDON, *May 9th*, 1858.—We met the 3 eldest Miss Fortescues after service, all alike : sallow, long-nosed, brown-eyed individuals. The third is just out. Althorp was at church, and so was Miss Seymour, but we didn't see her, much to my disappointment.

LONDON, *May 10th*, 1858.—We tramped waiting in vain for a sight of the Queen. The dear Princess Royal begged Lady Raglan to tell Granny how happy she was ; she is extremely popular, and loved by everyone. God bless her !

LONDON, *May 13th*, 1858.—We saw Cotton, Bishop of Calcutta, consecrated in Westminster Abbey, by Canterbury and 8 other Bishops. Most beautiful to see the united hands blessing the new Bishop, and much indeed does he need prayer and blessing for the weighty and responsible work before him, in that troubled and rebellious land.

The service lasted 5 hours, for there was a somewhat tedious sermon, and the Holy Communion, at which there were 400 ; it was very striking and perfect, in that glorious old Abbey, fit indeed for high services offered to God in the beauty of holiness, as to-day.

[1] This, I think, means a meeting of the Breakfast Club, a society of " intellectuals " who breakfasted together from time to time.

LONDON, *May 24th*, 1858.—Papa came back from Eton, so pleased with just coming in time for Charles' innings at cricket, where he stayed in for an hour and a half against the best bowler at Eton, and got 57 runs, and 13 later.

LONDON, *May 26th*, 1858.—Many spoke of Charles' noble play, which has been mentioned in the *Morning Post* as some of the best ever seen ! ! !

LONDON, *May 29th*, 1858.—Glorious summer heat, hazy and dazzling, with soft fragrant wind. We went with Aunts Coque and Kitty and Uncle Spencer—such an odd party—to the Crystal Palace, where I have only been once before, 3 or 4 years ago. It was lovely : the trees and grass in early green, and the masses of rhododendrons in flower. We came in for the playing of the fountains, and also heard " Der Freischütz " on the noble organ, and many rather dull things by a brass band. We also dined there, and had delicious strawberry cream ice. The heat was great : over-powering I may say at times, but so beautiful. We stayed till 6, then rushed off in frantic hurry to be in time for the Princess's at 7. We actually were in very good time. Much we admired the marvellous scenery, which is the very best that ever was, and this helping out the noble words of the great play (" King Lear ") made it delightful. But I can't abide the acting. Surely it ought to aim at being natural, not perpetual forced gestures and voice, affected and ranting. Yet we saw Kean, who is reckoned capital.

LONDON, *June 1st*, 1858.—The great Rubens out of the billiard-room came up to be valued, as Papa wants to sell it.

LONDON, *June 11th*, 1858.—I dined with Papa at the Bp. of Worcester's, M. being still feeble, where for the first time I was bowed at to leave the room, and taken in by the Bishop ! I didn't know if I was on my head or my heels.

HAGLEY, *June 23rd*, 1858.—I rode a grey mare in the morning, which Papa means to buy, for my riding, the boys', and his own when necessary, and also for hunting and to go in the gig. Therefore is she to be yclept

"The Mayde of Alle Worke."

HAGLEY, *June 29th*, 1858.—Every paper is full of outcries about the filthy state of the Thames, which has reached an appalling climax : affecting the Imperial Parliament of Great Britain itself, which accordingly sticks chloride of lime in its windows, and has stomach-aches nevertheless. Therefore we may hope that something more effective may be done : filthy lucre should be no consideration in the case of filthy smells.

HAGLEY, *July 4th*, 1858.—I told Bobby about the Creation, and with some difficulty made him attentive and interested ; when I was describing the empty world with no animals in it, he added : "No stable-yard."

HAGLEY, *July 20th*, 1858.—I ordered dinner for the very first time in my life. Oh dear !

HAGLEY, *July 30th*, 1858.—Heard of the first omnibus appearing with honours in New Zealand.

HAGLEY, *August 5th*, 1858.—This day month I shall be seventeen, and shall come out of the school-room ! Oh dear, my old journal : "I'm 13 years old, I wish I was only 12." "Fourteen years." "I have lived fifteen years." "The beginning of ' mortal woe ' with me at sixteen." I recall perfectly each of the days on which I wrote those words, as well as if I had written them yesterday. Oh, the deep sadness of the flying years !

HAGLEY, *August 11th*, 1858.—Mr. Girdlestone came for two nights, and we had a pleasant evening, combining words, poets, concertina, whist, reading, and conversation.

HAGLEY, *August 18th*, 1858.—Aunt Wenlock came, and played whist with us, graciously bearing with our third-rate powers. The first message arrived in 36 minutes by the Atlantic telegraph : "England and America are united. Glory to God in the Highest, and

on earth peace, goodwill towards men." Amen, from
the bottom of my heart !

HAGLEY, *August 20th,* 1858.—Spencer and I went
a seventeen-miles ride with Papa to Kinver Edge, most
lovely : a hill from which we looked down about 600
feet, as perpendicular as the cliffs of the sea, and the
cliffs at the bottom are covered with fern, gorse, and
heather, a mass of warm, picturesque colour. A bright
view, and such a stirring fresh breeze, all fragrant with
heath, the horses enjoying it as much as we.

HAGLEY, *August 28th,* 1858.—Seven of us, from me
downwards excluding Charles, went to Bewdly with
Papa, and Miss S. and Uncle Sp. to see the Bakers,
and go up the Severn in a barge to Arley Castle, all
which was accomplished most satisfactorily. Arley
was in our family, but was given away by naughty
Tom [1]; we saw some family pictures and monuments.
Such a hideous little church. Beautiful wooded banks
and islands up the Severn : I never gave it credit for
such beauty.

HAGLEY, *September 12th,* 1858.—Tallee and I read
and talked poetry together, in the most romantic
fashion, very greatly to our mutual enjoyment. We
saw a comet and a meteor.

HAMS, *September 21st,* 1858.—And here am I going
out on visits ! Oh, there is something forlorn in us two
alone with poor Papa ! It goes to one's heart his taking
care for us, and fetching us to go down with him.

HAMS, *September 22nd,* 1858.—I am exhausted with
behaving properly, and feel as if we had been away
from home a week !

HAMS, *September 24th,* 1858.—They gave us an interesting report of a wonderful Orphan Home in Glos-
tershire (managed by Mr. Müller, a Plymouth Brother),
which is flourishing and increasing, though he has no
certain money whatever. His strange one-sided re-

---

[1] The second Lord. " A nobleman," as Sir George Trevelyan has
said, " who, rather by contrast to the others of his name than for any
exceptionally heinous misdoings of his own, goes by the sobriquet of
' the bad Lord Lyttelton.' "

ligion is sad and unfortunate, for one can hardly tell what *lasting* and sterling good he may do ; and with such noble singleness of mind and faith, how one longs he should teach *all* that's right. Then it seems there would be no end to the good he would do. He has nearly 1,000 orphans. If they did but all turn out high-principled, right-minded Christians and Church-people ! This they can hardly do, as Plymouth Breth-ren, poor things, are not allowed to say their prayers till they are converted : what a horrible idea, that one has been a heathen for exactly fourteen years, 11 months, and 364 days, and that then on the 31st of December 185– one becomes a Christian for life ; for this it seems they think happens regularly. And the calm, com-placent way in which he talks of the converted and unconverted, those who are Christians and those who are not, settling them up in respective little packets as it were. Who are we to judge our brothers ?

HAGLEY, *September 25th*, 1858.—Three cheers, we came home, having been much pleased and amused with our visit. I am amused at everything, dulness and all, and in part it has been very pleasant. Oh, the refreshment of coming into the glowing evening beauty of Hagley, and its dips and rises, even after three days of country as flat as a pancake, and as dull as ditch-water !

HAGLEY, *September 27th*, 1858.—The papers are all wrangling over the new quarrel about confession : how odd people are ! What can be easier than the gentle and wise directions of the Prayer Book to ask advice and guidance when in difficulty, or oppressed with some sin, of the clergyman who has authority to declare forgiveness in the Name of Christ ? And why shd these directions lead clergymen to *force* their parishioners to *unwilling* confession ? Or why shd they be made stumbling-blocks and be reckoned popish, as long as St. James' words stand : " Confess your sins one to another " ? Marvellous extremes people fly to ! on whichever side, missing the truth, which is Scriptural, temperate, and wise. In difficulty, with something on your conscience, go to a clergyman ;

without a difficulty, without anything on your conscience, do not go.   Who wouldn't say Amen to that ?

HAGLEY, *September 28th*, 1858.—Baby a bad stye :
he kisses his hand to wish good-bye, says please, makes
little bows and curtseys, understands all you say to
him, pretends to read, takes everyone and everything
for horses, clicking to them like a jockey, and talks much
in his own way with many intelligible words.   But it
is impossible to describe the " winsomeness " of him.
Newmany has taught him to know and kiss Mamma's
picture in the dressing-room and study, and to call
her name when he goes there, in a little sighing plaintive
voice, oh, so darling and so deeply mournful.   He will
never know anything but the shadow : poor precious !

ESCRICK, *September 30th*, 1858.—A pleasant dinner
and evening, with a round game, in which for the
first time in my life I played for money.

ESCRICK, *October 1st*, 1858.—Lord Boyle turned up
in the evening, and we sat up till nearly 12 with a
round game, whereat I won four shillings.

ESCRICK, *October 2nd*, 1858.—I haven't spoken of
the people that are here : three daughters of Sir Guy
Campbell, one married, Mrs. Preston, *the* most fascinat-
ing beauty I have ever seen : shady deep eyes, all
expression and grace ; and such a lovely classical mouth ;
figure and manners most winning and refined.   All this
in spite of a strange impediment in her speech, which
makes it a sort of nasal prolonged drawl, but which
one does not care for in the fascination of everything
about her.

ESCRICK, *October 4th*, 1858.—We had a 60 miles drive ;
to Riveaulx Abbey, four-in-hand, changing horses
twice, in the drag.   So very delightful : Cousin Ebbett [1]
and I on the outside : the aged Meriel within.   There
came also Papa and C. Dicker, who drove turn about ;
Lord Boyle and Edward Neville.   I never saw finer
country or such perfect and beautiful Early English
ruins.   We set off at 9 and were home at 8, I remained
outside the whole time.   Pouring rain nearly all the

[1] Lady Wenlock.

morning; but a beautiful afternoon and night. I saw the heavy bank of clouds that had overhung the sky all day roll off into nothing at nightfall before the stars as they shone out one by one, and the marvellous comet with its sweep of pale light, curving high upwards, like a great white plume, all one line of beauty.

ESCRICK, *October 7th*, 1858.—Pleasant windy day, warmer; damp, but no rain. I rode with the three children to Morby, where we saw Mrs. Preston. I was on a nice fast pony, and greatly liked it. For the evening came Mr. and Mrs. Duncombe and her two sisters, who made most beautiful music, singing Italian together in such harmonious unison, with soft full voices. There were also two comic songs, and to wind up, the most capital jig, performed by Lord Boyle and Cousin Bick. Oh, the fun of the former!

ESCRICK, *October 8th*, 1858, or rather the 9th, for it must be past two.—We have all sat up to this unconscionable hour at Lord Boyle's earnest request to Cousin Ebbett, put in irresistible Irish, under the promise of something amusing at the end of the evening. So we had playing, the Miss Grahams' glorious singing, three comic songs, a round game, from whence I was 10*s.* richer, and finally a jig by Lord Boyle, in a coat with one tail, tucked-up trousers, and all etcs., to make him a perfect tipsy Irish post-boy. He kept us dying with his brogue for some time: amazing fun, but perfectly gentlemanlike all the time, and looking too absurd. I rode with Bingy, Papa and Edward. We saw some of the shooting. Bingy paid me a most elegant compliment. He asked me if I liked his mother. I said: " Do you think anyone can know her without liking her ? " Says he : " No ; and can anyone know you without liking you ? " He is a pleasant, bright boy, and the pink of courtesy. Papa has sold the Rubens for £500.

HAGLEY, *October 11th*, 1858.—We came home, after a most delightful visit, full of much pleasure, and giving me a very happy launch into the world. I have enjoyed it greatly and kept quite clear of all scrapes.

I—8

In fact, C. Ebbett has paid us both compliments **as** to our manner, etc. This is very nice to hear : it is what would have pleased Mamma.

HAGLEY, *October 12th*, 1858.—I invested four shillings of my gambling money in a new pack of green-backed cards, with a gold ivy pattern on them, wherewith we played at whist in the evening. I trust they are not intensely vulgar !

ANTONY, *October 18th*, 1858.—We went to Church, view [1] St. Luke, and drove with the Carews and young Captain Rice to the top of and all round Mount Edgcumbe. The steep descent below us was one mass of evergreen, tier above tier, and at its foot spread the open sea, lit up with one of the transient gleams of sunlight, which just caught the white crests of the waves ; while to the left lay five stately ships of the line. This broke suddenly upon us, and the beauty was such that I had a wild impulse to fling myself down into its arms as it were.

ANTONY, *October 20th*, 1858.—The most delightful day of all. We went in a boat across the Sound to the Breakwater, towed by a gunboat most of the way, and going 7 or 8 miles an hour. We went along the breakwater to the lighthouse, in spite of the sea breaking slightly over it. We climbed up the lighthouse, and going back had a sort of race with the waves, which as the tide was rising deluged the breakwater every moment. M. with her accustomed sang-froid, wouldn't go above a foot's pace, and got drenched up to the knees ; all of us were wet ; it was great fun. Then another delightful row, with the sails up, and all over the dockyard, where I first learnt to appreciate the enormous size of the ships, by their masts and yards. Also saw a $\frac{1}{2}$ penny reduced to pure copper ore by the blow-pipe, and soldering by the same. A delightful row, and pleasant walk home with the elder C. Rice.

ANTONY, *October 21st*, 1858.—We both greatly like the two Captains Rice, who seem sensible and good,

[1] Appendix A.

and are very amusing. We had an exciting morning of battledore and shuttlecock.

ANTONY, *October 22nd*, 1858.—We had great fun in the carriage parodying Scott, and singing all the old songs we could rake up.

ANTONY, *October 24th*, 1858.—A very pleasant last day. We went for morning service on board C. Rice's ship, the *Royal Albert*, which we went all over. The service was most striking : the middle deck covered with sailors : 1,000 of them, all very quiet and attentive, the sermon excellent. All the passages in the Liturgy about the sea coming in with such meaning, and the beautiful Navy prayer. I was positively awestruck at the enormous size, depth, and complication of the ship ; with the mighty mysterious machinery, the swarms of sailors, the beautiful incomprehensible rigging, etc., etc. It has the heaviest broadside of any ship in commission. And all as clean as a pink. C. Rice, with other officers, pioneered us about, and we *did* it as thoroughly as possible in so short a time. We had luncheon on board, and then home, and to afternoon church at the School. A very nice evening of talk, music, and singing.

LANHYDROCK, *November 4th*, 1858.—Dim, grey day, cold and autumnal, with no distance. We drove with Papa and Mr. Robartes in a post-chay and two, a 40 miles drive to Tintagel and back. The drive was bleak and desolate, over dreary moor, with stunted trees, few and ruinous cottages, and not a human creature for miles ; nearly went melancholy mad. At length we came within sight of the church, standing nakedly up on a hill against the sky, and then by a most un- prepossessing approach to a pretty little parsonage smothered in creepers. Here the brisk little Vicar received us with a rapid flow of words and welcomes, and carried us off to the church. I never saw such an interesting one : much of old Saxon architecture, so supposed, Norman, E. English, and a bit of Decorated and Perpendicular : a side-chapel with a stone altar 1,000 years old, with crosses cut upon it, ancient carved wood, and little single lancet windows, with deep splayed sides. We returned to a sumptuous and highly peppered luncheon, and then—— Now for the beauty that forms a fit crowning-point to all that we have seen in this beautiful county.

We went down a rocky valley with a stream running along it into the sea. Then we turned to the left and saw before us a steep path up one of the cliffs, which stood up grandly round the bay, all craggy and broken. The sea was deep emerald-green, far below us. We climbed higher and higher, among the scanty ruins of the Castle, old beyond all date, and said to have been King Arthur's. No use trying to do justice to the greatness and dignity of these perpendicular cliffs, and the sea four hundred feet below, warm with that wonderful colouring in spite of the grey November sunlessness, which, alas ! prevented us from seeing the glorious expanse of horizon.

We saw a peak standing apart, like a needle ; rough and craggy ; and on the flat top is a cross carved, still easy to be seen, and having a look of solemnity, as if the wild rocks and sea would speak of One greater than they. As indeed they do !

HAGLEY, *November* 10*th*, 1858.—I wrote to Agnes, who is going with her parents to the Ionian Isles, he [1] as Lord High Commissioner on some knotty point. Very delightful, but they will miss Willy's first Oxford vacation, and be away for Xmas, which is a pity.

HEWELL, *December* 1*st*, 1858.—Two young ladies Bridgeman have been frightfully burnt, through some carelessness. One, Lady Charlotte, died on Saturday. They are daughter-in-law's sisters to Lady Windsor, and very intimate. Hence we concluded that our invitation to Hewell would have been blown up. That not being the case, however, we drove here in the evening, doubting and wondering, 1st whether a letter had been written and miscarried, 2ndly whether we had been altogether forgotten, 3rdly whether we should find the whole party gone to the funeral, or going to-morrow, 4thly whether we were unaccountably reckoned such old shoes that they didn't mind our sitting, dullissi-

---

[1] Mr. Gladstone was sent on a mission to the Ionian Islands in 1858.

mus,[1] benumbing,[1] with them, 5thly if they had taken it for granted we should not come. In all which surmises we were mistaken. We found the Lady Baroness and two daughters in quiet but placid spirits, and happy coloured gowns, quite ready to entertain us, which, with the help of the Revd. Mr. Dickens of Tardybigg, they successfully did till 11¼ at night when we went to bed.

HAGLEY, *December 4th*, 1858.—Soft and pleasant. We made much of the boys : blew soap-bubbles with them (one of mine, by the bye, floated from the perron to the witch elm, where we lost sight of it), played draughts, whist, and backgammon in the evening. I marched in solitary state at 8 to church, which Cooper and I divided between us. Uncle B. reconnoitred from behind the curtain : looked at me in the foreground, dim emptiness behind me, and retreated. After a pause of agitating suspense, Papa and Mr. Boyle came. In due time both clergy walked into the reading-desks, where they stood for full 3 minutes. The silence was appalling. It might have seemed sublime ; but somehow 'twas only ridiculous. After those ominous minutes, Rector and Curate stalked back to the vestry, and Papa and I and Cooper returned to our respective homes.

HAGLEY, *December 15th*, 1858.—Papa and Charles hunted, and came home looking mildewed with fog, having found nothing.

HAGLEY, *December 30th*, 1858.—The great event of our first ball came off at Stourbridge, and we much enjoyed it ; chaperoned by Papa and Aunt Coque. The thought *would* come of how Mamma would have liked taking us ; and it must have made it sad to Papa. But I think he enjoyed seeing us dancing, and greatly we liked it. We were not in bed till past 3, nor up next morning till 11½ ! It felt so dissipated.

HAGLEY, *January 11th*, 1859.—Papa lectured in the evening on New Zealand—as none but he can ; clear, true, full of bits of his peculiar irresistible fun, and sus-

---

[1] Appendix A.

taining one's interest perfectly. He left one with such a happy, satisfactory idea of it all, and with proud thrills over its English-born goodness and prosperity. The end was a dear, beautiful allusion to the cloud " abiding "—yet not without light—over his life, and which he likes to speak of—as to those who can know and feel—to his neighbours and people at home. And surely it has gone into all hearts.

HAGLEY, *January* 14*th*, 1859.—I have just read the Bp. of London's charge, which is everywhere reckoned admirable : temperate, wise, careful, showing active knowledge, research, and appreciation of what there is to do, with a humble un-self-asserting tone. May he only act up to it ! The India troubles seem settling down. Our Princess Royal's confinement is daily expected. There is talk of a war between France and Austria.

HAGLEY, *January* 26*th*, 1859.—Corfu news : horrible fear that his Xcellency [1] will stay indefinitely, in which case he will miss all or a great part of the session, and oh ! result to shake all plans and politics ! we Shall Not Be Able To Come Out ! !

HAGLEY, *January* 27*th*, 1859.—East Worcestershire has lost its member, and there's to be an election : Calthorpe, Liberal, against Pakington, Derbyite : goodness knows which is best !

HAGLEY, *January* 28*th*, 1859.—The Princess Royal had a son yesterday at 3 a.m., being of the mature age of 18, bless her ! The little Queen a grandmother, Princess Beatrice an aunt ! ! The Duchess of Kent a great-grandmother ! ! ! Princess Alice wrote the news to Granny : " My *dear dear* Laddle "—such a happy, natural letter.

HAGLEY, *February* 3*rd*, 1859.—Some frostiness. The hounds met in front of the house, and they had a run over the place, which later fun, alas ! we missed. I have been in at the death ; it would have been but reasonable to have seen full cry.

HAGLEY, *February* 23*rd*, 1859.—I rode in the brilliant and exhilarating soft weather, through the sprouting

---

[1] Gladstone.

wheat and up lovely hill and dale, with Mr. and Amelia Claughton, and Arthur who fell flump on his back once. Most pleasant. Oh, the view from High Down !

HAGLEY, *February 22nd*, 1859.—As a counterpoise to this excellent news, Mr. Calthorpe came in by a majority of 320 odd.

HAGLEY, *February 25th*, 1859.—Aunt Emmy came, and we talked parish matters, which are unusually exciting with illness : 6 people prayed for ; 4 expecting babies, 3 of whom are anxious cases ; my old Priest ; little Wright children with disgraced father, mad mother, and no money ; little Shilcocks ill with the dregs of scarlet fever ; and to wind up, a bewildering bother about Annie Farmer—who we trusted was off our hands. I drove the children exploring.

HAGLEY, *March 1st*, 1859.—Delightful day, exactly the spring of books, which I used to quiz as never existing. Hedges breaking out here and there into precious little ducky tender green baby leaves : three little tiddly lambs, with only one mother, three calves, rose leaves appearing, primroses, and a scrap of (forced) mignionette.

HAGLEY, *March 4th*, 1859.—Most deliciously soft, with dark blue distance, and gleaming sun : coming out of church was like emerging from a well into full summer. A very pleasant day : we went an uproarious and boggy driving-and-riding expedition up the obelisk hill, whence the view [1] *was*. Thence set off for St. Kenelm, but a much tormented spring of U. B.'s [2] carriage broke, and we all turned out. Great and high was the facetious-ness of the party, in course of which, by an awful absent thoughtlessness, what should I do but call Mr. Pepys Herbert ! The evening is memorable for the surpassing beauty of the singing, which came off in the hall, and for an exciting game of Commerce and Fright. The Miss Yorkes have won our hearts ; especially I like Bertha, who is decidedly pretty.

HAGLEY, *March 17th*, 1859.—Ceaseless rain till sunset, when soft glowing light broke over everything :

---

[1] Appendix A.   [2] I.e. Uncle Billy's.

too beautiful, contrasting with the heavy clouds. I took advantage of the evening beauty for a 6 o'clock trapes [1] thro' the mud into the villages : hedges quite green in parts. Congregation 10.

HAGLEY, *March* 29*th*, 1859.—Every expectation that Ld. Derby will go out, and Radicals come in for good ! ! ! Thunder ! ! ! Uncle Billy lectured on Bodies again.

HAGLEY, *April* 2*nd*, 1859.—Oh, bliss ! the dear soft glorious air again : exit snow, exit frost, exit the last remains of chilliness, but pouring rain all day. I adventurously took pudding and barley-water to the Pratt child ; which is recovering from croup, as none but a poor child would at 6½ : warm, green, and delicious.

HAGLEY, *April* 4*th*, 1859.—I hope we appreciate this beautiful early summer : larches, sycamores, in full leaf, everything all life and warmth and loveliness.

HAGLEY, *April* 6*th*, 1859.—It is hot and fragrant ; summer in the sun and air and scents, early spring in the leafless beeches, oaks, and elms, winter in the here and there nipped young leaves, consequence of this day week's frost and snow.

HAGLEY, *April* 7*th*, 1859.—I rode till 6 with Arthur, over Clent Hill, by Hunnington and Halesowen-Birmingham road and Wassell road home. Delightful ! The child asking all manner of questions about macadamized roads, poor-law guardians, fire insurances, etc.

HAGLEY, *April* 16*th*, 1859.—I finished Bourrienne's " Napoleon " : very interesting and apparently trustworthy. It is curious how he declares a free government to be indispensable to France, and yet it has never succeeded under one ! On the contrary, this grinding despotism seems the only thing for it. Oh, one has a sort of feeling as one thinks of that, and hears of the decrease of the population, that the everlasting stain of Louis XVI revolution, and the slow murder of his saintly little son, has robbed the nation of all vigour and healthy prosperity.

HAGLEY, *April* 29*th*, 1859.—Granny began yesterday to spout to us the new novel about which the world

---

[1] Appendix A.

raves, " Adam Bede," to be duly bowdlered for our young minds. (Only 1 chapter was missed out.[1]) So nice.

HAGLEY, *April 30th,* 1859.—Bright has beaten Mr. Acland at Birmingham by 3,000, and has made a magnificent speech, the wretch.

HAGLEY, *May 7th,* 1859.—The first new drinking-fountain in London been inaugurated.

HAGLEY, *May 8th,* 1859.—Most lovely clear and bright, many of the trees, sycamores and chestnuts, with quite a depth of foliage, the others the tenderest green : yet a " soupçon " of N. in the wind : the park too beautiful. We went, 8 strong, excluding that most pintoed M., up Sparry's and Obelisks Hill.

HAGLEY, *May 11th,* 1859.—" Adam Bede " is full of dreadful interest. C. Jem Wortley has been beaten for the W. Riding by 2,000 : not a large majority. The Leeds people are wild with fervour at Dr. Hook; Unitarians and Dissenters speak enthusiastically of him. The school eat up yesterday's remains. There is a new cart foal.

HAGLEY, *May 13th,* 1859.—Granny finished " Adam Bede " to us. It is a heart-rending book, with its stern true moral of the irrevocableness of sin.

HAGLEY, *May 14th,* 1859.—One of the village girls has been led into evil : such a rare thing in this parish, that it is extra horrible.

HAGLEY, *May 18th,* 1859.—After a most smutty journey, for we travelled in the open britschka, we arrived prosperously in London, Papa the complexion of a stoker, having faced wind, rain, and dirt on the box. Found Atie P. very well. Papa and M. dined with At. Wenlock, I was begged off, being the colour of a blotchy turkey-cock from having to wash my face with cold water.

LONDON, *May 23rd,* 1859.—It's 1.15 on Tuesday morning, for we are just come in from our First Party at the Admiralty, where little Sir John Pakington looked

[1] Added later.

Hagley-ey, and where we saw the great Sir John Lawrence, who saved the N.W. Provinces of India, Capn,
Mrs. and Miss Gladstone, Lady Raglan, so thin and
changed, the Saxon minister, Ld. Carnarvon, Lord John
Manners, Dean Trench, Miss Leigh, Mr. and Mrs. Adderley, Drummonds, and what not. I believe it was a
dull party, but we were much amused, and struck with
the almost invariable ugliness.

LONDON, *May 24th*.—A little past 3 a.m. ! Our first
ball is over. We danced much more than I expected :
M. 6 times and me 4 : twice with Reginald Yorke,
Ld. Skelmersdale, and Mr. Something Stone. It
was fearfully crowded. I saw Wilbrahams and War-
burtons, Mary War., just come out, and very pretty,
Ld. Mahon, J. Gladstones, A. Woods, Mr. Rolle, Ldy.
Constance Grosvenor, etc. Shall I ever remember
them all !

LONDON, *May 25th*, 1859.—Midnight : going to bed
after " Henry V " at the Princess's. It's strange the
strong charm a play acted has for me, viewing that I
dislike more or less all the acting, which seems to me
invariably " outré," unnatural and vulgar. But oh,
dear ! the scenery and some feeling which makes
it almost seem real, and brings the olden time before
one. Before this, we went to a very pretty amateur
concert at Ly. Barrington's and toodled about Covent
Garden etc., with Atie P. Black Miss Brown and a
maukin [1] called in the morning. There has been a
battle at Montebello, the Austrians beaten, it is said
with great loss. The Duchess of Kent is ill. Princess
Royal is visiting the Queen. 6th of the 10 babies born :
Mrs. Bradley's. My poor old Preece is dead ; I shall
never read to him again ! But please God, I shall see
him again ; and he me, with opened eyes there, in the
Light that sorrow can never dim.

LONDON, *May 26th*, 1859.—'Tis 1 a.m. after a most
delightful party here, of which I must at once tell the
great event. I was introduced to the Duc d'Aumale,
the descendant of the old race of French kings. Low
was my curtsey, most gracious was his bow, and oh !

[1] Appendix A.

he spoke to me, and I said, " Oui, monsieur ! " I
thrilled. We also saw the nice Escrick Grahams,
Warrens, Wilbrahams, and all the usual people, and I
was introduced to Lord Clarendon, Lady Manchester,
crazy Lord Crewe, Ly. Constance Grosvenor, Duchess of
Sutherland, etc., etc. There were there besides Lord
Palmerston, Dean Trench, who is going to send us
tickets for Handel at the Abbey next month—Bliss !—
many ambassadors and Indians, Ld. J. Manners, etc.,
etc.

LONDON, *May 28th*, 1859.—About 1. We've been to
the Opera ! *Gazza Ladra* at Covent Garden, Lord
Ward's box. There being no ballet, Papa let us go.
I believe I was slightly disappointed, but it was because
I don't know the music well enough, and I must always
know it well to be properly worthy.

LONDON, *May 29th*, 1859.—Papa and I walked after
luncheon, in spite of rain, to St. M. Mag., Munster
Sqre., where we had nothing but the Litany for the
second time, gabbled so bewilderingly that, without
my book, it might have been the Alphabet for aught I
heard. Disgracefully irreverent and distressing. And
I hate missing Evening Service. Dined quietly at
Granny's. Tho' our services weren't perfect, the Psalms
and everything that no hitch can alter were so beautiful
and helping to remember in London whirl. I hope I
shall keep such things in mind.

LONDON, *May 30th*, 1859.—In the morning we went
to the Exhibition, where there are not many beautiful
pictures, and a host of glaring absurd Pre-Raphaelites,
with every face bright pink, and every sky of lilac,
tin leaves and grass like coarse stuffs, and a lunatic
attempt to render every atom as it *is*, instead of as it
looks. The result is like the sign of an inn ; a laboured
and vulgar finish, with a dazzle of ill-assorted colours.
Pah ! the refreshment of turning to Stanfield's fresh
and living landscapes with soft blending light, and *wet*
water.

LONDON, *May 31st*, 1859.—We went with Papa,
Aunt Kitty, and Johnny to a very low diversion,

Christy's Minstrels, full of excessively broad vulgar fun, with one or two pretty things.

LONDON, *June 3rd*, 1859.—¼ 4 a.m.! and this is written, ill or well, by the light of dawn : mad and dissipated I feel. We have been to Ly. Derby's ball, which, truth to tell, was very dull : hot crowds of chaperons and old gentlemen, and the dancing a fierce struggle with all-surrounding petticoat, and I only danced once, at about 2, with Johnny, who turned up when I had quite given up. This was pleasant, for the room was thinned, and we had the space of a hearthrug. Duke and Duchess of Cambridge were there, and Princess Mary,[1] who, in spite of her imposing size, danced and valsed beautifully.

ETON, *June 4th*, 1859.—Our first 4th of June at Eton ; we must have brought ill luck, for it poured heavily, after great morning heat, and a grumble or two of thunder, from 7 to 9, just the time when the boats were afloat. We saw them start, with their bright uniforms, very successfully, but shortly after had to take shelter in a little room, where we resignedly sat, with Mr. Wynne and his sisters, Reg. Yorke and Mr. Cocks, relation of the Antony one. We talked pleasantly, and the time didn't hang heavy. But the unhappy boats' crews had to walk home from Surley. There is horrid drunkenness in the boats now, the Captain (Wynne) says his greatest difficulty is to keep them sober. I'm so glad our boys are dry-bobs, in spite of the delightful look of the arrowy boats and brilliant dresses, only I trust cricket will look up under Charles's captaincy, and not be everlastingly beaten by Harrow. We had luncheon with the Provost, and I was taken in by Mr. Walpole,[2]—such an honour !—who was most agreeable.

LONDON, *June 5th*, 1859.—My energy is certainly great. I walked to Trin. Ch. Vauxhall in the morning with Papa, on the top of yesterday's perpetual tramp, and the night before's dissipation. Ain't a bit tired. A thundery, languid day. In the evening to a special service at the Abbey, where the singing was beautiful

---

[1] Afterwards Duchess of Teck and mother of Queen Mary.
[2] No doubt Spencer Walpole, afterwards Home Secretary.

from the fine voices, but slow and unambitious and the
trebles drowned. Striking but not altogether perfect
sermon by Mr. Milman. We dined with Granny, and
met the dear Rectors. The Abbey is gloriously cool
and lofty ; there is nothing like it : crowded.

LONDON, *June 6th*, 1859.—A little past two, after *the*
pleasantest home ball, that's to say dance, for it was
carefully distinguished from a ball by its smallness,
absence of champagne, and substitution of modest
p.f. and harp for band. Moreover, it came after a
child's ball, where the little things toddled about so
prettily, and which was honoured with the presence of
the young Prince de Condé, a gentle, grave, and most
courteous boy of fourteen, with whom I danced twice,
" Altesse Royale " and all. His mother, the Duchesse
d'Aumale, was there too, and was introduced to us.
I danced everything but one, valses of course excepted,
but I can only remember 5 partners. I think I must
have danced more than that. R. Yorke, Mr. Majendie
(of happy Oxford memory), Mr. Burgess, Mr. Le Fevre,
and Lord Sudeley ; they were all more or less pleasant ;
Ld. S. knew Charles at Eton. All day we were up to
the neck in the work of titivating the rooms, which
indeed looked lovely. Warm and thundery. There
has been a battle of Magenta, the Austrians completely
defeated, and Paris illuminated.

LONDON, *June 7th*, 1859.—It's of little use my writing
small : I must take up space when there's so much to
talk about. In the morning, what did I do but go to
the Opening of Parliament ! ! ! The beauty of the
tiers of bright colours and sparkling ornaments first
struck me, as we went in, and Papa, delighted to get
rid of me, hoisted me into a capital place next Ly. Ger-
trude Talbot, where we waited for about 3 qrs of an hour,
amusing ourselves greatly with finding out the few
beauties among the fat and wizzy peeresses opposite.
Those we *did* see were Ly. Lothian, Ly. Raglan, Ly.
Mary Craven, and the Duchess of Manchester. The
peers kept dropping in in their red robes, looking for
the most part rather quizzical, but the rich colour nice
to see in dingy England. Papa looked vey comical.

I saw Ld. Spencer and Ld. Lothian, who has got a sort
of creeping palsy; so very sad, and his poor pretty
young wife! At last from the midst of gentlemen-in-
waiting and other attendants, I became aware of the
little Queen standing on the step of the throne, a diamond
coronet on her head, in her robes of state, the crown
held on one side of her, and the mighty sword of justice
on the other; while all stood up, and there was deep
silence. It was a stately sight. The Queen sat down,
everyone also sat down. What next?, I thought,
as several minutes passed in the same grave silence,
and the Queen looked at us, and we looked at the Queen.
I soon found out what was being waited for. There
was a scurry and rush outside the doors, which were
dashed open, and in poured the Commons, jostling and
talking like nothing on earth but a pack of schoolboys
or herd of bullocks. It was a curious contrast to the
red-robed peers, sitting in solemn order, and the Queen
in all her majesty. When as many as cd squeeze
in had jammed themselves against the rails, and after
some hushing had begun to hold their tongues, the
Queen, slightly raising her voice, said, " My Lords, be
seated." (This, however, they were already.) Then
she read her speech, with a low, clear, and most harmonious utterance, and so distinct that I heard perfectly. There was nothing interesting in it : " in spite
of her earnest endeavours, the peace of Europe had
been broken, we were to keep neutral, and at the same
time the fleet was to be done something to, etc., etc."—
things that are talked of every day. Then she gave her
paper to a maukin [1] near her, we all stood up again,
and she went away : there were no cheers in the House,
but plenty outside I hear, and I have actually seen
Parliament opened ! There was a little musical practice
in the morning. Meriel and I dined with Ats. C. &
K. at the Percys', immediately on returning from which
at 11¼ we found a note directing us to go to House of
Commons, which we did to my great delight, and heard
the greater part of an interesting speech of Ld. Palmerston's against Govt. The debate was adjourned, so
we were home by ¼ 1. An eventful day.

[1] Appendix A.

LONDON, *June 9th*, 1859.—Bishop of Brechin, Sir J. Lacaita, Messrs. Parker, Russell, and Monckton Milnes, Sir J. Coleridge, Ld. Alfred Hervey, and Miss Williams Wynne came to breakfast, and I heard much interesting man-talk.

LONDON, *June 10th*, 1859.—We went with Papa and the Talbots to the British Institution, where were beautiful Gainsboroughs, etc. We wrote and directed more than 200 cards for a concert. And in the evening I had a great delight, in the rehearsal by 1,600 voices of part of the Handel Festival, at Exeter Hall. I could apply to it nothing but the words of Revelation : " The voice of many waters, and the voice of mighty thunderings," the basses especially ; the absence of all instruments except organ, and now and then drums, only showing how infinitely above them is a great unity of human voice. Oh, if I could but give an idea of it ! One of the things was the Dettingen Te Deum, and it was almost appalling to hear : " We believe that Thou shalt come to be our Judge," shouted with that tremendous harmony by so many : of each of whom it is true. " We praise Thee, O God ! " and this *was* praise fit for the Lord of Sabaoth ! " All the earth doth worship Thee "—and indeed one cd fancy the whole world joining in that triumphant worship. And the end, so grand in its trust : " Let me never be confounded." It might be Heaven—only it is over, and *that* is for ever and ever.

LONDON, *June 11th*, 1859.—A very memorable day, with a strange, abrupt contrast between the morning and evening. We were presented at 2 o'clock ; and after all the frightful bathing-feel [1] and awestruck anticipation, behold ! it was a moment of great happiness to me. The look of interest and kindliness in the dear little Queen's face, her bend forward, and the way she gave her hand to me to be kissed, filled me with pleasure that I can't describe, and that I wasn't prepared for. She said to Auntie Pussy : " You have brought yr nieces to me," with great feeling : oh, so touching of her ! for no doubt she was thinking of our having no

---

[1] Appendix A.

Mamma to bring us. And to Aunt Coque : "I am so glad to see them : tell your Mother how nice they looked." I feel as if I could do anything for her !

FALCONHURST, *June 12th*, 1859.—My 2nd Communion in this church—how different from the first ! And yet —as I trust I could realize a little—alike in the highest ways—the Communion of Saints, through all chances and changes—in all time of our tribulation, in all time of our wealth : the same unalterable reality. I knelt in the same place, and the last time so filled my memory, that it was almost impossible to feel what a change had come over everything. And oh dear ! the sight of Mr. Hunt, the smell of the church, the sound of the singing : nothing is altered, except our own selves. Mr. Hunt's sermons were just what they used to be : the texts, " Have I any strength, that I shd hope ? " and " Quench not the spirit," are enough, I hope, to keep the sermons in my head.

LONDON, *June 13th*, 1859.—Ugh ! how nasty London looks ! Directly we were home, at $\frac{1}{4}$2 about, we had to turn our minds to a concert at Ld. Ward's, to which we were to go at 3½ having " nothing to wear." However Atie Pussy had bought us bonnets from Brighton, where she has been since Saturday, and by astonishing luck they fitted ; so after altering the green in them, as our gowns were blue, and digging out white scarfs, we went.

LONDON, *June 15th*, 1859.—Very lovely day. A torrent of people came to luncheon : Sir J. Lacaita, Mrs. and E. Talbot, C. Jane Wortley, Annie and Mary Gladstone, the latter of whom is strikingly handsome. Afterwards I went with Atie Pussy, Aggy, and the children to a breakfast (! ! ! ? ?) at that beautiful place, Wimbledon, where there was little to do, and less to say, but we amused ourselves looking at people, and guzzling as it seemed all the afternoon. Poor Lord Seymour looked very dismal, Ly. Blanche Lascelles, whom his parents wouldn't let him marry, being engaged to Ld. Boyle. We daundered [1] over Ly. Hermione Graham's lovely little children : Margaret-Frances,

<hr>

[1] Appendix A.

Violet-Hermione, Helen, Sybil, Hilda-Georgina, and Richard-James. We picked up all these flowery names from the little creatures themselves. The eldest isn't six yet, the babies being twins. Atie P. had many political talks with different great guns. I was a good deal with Tallee and the Miss Seymours, to whom I was introduced. We played at At. Sally with the Speaker (Mr. Dennison) and Lord Stratford de Redcliffe. I have a conviction I took Mr. G. Dundas for Mr. Rolle. Cousin Jane gave us beautiful parasols and sashes, and dear Mrs. Talbot *such* muslin gowns.

LONDON, *June 16th*, 1859.—Then Mrs. Talbot took us to George St., where we dined, and came back for that momentous event, our first concert, which was what glorious music always is, the greater delight because it began unpropitiously ; but each thing overtopped the other, till we reached a climax, with Ly. Agneta Yorke and Ly. Hardwicke, who sung together with a power and pathos beyond description, their whole soul in their angelic voices ! And there was Miss Connor with her glorious ringing, clear, and flexible voice. Moreover, I was introduced to young Ly. Spencer, radiant in her winning loveliness : talked to the nice Yorkes, to Althorp, and many other folk. Tallee was there, with At. Yaddy. It would be worth coming to London if only for this sort of thing.

LONDON, *June 18th*, 1859.—Breathless, thundery sort of day. A profoundly quiet morning. We went to a little breakfast at Ld. J. Manners', with children. This may be briefly described as Dull. His little boy [1] of 7 is a fine, spirited fellow, exceedingly tall, and in a violent state of excitement. The D. of Rutland was there, looking most depressed. It is said he has never got over not being allowed to marry his first cousin, now Lady Newport. Lord B . . . was present, strikingly like an attenuated baboon. M. dined with Granny and Co., I with Papa at Ld. Camden's, where, having expected surpassing dulness, I was agreeably surprised, being between E. Neville and extremely agreeable Ld. Overstone. Moreover, I was determined

---

[1] The present Duke of Rutland.

to extract some conversation from the proverbially
silent Ladies Pratt, and succeeded, tho' far from the
point of discovering any brilliance of conversation.
Still they brightened up, and said more than yes and
no.   Home by 11, for Sunday.

LONDON, *June 19th*, 1859.—We dined at Spencer
House with Granny. At. C., U. Spencer and wife,
Miss Seymour and her brother : a family gathering, view [1]
U. Spencer's birthday, but it felt wicked, and was a
bore, to dress up and go smartish out to dinner on
Sunday.

LONDON, *June 20th*, 1859.—Nearly ¼4 and daylight.
3 mortal hours and a half have we been at Mme de
Persigny's ball, and sorrow a bit have I danced.   Till
2 o'clock no chance of it ; then Ld. Sudley engaged me
for a quadrille, which he performed with another lady.
His next attempt was futile, as the era for quadrilles
was over, and the cotillon preparing.   One or two other
hopes were dashed for this latter reason, and only came
to mock me, for what is a cotillon to me !   M. danced
once.   It was a brilliant ball, for them as danced, and
pleasant enough to look at for a while, there being
hardly any but beauties present, on principle, for
Count Persigny asked U. W.[2] if we were pretty enough
before inviting us.   What that relative's answer was
will for ever be unknown.   Before this eventless ball,
we dined pleasantly with the Spencers ; only I am
troubled with a frightful access of deafness with regard
to Ly. Spencer's voice, which is indistinct to me, and
I answer nonsense to the questions that come from her
beautiful mouth, and could beat myself.

LONDON, *June 21st*, 1859.—Now I have a little breath-
ing-time to spare from accounts of our perpetual dis-
sipations, to tell of much more interesting things.   U.
William has taken office under Ld. Palmerston, and is
Ch. of the Exchequer, thereby raising an uproar in
the midst of which we are simmering, view [3] his well-
known antipathy to the Premier.   What seems clear
is that he considers it right to swallow personal feelings

[1] Appendix A.   [2] Uncle William.   [3] Appendix A.

for the sake of the country ; besides he agrees at present with Lord P.'s foreign policy, also he joins several Peelites. There is this question, however : why, if he can swallow Palmn., couldn't he swallow Dizzy, and in spite of him go in under Lord Derby ? I don't pretend to be able to answer this, but one can enough understand things to be much excited and interested, above all by the contest he will have to undergo for his Oxford University seat, his opponent being Lord Chandos. It is likely to be a near thing. If he isn't returned, good-bye ! I went alone with A. P. to a little ball at Ly. G. Balfour's : where of the 4 dances that took place while I was present, I danced one, and was asked for three : 2 being valses,[1] and the 3rd we were going. Very pleasant.

LONDON, *June 24th*, 1859.—M. was taken by Cousin Jane to the C. Palace, where she heard " Israel in Egypt." And I have lost the Handel Festival, and shall never live to hear another, if it's true that it's to be centenary. This is very dismal to think. " Du reste," M. was rather disappointed, from not knowing the music well : what struck her most was " God save the Queen," when the enormous audience all cheered, thinking the Queen was there, which she was not, as it is said, because she does not like Handel ! ! ! As far as we can see, fair hopes at Oxford : the Bp. thereof much cut up at the defection of his very intimate friend, the Warden of All Souls', with others. Oh dear, the quantity one has to write ! In the afternoon I drove with Auntie Pussy : we went over Downing St., but she probably won't move there this year ; it looked very familiar to us. We took Winny to a little child's concern at Ly. De Mauley's, and in the park and streets shot [2] several people we knew : Susy Clinton, Ly. Egerton of Tatton, dear pretty little Miss Graham, of happy Escrick memory, Ld. Bristol's daughters, etc. Also went to see after C. Ebbett, and she not being up to seeing us, we stayed in the nursery, making ourselves fools over the darling little blue-eyed infant : the comfortable nurse, the atmosphere of flannel, the cozy fire, and the baby's little crowings, bringing to

[1] She was not allowed to valse. [2] Appendix A.

my mind many memories of Mamma, so pale and lovely, with one of our own sweet babies; and the happy quietness of those old times.

LONDON, *June 26th*, 1859.—We went to St. Martin's, where we sweltered in inconceivable bore through a 52-minutes' sermon, for the most part inaudible, and of the remainder not a sentence worth hearing. People began dropping out of the church in considerable numbers, and in some invisible locality most astonishing wheezing, groaning, and cracking went on at intervals, like several large clocks running down. These two causes united provoked almost irresistible giggle, as the reverend person went mildly on, undeterred by either. The singing was brisk and decidedly good, and the Minuet in " Samson " played after service.

I went with Atie. P. etc., to Chapel Royal, where Maria Marchioness of Ailesbury dropped her parasol all the way from the imposing eminence of the Peeresses' Gallery.

LONDON, *June 28th*, 1859.—We went to the most beautiful ball conceivable at Ly. Egerton of Tatton's, a horrid woman ; but such a room, such lighting, and such delightful space. I had ever so many chances of dancing, but only did 3 times, what with the valses, galops, and being jilted twice. I saw and was delighted with the Comte de Paris : " King of France." Such courtesy and nobleness : tall and handsome. Home, walking ! ! from St. James' Square at 3¼.

LONDON, *June 29th*, 1859.—What with the manifold delights of this eventful day, I'm sorry to confess that, till this moment, the fact of its being St. Peter's feast and dear old Albert's birthday has never entered my head. To begin with, we went to luncheon with the Grahams (daughters of Sir James), which was extremely pleasant, as we are getting to like them both very much. And they sang to us till I could have cried with delight. The lovely little one has the most glorious voice, and " The Land of the Leal " and " The Last Rose of Summer," especially the latter, so went to my heart that the vision of them keeps coming back upon me with an indescribable thrill. There ! I hope I'm not high-flown : but great enjoyment ought to do one good, and so far it does indeed make me thank God for giving us such pleasures. " Thou hast anointed my head with oil, and my cup runneth over." It is indeed goodness and mercy following us all the days of our life that gives us these happy hours.   .

After they had sung till they were tired, nice kind things that they are, and after much conversation, Atie. P. picked us up, and we went again to Wimbledon, which was lovely : the smell of hay all round, and the pleasant fresh day perfect. Oh, how cd I forget : I dined as a face [1] with A. P. and Wortleys at Ly. Waldegrave's, where I saw and was introduced to the " King of France," God bless him ! The crowning-point of these many breaks was our first Queen's ball, Meriel's very first ; I, as before detailed at great length, have been to children's balls at the Palace. What a beautiful sight it is ! the glittering uniforms, the regal rooms, and the Royal presence. We made our curtseys rather ill I'm afraid, such a slippery floor, and difficult to take the Queen's hand from her eminence of two steps. However, we did better than most, for at all events we went low down, and the rest of the world made nothing but nasty little bows and inclinations ; so horridly disrespectful. Pr. of Wales was there just come back from abroad, decidedly grown, tanned, and more manly looking, with all the Royal courtesy and grace of manner. Pr. Alice quite pretty, so very much improved in looks. The brother and sister valsed together with marvellous grace and dignity, considering that neither is tall. They went round only once or twice, slowly, so unlike the fierce fluttering whirls in a tight embrace that one sees elsewhere. It was happiness to see the Queen dancing the quadrilles with her colossal uniformed partners, majesty and grace in every movement of her little form, and the Pr. of Wales standing near her, and giving his hand to her in the Grand Rond with beautiful respect. And all to the sound of such music !

Of course we never dreamt of dancing, nor had we one chance, but this didn't in the least take from my

[1] Appendix A.

pleasure. The only thing that did was that all the king's horses and all the king's men couldn't make Atie Pussy sit down again (what lovely poetry!) after a little bit of rest in one of the outer rooms, till about ¼1. The consequence was that M. and she looked at death's door, and even my back began to ache. However, after a peep at the gorgeous supper-room with its sideboard of plate reaching to the ceiling, we did get her into one of the tiers of seats under the orchestra, where we sat in bliss for about 25 minutes, when shooting [1] a splendid place to the right of the throne, we moved there, and lucky it was we did! Five minutes afterwards, the Queen rose, and stepped down. With one rush everyone stood up, while the old glorious music of " God save the Queen " struck up. The officers of state went before her, but facing her as they cleared the way. As she bowed to right and left all curtseyed low, and so, to the majestic time of the music, she went out in all her state. Oh! I thought my heart would crack with excitement! And so it was over. What a happy day! I was determined to give a full, graphic, and particular account of it, and I think I have done my duty.

LONDON, *July 3rd*, 1859.—Had luncheon at G. St. and aft. service at the Abbey, where everything was got through in the most disgraceful slovenly manner.

LONDON, *July 4th*, 1859.—We had a prim luncheon at Ly. Windsor's, where nice Victoria Clive sang all the tunes that all old cows have died of. For the first time, two balls; duty first, and pleasure afterwards: Ly. Mary Hoare's, and Mrs. Washington Hibbert's. At the former there were not 5 people I knew; nevertheless I danced once, with Mr. Dundas. Mrs. Hibbert's was the most lovely thing I have ever seen in its way: a tent in the open air for ante-room, from whence you descended by a flight of steps into the ball-room, at the top of which you could stand and see the dancing like a magic picture. A smother of flowers, and cool atmosphere. I danced with Mr. Turvil and Johnny, and was asked to valse ever so often. . . .

[1] Appendix A.

We shopped, and our great-uncle's sister-in-law, the first Ly. Spencer's sister, the second's stepmother, and the third's aunt, and Althorp's stepmother's stepmother, in virtue of her intricate relationship,[1] gave us lovely muslin gowns.

LONDON, *July 6th*, 1859.—We went to our last breakfast at Wimbledon, Papa coming to see the place where he lived so much in his childhood, before Granny's eldest brother sold it to get rid of the debts on the estate. There are two lots of old pencil measurements in the gallery, one of great-uncle George Spencer in 1804. Papa was so interested and pleased to see them there still. The Duc and Duchesse d'Aumale were there. We had Annie Gladstone with us. In the evening a brilliant party at Ld. Lansdowne's.

LONDON, *July 7th*, 1859.—A breakfast, to which came the Comte of Paris! And I thrilled at him thro' the door of the private, or, as it is called, jimmy staircase, as long as he was there. There also came Duke and Duchess of Argyle, Bp. of Oxford, Mrs. Norton, and the King's "bottle-holder." Meanwhile, while I think of it, Mr. Brewster has got a baby, and A Living! ! ! !

LONDON, *July 8th*, 1859.—We went to Lord's to see the humiliating Harrow match : our 11 are at the lowest ebb of bad play, and they remarkably good. Unhappy Charles only got 9. . . .

A very delightful ball at Ly. Mary Wood's, of which the following were the great events. The Comte de Paris was there, and he engaged Susy Clinton for a quadrille, and set off to find a vis-à-vis. He returned saying "Il n'y en a pas!" whereupon Atie. P. grabbed Sir C. Wood, and sent him off to find one. In the interregnum, however, I (who wasn't dancing) flew at Willy, and dragged him up to act vis-à-vis ourselves, for which the Comte gave me two beautiful little bows of thanks. This was happiness enough ; but after the quadrille the Comte came up and thanked Atie. P. for getting him a vis-à-vis, thinking it was her doing, and

---

[1] This lady of remarkable relationships was, I think, Frances Isabella Dowager Lady Clinton. But the Lady Spencer whose sister she was, was wife of the 4th Earl, not of the 1st.

she, with her wonted sagacity, told him what an honour I had felt it, and that I had a great enthusiasm for France. (Rather a lie that; my enthusiasm is for the old Royalty, not for that fidgety country.) Well, he didn't speak for a moment, as if he was pleased, and then asked if she thought I wd do him the honour of dancing with him. I didn't hear all this transaction, being out on the balcony airing myself. The next thing I saw was the Comte making a gracious bow to *M.*, and she with a most awestruck curtsey accepting him for the next quadrille. The fact was he had taken her for me! So I was made to take her place, and waited in palpitating excitement. After the valse that was going on, it was the turn for a Lancers, but they had a quadrille instead. The Comte, however, being engaged for that dance, couldn't throw his partner over, tho' it wasn't Lancers, and couldn't have me of course. So after it was over, he came up to explain. I stood up in unutterable bathing feel,[1] and he began in lovely French, and the extreme of grace in his manner, to say that he had expected the dance just over would have been Lancers, would it be too late for me to wait for the next quadrille? was I sure it wouldn't be? then " Mais, ne vous dérangez pas," so I sat down, thrilling; and a good deal more talk about dancing, the quantity of valsing, which he didn't like, the pity they never danced polka mazurka, how nice balls in the country were, etc. Oh! how delighted I was! The Fates decreed however that my quadrille should never come off. The next was Lancers, and then the stupid cotillon, so up he had to come again : " Je suis désolé," and what not. I managed to say : " Monseigneur, vous m'avez fait trop d'honneur en me demandant," and then curtseys and bows, and we went away. I cannot describe the nobleness of his look and manner, and the beautiful old French courtesy. And there he is, the descendant of that ancient glorious race, tho' it is a younger branch, still the same blood; banished from his country, and with that upstart Napoleon on the throne in his eye! What with awe, respect, com-

[1] Appendix A.

passion, and gratitude, I was nearly out of my mind. Certainly I have enjoyed this ball more than any other.

LONDON, *July 9th*, 1859.—We went again to Lord's with Mrs. Talbot and sons : the play was a little improved, and there were some fine leg hits ; but oh ! Charles was out third ball, by a brilliant shooter, lightning swift, middle stump. We immediately drove off, in a raging state of disappointment. Home a little past two, luncheon, dressing, and then we went by the 4 o'clock train to Ly. Marian Alford's beautiful breakfast.[1] The train was 20 min. late, and the journey horrid with the dust, which grievously dirtied my new gloves. At Tring, where carriages were to be provided by Ly. Marian, we had to wait an hour before they came, then such a scramble for them. We got off at last in a break with Ly. Clarendon and the Villiers, but didn't arrive till 7. Such a beautiful drive, and the place glorious : 800 people were there in the course of the day : heaps that we knew. We sat, walked, and talked, eat some cold dinner and listened to the splendid Grenadier band. At dusk, the band moved under the windows, and some dancing began. Ed. Neville turned up, and carried me off for a quadrille, a capital one, of 50 people, but plenty of room. Then we sat in the beautiful darkness on the terrace, looking at the pretty illuminations in the garden, and finally, who shd I shoot [2] but the Comte de Paris ! ! Atie. Pussy, flying into activity, plunged after him ; we watched him thro' a quadrille ; and after it, he saw us : profound was my curtsey. He engaged me for the next Lancers, which he'd no sooner done than I missed my pretty chrysoprase bracelet, which took away nearly all my pleasure. Well, I took off my bonnet, to look my best, but then, to my anguish, he passed me two or three times without recognizing me. Also the room emptied, and it looked as if there was to be no more dancing. All that, however, came right, he came up at last rather dubiously, and looking doubtfully at M. all the time, said the Lancers were beginning in another room,

[1] At Ashridge. Lady Marian was the mother of the late Earl Brownlow.   [2] Appendix A.

hooked me, and off we went !—oh, bliss !—M. following with Ed. Neville. We got them for vis-à-vis, and were only late for one figure. He talked of the House of Commons, asked if I ever went there, said he often did. I told him how I heard Ld. Lyndhurst, and we danced the 2nd figure. In the third, he began the visiting, when it ought to be the curtsey one, and we'd hardly got that right, when there was a general rush to the window, to see a very flat little firework. So as I remarked to him, " La destinée ne veut pas " that we should ever dance a thing through. For it all broke up, and he hooked me again, and we marched, half over the house, looking in vain for Atie. Pussy, which gave occasion for another beautiful bit of French from me : " Mais, Monseigneur, je crains bien que je ne gêne votre Altesse Royale." " Pas du tout ! " of course was the answer. Then I said, à propos of his asking me, " C'est pour moi un grand honneur," to which he answered something about " pour moi un grand plaisir." At last M. and Edward, who were following us, proposed that I should stay with them, for I was quite hot at keeping him ; " Mais je voudrais vous ramener à Mme Gladstone." " Monseigneur, je crains de gêner votre Altesse." " Pas du tout. Mais où resterez vous donc ? " " Ma sœur est ici, Monseigneur." " Ah ! c'est bien donc." A beautiful bow, a deep curtsey, and that most exciting and delightful trans-action was well over. We stayed till about 10½ looking into the beautiful solemn chapel, full of very old sober-coloured and stained glass, so profoundly quiet after the crowds outside, but almost too near the room where they were valsing, so that the music followed one to the threshold. We crammed 13 into a break, with Ly. Schomberg Kerr and Ly. Constance Grosvenor, the others invisible in the dark, and had great fun bumping down the long steep hill, feeling very near upsetting now and then. At the station, to my very great delight, my bracelet turned up again, found by a poor man, to whom I gave 6s. on the spot. We waited in the train an hour before it set off, with the nice Wilbrahams who were with us, then everyone went to sleep, except me, who only succeeded in getting muzzy and uncomfortable, and we arrived at home at 2 on Sunday morning, feeling wicked. Eat some cold mutton at that dead hour, and went to bed, everyone hideously tired except me. Wretched Willy, who was to have gone to Eton from Tring, missed the train and had to go early this morning.

LONDON, *July 11th*, 1859.—Big Ben began striking the hours in a deep melodious tone, with an endless echo.

HAGLEY, *July 29th*, 1859.—Thank Heaven, we came safely home to the dear bright snug quietness of green summer Hagley. I think I never so much appreciated the sight of the six flourishing children who stood on the steps, or ever felt so thankful that darling Papa can look at our band unbroken, and not see the sad gaps among little faces that haunt one at poor Hawarden.[1] They are all blooming, except little Edward, who is puny as Albert was, tho' far less ill than he, and tanned, which makes his small phiz look healthier. As for that young plant Alfred, his size and height and figure are splendid! such a neck, chest, and forehead, with all the good points of Charles, Nevy, and Arthur in his noble little head and face. Fluent though happily still broken conversation, and such fun, memory, and sharpness. O bless him, for a gladdening sunbeam! Bobby enormous, and not very evidently more intellectual. May, I think, a degree less ugly! Win and Arthur very charming. Much talk with Miss Smith; and I went in the twilight to see our *own* Church, and look at Mamma's beautiful E. window, shining thro' darkness, as the thought of her does, in all that happens.

1 Where one of her Glynne cousins had just died at the Rectory.

BOOK VI
DECEMBER 1860—JUNE 1862

INTRODUCTION TO BOOK VI

THE fifth volume of the diary, which covered the rest of 1859 and nearly all 1860, was lost almost as soon as it was written. The first entry in Book VI refers to its loss, and the letter to the Cab Office mentioned in the first extract was an enquiry about it. It was never recovered. Its great event must have been the marriage of Meriel, Lucy's eldest and very intimate sister, the " old thing " of the diary, to John Gilbert Talbot, afterwards for many years Member for Oxford University. The present volume shows Lucy taking her sister's place as mistress of Hagley and mother of the younger children, so far as a sister can play a mother's part. She is all through endlessly occupied with the health and the characters of all her brothers and sisters. Albert's illnesses fill many pages, and cause much anxiety; his character, on the other hand, none at all. She gives her views at some length of all the others: shrewd and observant, always very affectionate, by no means exclusively complimentary. One of these is quoted, that of Arthur, the Queen's Page, who, alone of Queen's Pages, ended his life as a Bishop. One person, too, of the generation younger than her brothers occupied a good deal of space—her first nephew, George, now Mr. Justice Talbot, all of whose baby doings and sufferings are minutely and admiringly recorded. I incline to think that I am respecting what would be his wishes in leaving these pages in the seclusion of manuscript. They are, indeed, unique in the Diary; for Lady Frederick never had a child of her own; and Mrs. Talbot, though in no hurry for babies, as her sister records, did in fact have so many of these best of all possessions that even the most affectionate of aunts could not be expected to receive the later arrivals with the enthusiasm with which she greeted the first.

For the rest, Lucy Lyttelton's life goes on here much as before, divided between Hagley, country-house visits, and London. When in London she stays at 11 Downing Street, whither the Gladstones had removed from Carlton House Terrace, apparently not taking Mr. Gladstone's books with them: for she complains of it as a " bookless house " when she had typhoid fever there in May 1861. The London life, of course, repeats in general that of her first season. There are a great many parties and balls; and certain names, especially those of Lord Cowper and Sir Charles Mordaunt, recur very frequently as partners. But there is not the slightest hint of any special feeling of interest in anybody as yet ; and I doubt whether several mysterious allusions, in September and October of 1861, to suspense and anxiety and the desire for guidance, refer to anything of that kind. If they do, the reference is probably to another young man, a friend of her eldest brother's whom she frequently met and always liked meeting.

Besides the balls and parties in London there were occasional operas and theatres, though she was not allowed to go to the opera when it included a ballet. She visits picture-galleries, and after visiting South Kensington Museum records her opinion that the pictures of Turner's middle period are " beauties," but that his later ones should all be inscribed " Fire in a Fog " ; while her impressions of the Academy in 1862 are of " overdone lurid glows, glaring colours, solid gold cornfields, manufactured heather and herbage, woollen water, and a general air of papier-mâché tea-tray," all of which shows that there is nothing new under the sun, not even in the writings of the newest and most advanced criticisms of the Academicians ! She attends a Drawing Room (as Queen Victoria's Courts were called), and has the disagreeable experience of being taken very sick on arrival and having to retire to the ministrations of the Royal housekeeper, who had " everything handy for such an emergency." However, she was soon duly " bolstered up " for the Presence and all went well. " The Queen shook hands with me and asked after Meriel." She continually rides in the Row at the then fashionable hour of half-past twelve. She is often present at what she calls the " clever breakfasts " ; at which she sees and hears such men as Bishop Wilberforce, Lord Houghton, Lord Acton, Lord Dufferin, and other notable intellectuals of that time. At one she met two Frenchmen who talked of French schools " where the boys would stab right and left with pen-knives if they were flogged, as they richly deserve to be ! and of which one of my neighbours said he retained such a dismal impression that for a long time he dreamt of school whenever he had the nightmare ; where also they haven't space for cricket ! "

There is a great deal about the death of the Prince Consort, which darkened the season of 1862, as her own illness had, for her, rather spoilt that of 1861, taking up all May, and causing the first half of June to be spent recruiting at Sheen, the house of her cousins the Wortleys, the youngest of whom was afterwards to marry her brother Neville. But she was very content there, the country and the spring and the feeling of recovery all helping to make her happy. Her entry on June 11th is : " Oh, so lovely, like poetical May ; and how shall I describe my enjoyment of the soft brisk wind and fragrant lanes this morning when I drove a mouse of a pony, in a bit of a carriage, with Mary to Wimbledon Common ? Oh, the treat of reins and whip in my hands again ! " Mrs. Wortley afterwards forbade this driving when she heard of it : either thinking Lucy not strong enough for it, or perhaps not thinking it " proper." The limits of propriety were strict in those days. The diarist walks alone on the pier at Brighton, but records that it " suddenly struck " her as " scampish " ; and we hear of her and her cousin Agnes Gladstone walking

I—10

from Downing Street " over to Stratton Street " (her
grandmother's house) " after breakfast with footman,"
which she describes in brackets as " rather scampish,
but it was early and the streets empty." It sounds
almost as if they had breakfasted with the footman,
which would have been " scampish " indeed ; but it
was evidently bad enough to venture without any other
protector on this bold and dangerous walk !

In the country, too, there are things recorded which
have an antiquarian interest to-day. In a pen-sketch
she gives of the skating at Hawarden in December 1860
the men wear top-hats ! She records that at Hagley
five-o'clock tea was then a luxury reserved for Sundays.
Probably the dress she wore as bridesmaid at her cousin
Reginald Yorke's wedding will seem to connoisseurs
as out of date as tea only once a week ! She describes
herself as " figged out in tarlatane trimmed at the
bottom with light green *battlements*, a geranium
wreath, a tulle veil flying behind, and a pretty locket
presented for the occasion." Nor are some of the
amusements recorded any longer in vogue. Cricket
and croquet and billiards, all of which she records
herself as playing, are indeed still popular ; and girls
hunt and fish to-day at least as often as she did. But
ordinary riding has almost disappeared from roads
overrun by motors ; and archery and its accompanying
" bow meetings," though not perhaps unknown, are
no longer often heard of. Nor do many young people
now know enough poetry to play the game of " capping
verses," which Lucy Lyttelton is always playing, both
before and after her marriage. In this volume she
describes herself as going a twenty-mile ride with her
uncle, the last twelve miles of which were done under
pouring rain, so that they arrived home soaked to the
skin. But " we came the ten miles home within an
hour, capping verses to keep up our spirits."

Nor does anyone, so far as I know, now practise a
curious sort of game which she describes herself as
going in for at Lady de Tabley's, with touching results

which she no doubt kept to herself. "Lady Jane
Levett set us all off feeling each other's pulses to discover which, of three individuals thought of, the person
whose pulse is being held loves most. Very little could
be made out of my odd feeble pulse at first ; but at last
I thought of some indifferent person, and then of darling
Mammie, and the change was from a small weak pulse
to a very quick one. A proof I can't help liking that
one's love is not vague and unreal, but actually affecting
one's nature." Strange that she should have fancied
she needed any proof of the sincerity of her love, not
only of the dead mother but of the living father and
brothers and sisters. It is written plain in almost every
page of the Diary.

POSTSCRIPT

Since this was in type, I have been lent a little
volume written in 1862 in place of the lost fifth book
of the Diary. Of course it only relates a few doings
which stood out enough to be remembered after two
years. There is a visit to Althorp, where she says of
the new and beautiful Lady Spencer—"Spencer's
Fairy Queen," as she used to be called—" I am falling
head over ears in love with Charlotte. Mr. Leslie is
painting her : but does he hope to do justice to her
lovely expression, her dancing ingenuous eyes and indescribable winsomeness, etc ? Sanguine ! " She met
Lord Derby, the Prime Minister, at Witley (Lord Dudley's) and describes him as " beyond anything agreeable " ; adding that he " flirts with me in a way that
does me honour." At Witley, too, we hear that she
walked ten miles to church and back " through mud,
up hill, with an immensely heavy poplin gown to hold
up." She finds Cliveden " full of dignified and courteous
grandees " who fill her with " portentous shyness ":
" the old Duke " (of Sutherland) " still very grand
looking but as deaf as a post." And there is a Royal

Ball at which she danced with Lord Cowper, who is described as " a grand partner."

But of course the chief event mentioned is her sister Meriel's engagement, which took place on an expedition to the Crystal Palace, on May 26th, 1860; and her marriage, which followed on July 19th at Westminster Abbey. There is nothing to quote in her account of it, unless it be this: " I don't think darling old Meriel and I slept very calmly on this our last night together, after all these happy years of sisterhood."

DIARY, DECEMBER 1860—JUNE 1862

HAWARDEN, *Friday, December 28th*, 1860.—Same weather. Church at 11, after some effort, after ball hours. Capital sliding and skating, when everyone tumbled over except Ld. Jermyn, Willy, Mr. Ryan and me ; Ld. Clarence [1] fell on his head, Mr. Layton on his cheekbone, Agnes on all-fours, Atie. P. and Selina Lascelles on their knees, the children in all directions, and Ld. John Hervey promiscuous. The latter, whom I tried to cultivate, viewing Charles's friendship, is nice and engaging. I wrote to Papa and the Cab Office. Pleasant evening, ending with Lancers.

HAGLEY, *Tuesday, January 8th*, 1861.—The distress at Coventry is quite appalling ; a once well-to-do tradesman stole meat from a butcher's, and was found with his family tearing it to pieces like wild beasts.

HAGLEY, *Tuesday, January 15th*, 1861.—Wild March wind, driving the snow in all directions : quite good-bye the thaw. The poor people at the club and everywhere speak of the hard times : borrowing money for actual food.

HAGLEY, *Friday, January 18th*, 1861.—There seems a cry of distress all over the country, London they say as bad as country ; everything at a standstill. £80,000 [2] nevertheless will first and last go to Coventry ! I shd think anything cd be done with that.

HAGLEY, *Saturday, January 19th*, 1861.—Some talk about the dreadful Oxford Free-thinking.

HAGLEY, *Tuesday, January 22nd*, 1861.—At. C. writes of the hungry Bedworth people, kept alive by diligent care from day to day ; and, as far as one can see, nothing else before them.

---

[1] Lord Clarence Paget.   [2] Or £30,000 : the figure is not legible.

HAGLEY, *Monday, January 28th*, 1861.—Messrs. Claughton and Pepys ; the former lectured on Poetry, reading extracts from Crabbe and Spenser quite beautifully. But too little variety.

HAGLEY, *Friday, February 1st*, 1861.—Aunt C. came back from her gallant hard work at Coventry none the worse, and having evidently been invaluable. They have hope of the trade looking up in a month ; meanwhile daily feeding and clothing amongst misery, cheating, and starvation goes on.

ESCRICK, *Thursday, February 7th*, 1861.—Our precious blossom, Alfred, struck four. Each year in his sunny little life marks more than anything the distance between the present and the cloudless Past. Four years ! He wd rejoice Mamma's heart, with his bright generous temper, his amazing winsomeness, his quickness and noble looks.

ESCRICK, *Monday, February 11th*, 1861.—Dr. Vaughan pioneered us [1] : I greatly dislike his curious, silky, feminine voice.

HAGLEY, *Ash Wednesday, February 13th*, 1861.—After what seemed a lull, the distress at Bedworth has broken out again awfully : one poor old woman tried to kill herself, from " clamming."

HAGLEY, *2nd Sunday in Lent, February 24th*, 1861.— Albert wrote to John, saying Edward's tutor Curgenven seems bitten with these horrible " Essays and Reviews," which some sound theologian ought to answer.

HAGLEY, *Saturday, March 2nd*, 1861.—Heavy stormy rain, thro' which At. Emy and I were pleased to walk parochially. Tommy Morris came to the Rectory and sang to us, that we might decide if his voice is good enough to compete for a choir place at Windsor ! Part of the Crystal Palace was blown down. To-morrow morning all the Russian serfs will be free men ! A grand thing.

HAGLEY, *Saturday, March 16th*, 1861.—At. C. came

[1] In a visit to Doncaster Church, of which he was Vicar. He was afterwards Master of the Temple, where, in spite of his " curious silky " voice and manner, his sermons, which were not at all " silky," attracted great congregations.

back from Bedworth at last looking blooming, and saying there is a slight improvement in work just now, but *very* little. Also bringing some presentation sausages from a poor man whom she has helped to start with that commodity. Tantalizes me with accounts of the quickness and earnestness of some of the people, which really leads to some good coming of working amongst them. One hardly ever sees any results in stolid country poor.

BRIGHTON, *Tuesday, April 2nd,* 1861.—I walked alone on the pier, which it suddenly struck me was scampish.

BRIGHTON, *Thursday, April 4th,* 1861.—Went to St. Paul's for 8½-o'c. service ; having to walk back alone, I pretended to belong to two elderly ladies in succession, who I don't think found out that they were escorting me.

LONDON, *Thursday, April 11th,* 1861.—There departed to-day Charles and I to London for the ball, which came off at Carlton Terrace with great success : I can't remember all my innumerable partners ! One, however, I do remember ; the " King of France " (Comte de Paris) asked particularly after me and danced with me : stomach-ache of thrill ! For the rest, Messrs. Trefusis, Ryan, Le Fevre,[1] Hope, and Capt. Grant, Mrs. Percy's distinguished son, are all I remember. Charles was quite the handsomest man there : enjoyed himself, and danced with Warrens, T. Gladstones, and Sybil Grant. Introduced me to the D. of St. Albans with great propriety ! Declares he will learn to valse ! ! Everyone looked well in white and black. The house recalls the days of courtship [2] and matrimony wonderfully !

BRIGHTON, *2nd Sunday after Easter, April 14th,* 1861. —We all went to St. Paul's in the morning ; fine singing ; anthem, Spohr's " Blessing and honour." S. Mary's aftn., sermon by Mr. Elliott on the tremendous Indian famine : he got £73 from his morning congregation !

[1] No doubt G. J. Shaw-Lefevre, afterwards a Cabinet Minister and now Lord Eversley.
[2] Presumably referring to her elder sister Meriel's marriage.

BRIGHTON, *Tuesday, April 16th*, 1861.—I went with Papa over S. Mary's Home ; a penitentiary, hospital, sisterhood, school, and nursery all in one, under Mr. Wagner. The Lady Superior showed us all over ; a cheerful, pleasant woman. The penitents do all the household work. Everything beautifully arranged, clean, bright, and airy. The sick children's room very touching ; one poor pretty little fellow, hopelessly ill with abscesses, knitting in his crib, with such a placid angel look in his small wasted face. There were some things rather shocking to one : a picture of the Blessed Virgin crowned, with the words in Latin, " Holy Mother of God, pray for us " ; which I trust was only there for ornament ; otherwise it goes beyond mere sentiment. Also a large crucifix in one of the sisters' rooms. But it is a wonderfully good and great work, and one must believe it is done in the full strength of the text which was in nearly every room : " The love of Christ constraineth us."

Nevy, Spencer, and I had an hour's boating. Papa said (of St. Mary's) that it was always a striking thing to go among people who were in the very *straightest* road heavenwards.

LONDON, *Tuesday, April 23rd*, 1861.—I dined [1] there, and then came to Downing Street,[2] where Atie. P. and Aggie were looking well. I am so glad it ain't Carlton Terrace : grim grandeur, and how I shd hate it without Meriel ! A first-rate ball at Ly. Egerton of Tatton's, where we both danced plentifully. My partners were Ld. Carnarvon, Althorp (oh, little Charlotte ![3] I fell over head and ears in love as usual), Mr. Wortley, Lord Cowper, and Mr. Sarin. Home abt. 3. So off we go !

LONDON, *Wednesday, April 24th*, 1861.—A squash at Ly. Derby's, which was very amusing ; he in immense spirits, poking fun at Atie. P. about the Budget, which, however, it is expected will be accepted and approved : 1*d.* off the income tax, duty off paper, but left on tea

---

[1] I.e. at 10 Great George Street, her sister's house.
[2] To which Mr. Gladstone had now moved as Chancellor of the Exchequer.
[3] Lady Spencer, wife of " Althorp."

and sugar, which I believe I ought to rage at, being a Conservative ! Am I ? I don't quite know.

LONDON, *Monday, April 29th*, 1861.—We went with Atie. P. to the House and stayed till 2 ! Uncle W. spoke quite admirably in defence of the Budget, and Dizzy admirably against it ; so I am left in the wood.

LONDON, *Tuesday, April 30th*, 1861.—Uncle W. in rollicking spirits over his Budget, and very kind to me.

LONDON, *Thursday, May 2nd*, 1861.—The Duke and Duchess of Argyll dined here and Mr. Norton, and I at once fell into a fit of Cliveden [1] shyness. Uncle W. was hoarse after another great speech, Atie. P. silent, and the three guests would speak below their breath, so we were sotto voce to a painful extent.

LONDON, *Tuesday, May 7th*, 1861.—We went to Miss Coutts's [2] to hear the tragedian Fechter (whom everyone raves of) read a particularly scampish French play in the most beautiful way. Poor Miss Coutts sat on thorns, not anticipating the scampishness, and a Bishop or two stalked out ! Aggy and I dined alone.

LONDON, *Tuesday, June 4th*, 1861.—Slept like a top, and eat vigorously, but I had a nice upset with Wheeler's proceedings. She has for some days been tiffy with the nurse, thinking she (Wheeler) was reckoned a p.h., [3] and such-like nonsense, and has treated me to one scene, for which she begged pardon afterwards. But now it has been settled that the nurse is to go to Sheen with me : two can't go, so the Grim One must stay behind. She should have had a holyday meanwhile, but she flew into a passion with Atie. P., and gave warning to me rather impertinently, so as I ain't a horse yet, I was put into a regular tremble and heart-beatings. It's a most lamentable thing, the want of common Christianity in servants. Suppose it was an unnecessary fidget to take the nurse (which it ain't, as Atie. P. won't be much there and there's no doctor near), one shd think it a very simple

---

[1] She had met the Duke and Duchess of Argyll at Cliveden, where the Duke of Sutherland lived.
[2] Afterwards Baroness Burdett-Coutts.
[3] See Appendix A.

duty to give up one's own wish and swallow one's own pride rather than kick up a dust, especially with a Hinvalid [1]; but they wd never dream of such a thing. I could kick her.

SHEEN, *June 6th, Thursday,* 1861.—Wheeler at the last moment ate humble pie; and was received back into favour with dignified condescension.

SHEEN, *Monday, June 10th,* 1861.—For the first time a potation of port wine flew into my head, so 3 cheers, I am to leave it off. When I was ill I actually drank what wd amount to a tumbler full in the 24 hours! besides quinine. And the nurse tells me they give wine or brandy in every fever. The great Cavour has died of typhus or some such thing, because the doctors wd do nothing but bleed. They say there will be a rumpus all over Europe.

LONDON, *Monday, June 24th,* 1861.—Most tremendous accts. of the fire in the papers: the greatest since 1666! It is along a whole line of warehouses on the banks of the river, full of every sort of store—oil, tallow, cheese, bacon, sugar, cotton, hops, saltpetre, and what not; and so fierce that the " fireproof " buildings seem to become red hot, and are of no avail. The neighbouring street (Tooley St.) is ankle deep in hot tallow and the Thames itself blazing with masses of burning oil. The ruins are glowing with white heat, the engines were entirely useless, and the excellent head fireman, Braidwood, is killed, with others. They hope to keep it now from spreading further, but if the wind rose I believe it wd be impossible to check it. Providentially it has been perfectly calm weather hitherto. About 2 millions' worth of damage done.

LONDON, THE COPPICE, *Saturday, June 29th,* 1861.— I came to the Coppice with Mr. Phillimore: pleasant breezy weather, which makes the trip to this nice green place very enjoyable. The 2 eldest girls have outgrown their looks, but Catherine and Lucy seem extremely intelligent and sharp, with a strong turn for

[1] She had just had typhoid fever.

quizzing, inherited ! Walter [1] a nice fellow and quite awfully clever.

LONDON, *Tuesday, July 2nd*, 1861.—Charles has been playing well in Gentlemen agst Players : got 3 of the best wickets. Papa deep in " The Woman in White." A comet was visible. Meanwhile the great fire goes on, being fed by vast underground stores.

LONDON, *Wednesday, July 3rd*, 1861.—Delightful home ball (my last dancing was on May day !) ; not too crowded nor too empty, and everyone enjoying life peculiarly. Many grandees, however, missed fire : my partners were beyond dowdyissimus [2] ! Messrs. Ryan, Hope, Majendie, Willy, Wynne, Yorke, Baker, and Edward Neville. From 11 to 3 ; and I went to bed as fresh as may be.

LONDON, *Monday, July 8th*, 1861.—I was treated in the evening by Mrs. Talbot to the greatest treat I have had this season : " Hamlet " at the Princess's with the admirable German actor Fechter. In spite of his very evident foreign accent, he did the part most beautifully ; the acting throughout being perfect, and an entirely new delight to me in these days of no good tragic actors. Oh ! what an absorbing, exciting delight it is to see !

HAGLEY, *Friday, August 30th*, 1861.—Ld. Sandon is to marry Ly. Mary Cecil, refreshing and satisfactory after the Misses . . . and . . . marriages. O if they were profligate Brown and Tomkins instead of profligate Marquis and Viscount, how loud wd be the horror and disdain of the world !

HAGLEY, *Wednesday, September 18th*, 1861.—A horrid business turned up : the girls' Swiss maid, Henriette Descoster, has been thieving and is to be prosecuted, as an example to others and a warning to herself.

HAGLEY, *Thursday, September 19th*, 1861.—The horrid business of Henriette's being taken into custody took place, Mr. Marcy coming over about it. She showed strangely little feeling ; some loud crying, but did not beg off or defend herself, or say she was sorry.

---

[1] Now Lord Phillimore.   [2] See Appendix A.

Went away with the policeman very quietly, tho' rather red in the face. But my spirits are low, thinking of her loneliness and disgrace to-night.

HAGLEY, *Friday, September 20th,* 1861.—Wretched Wheeler went to witness against Henriette, who was sentenced to 14 days' prison and hard labour, after Wheeler had been well badgered by a rascally attorney, who got Henriette to engage him in her defence.

HAGLEY, *Saturday, September 28th,* 1861.—Went with John [1] to see wretched Henriette in Worcester gaol. Found her in strapping health and unchanged in manner, only I discovered she cried for the first time after I had spoken to her. Has needlework to do. We were taken over the gaol and were much edified : the prisoners looked subdued but not sullen, all busy at something or other, everything as clean as it's possible to be, and beautifully ordered. But what an oppressive thing to feel oneself under that irresistible overlooking and coercing power and obliged to revolve in that invariable round !

HAGLEY, *Sunday, September 29th,* 1861.—Anxiety and trial are before me ; but I think I have strong hope and trust about whatever may happen.
" So long Thy Hand hath bless'd us, sure it still will lead us on."

HAGLEY, *Wednesday, October 2nd,* 1861.—I wish I could stay a little while longer among these quiet days —that this calm sort of pause in our life might last a little !

HAGLEY, *Friday, October 4th,* 1861.—Very mild and pleasant. Church ill attended. I walked with At. C. towards the Rectory, to Mrs. Preisse and to croquet : 1 game ; a little accounts, Peerage corrections (of which I make, I suppose, on an average 1 every 2 days), little boys' Bible and singing, *Promessi Sposi,* 5 o'clock sit with Granny, 6 o'clock ditto with schoolroom ; whist, reading and At. Coque's music ; so I filled up the quiet day, which had, however, its worry and

---

[1] I.e. John Talbot.

distress, over and above the strange sense of suspense just now.

Letters from C. Neave, and (dreadfully angry) Miss S. ; to C. Neave, Arthur, and Mrs. Oxley (not sent).

HAGLEY, *Saturday, October 5th*, 1861.—I keep myself to a wonderful extent from looking forward.

HAGLEY, *Thursday, October 10th*, 1861.—All the suspense and anxiety of the last days is taken away and I feel proportionably light-hearted.

HAGLEY, *Wednesday, November 20th*, 1861.—Went with Papa and Uncle Henry to see rifle shooting at 900 and 650 yards. Only one man got in at 900 while we were there.

HAGLEY, *Friday, November 29th*, 1861.—Those precious Yankees have stopped a merchant ship of ours (the *Trent*) and carried off, from under her flag, certain accredited commissioners, which proceeding excites great uproar. I spouted the *Times* account and leading article.

HAGLEY, *Tuesday, December 3rd*, 1861.—We shall go to war with America if the Govt. doesn't apologise ; which it is far from likely it will do. On the side of the slave-owners too.

HAGLEY, *Wednesday, December 18th*, 1861.—Sullen, dark, dark weather. Poor Granny received many sad and touching letters which took out of her grievously [1] ; and the service was strangely overpowering ; the familiar prayers for the Queen full of deep pathos ; the funeral Psalm, some parts of the 1st lesson curiously appropriate, and greatly moving one ; and then the missing of his name, and the Prince of Wales' coming alone, reminding one of his altered and responsible position now, left fatherless to be the stay and support of the desolate Queen. God enable him to be so ! We heard that Her Majesty is still calm and, thank God, can sleep, and cries much : finds consolation in her children ; and Prss. Alice, whose " life was bound up in her father's," is an Angel in the house. Miss Hild-

---

[1] The Prince Consort had died on December 14th.

yard's letter one almost dwells most on; none knew
the Prince better than she and Granny, and accordingly
there are none who so loved and looked up to him.
But indeed, everyone does that in proportion as they
knew him.   Miss H. said that a hasty word was never
heard from him.   His last words to Prss. Alice were :
" Good child."   She will love to remember them !
When someone mentioned Granny to the Queen, she
said, " Ah, she knew our happy, happy life."   Most
nobly and patiently she seems to be taking up the
cross, set upon doing what would have pleased her
husband, and saying : " I will do anything "—showing
that she accepts the dreadful change with meekness
and courage.   I can't help going on about it all, for
the cloud over the days is ever before me, and it is
such a great, solemn, and awful thing.

HAGLEY, *Thursday, December* 19*th*, 1861.—Granny
heard from Atie. P. ; she quoted from the Dean of
Windsor (who was present) the most interesting and
pathetic account there has yet been.   He says he
cannot speak of the last scene without tears.   " The
Queen threw herself on the Prince with one fervent
kiss, and then let herself be led quietly away, with such
a look of despair on her face !   She then went to the
younger children, who were in bed, and kissed them,
and took little Princess Beatrice to her own room."
Those were (nearly) his words.   The simplicity of this
makes it more touching, and brings her deep, gently-
borne sorrow most piteously before one.

HAGLEY, *Thursday, December* 26*th*, 1861.—Troops
have embarked for Canada, amongst others, Edwd.
Neville.   There is scarcely a doubt that there will
be war;   altogether this year goes down in gloom.
Willy Gladstone has heard from the Prince of Wales,
who says " the Queen is sadly shattered."   But her
patience and calmness seem not to desert her.

HAGLEY, *Friday, December* 27*th*, 1861.—Ly. C.
Barrington wrote from Osborne with good accounts
of the Queen.   I had pleasant sensible talk with old
Nevy, who I fancy is rather softer than usual : much
more civil they all are.   Walked parochially and

pleasantly with Win and May visiting Mrs. Ince and her new-born baby girl.

HAGLEY, *December 30th*, 1861.—Granny heard from Mrs. Talbot a most characteristic and touching saying of the Queen's. She said to Ld. Granville : " He taught me how to reign. I hope I shall show that I can do it."

HAGLEY, *Tuesday, December 31st*, 1861.—And now this troubled and saddened year is past ! Never in my recollection, and I should fancy hardly ever in any recollection, can there have been a year so full of awful events. It opened with the Coventry famine. Then the death of the Duchess of Kent, the great fire, the deaths of Lord Herbert, Sir J. Graham, Cavour ; the Indian famine ; the death of Lady Canning, and finally of the Prince—all these have darkened this year, besides the American war, and the almost certain prospect of ourselves being dragged into it. The sun may well go down in total eclipse to-night, as it does, tho' unseen by us ! The Future is most dark, great troubles seem coming, and much of the wisdom and strength that would have faced and overcome it is lost to the country for ever. And the overwhelming thought of our Queen now setting out on the untried sea of loneliness and affliction—this is the greatest grief of all.

Thank God, when all is sad and clouded, we can lay hold the more steadfastly of the Hand that can lead us safe through storms and danger ; and the darker the way before us, the more serenely shines the Love of God to be our beacon. To that Love we may leave our widowed Queen, our sorrowing country, in sure and certain hope ; and He will not leave us nor forsake us.

HAGLEY, *Thursday, January 2nd*, 1862.—Still no answer from America.

HAGLEY, *Epiphany Monday*, 1862.—The poor Queen has had to hold a Privy Council to-day ; so soon to be obliged to take upon her the regal duties alone and unsupported ! Papa wrote a beautiful address of condolence for the county.

HAGLEY, *Tuesday, January 7th*, 1862.—Little Arthur struck 10 ; he is in a very satisfactory phase this holy-days, frank, sweet-tempered, full of fun and intelligence, particularly nice to read with, from his quickness and interest, easy and pleasant to manage : gets on better with the big boys who have left off quizzing him unmercifully, and much run after by Bobby. Rather a bore from incessant chatterbox and perhaps a touch of affectation ; but a very nice bright little fellow. Keeps his good looks tho' short, only 4 ft. 7 ; but his open forehead and intelligent expression make up.

HAGLEY, *Thursday, January 9th*, 1862.—At length the precious Yankees give up the Commissioners and it is Peace. But they have given themselves a name for ever, I shd think, for insolence, bragging, and absurdity. For the bluster ending in backing out is just contemptible, tho' certainly better than fighting.

HAGLEY, *Friday, January 10th*, 1862.—The American Government seem to have been for peace all along, the newspapers being nothing but mob brag and insolence.

HAGLEY, *Tuesday, January 21st*, 1862.—A frightful colliery accident at Shields.

HAGLEY, *Wednesday, January 22nd*, 1862.—There is little hope for the poor colliers.

HAGLEY, *Thursday, January 23rd*, 1862.—The 200 Hartley colliers who have been buried in the pit 7 days have been found all dead. The Queen had sent a telegram, which said " her heart bled for them, " to ask abt them. Atie. Pussy managed to get Papa's beautiful thing in the Parish Magazine shown to the Queen who liked it.

HAGLEY, *Tuesday, January 28th*, 1862.—In the paper a letter from the Queen to Shields about the poor colliers, most touching and beautiful in its tone of real sympathy, coming from a heart so broken, but yet so loving and thoughtful for others' grief.

NEWNHAM PADDOX,[1] *Wednesday, January 29th*, 1862. —And so, off I set, at 10¼, chaperoned for the 1st time

---

[1] Lord Denbigh's.

by old Meriel! with her and John, to this place, stopping
on the way and mightily enjoying ourselves at Coventry,
having luncheon there, and seeing the glorious churches
and a bit of the town. Working men standing about
idle, and empty factory windows, speaking silently
of the still bitter distress. Arrived at this stately
mansion abt 4, find swarms of people, all of whose
names I shall perhaps pick up by the time we go.
Lively ball, M. dancing again, but looking amazingly
matronly! I danced with Ld. Feilding, his brother
Percy, Messrs. Sykes, Cameron, etc., etc. : maukins.[1]

NEWNHAM PADDOX, *Thursday, January* 30*th*, 1862.—
Same weather: aftn. pour. We had a paper hunt;
Col. (William) Feilding and I being hares. I never
went such a dance : over two miles across country, of
which a mile was mostly running ; and though I shirked
many fences, there was plenty of moderate scrambling.
We baffled the hounds (most of the remaining guests,
etc.) ; and after the first loss of breath I got on very
well. Learnt for the 1st time what getting one's 2nd
wind was. Lovely singing in the aftn. Mem. : " The
Reaper and the Flowers," sung by Ladies Mary, Ida,
and Adelaide Feilding, and Capt. Palisser ; and " Sing
me to Rest," Ly. Mary. Charming dancing in the
evening : Lancers with 10 people, and Sir Roger de
Coverley to end with : immense fun. There were
here, Lady and Misses Mordaunt, Admiral Erskine,
a brother of Ld. Denbigh's, Lord Welscourt, Sir Theo-
philus Biddulph, host and four daughters and two sons,
of whom the hare is particularly pleasant. The rest I
shall remember to-morrow, I hope.

Letter : from Nevy ; to Papa.

NEWNHAM PADDOX, *Friday, January* 31*st*, 1862.—
A delightful and memorable day ! I went out hunting !!! Ld. Denbigh and his sons and 2 daughters
went and when they offered to mount me, and supply
me with habit, etc., and old M. encouraged me, could
anyone refuse ? No ! so off I went on a glorious old
hunter of 21, called Marmion, his action free and beautiful, and his gallop like the South Wind, so easy, yet

[1] Appendix A.

I—11

so rapid and strong. I saw the fox break away, I heard
the music of the hounds, and horns and halloos, I careered
along to the sound of the scampering hoofs with the
delicious soft air blowing in my face. I flew over 2
or 3 fences, too enchanted to have a moment's fright;
in short, I galloped for $\frac{1}{2}$ an hour in all the glory of
a capital run. O dear! if I don't take care I shall
pine for it every time Papa goes out, and that won't
do! However, I had my sense enough about me to
keep with Lady Ida (losing sight of the others, and no
wonder, in a field of about 150), and when her saddle
turned, her hat blew off, and she spoke of going home,
I nobly went with her, tho' I cd have gone on for
ever. But really I think it was the most glorious
exciting enjoyment I have ever had; and that says
a good deal.

Some theatricals in the evening, which wd have been
deplorably bad, but for Col. (William) Feilding's wonderfully good acting of an old Frenchman. I had a long
sit with nice little Ly. Katharine, who spoke of their
great grief, the conversion of Ld. Feilding, who is an
enthusiastic Romanist; O how awful a trial it must be!

ALTHORP, *Wednesday, February 5th*, 1862.—Delightful day. Althorp mounted me on a nice, spirited,
high-stepping little horse called Friar Tuck, and (driving
to West Haddon) I joined Tallee and we went to the
great meet at Crick. There must have been nearly
300—I didn't see the fox go away; but it was almost
as beautiful to see the sudden unanimous start of the
whole field, without apparent cause, and away we
streamed at a gallop. But alack! Tallee's horse
wdn't take the mildest ditch even, so we came to a
stop in the 2nd field, not however before freely enjoying
the glorious start, and seeing many leaps, and more
than one tumble. It didn't much signify, for anyhow
we were not going to follow any distance. So we
resigned ourselves with tolerable philosophy, and had
about given up hope, after quite losing them and having
half an hour's meandering in the field, when suddenly
we came right upon them again, followed during a nice
little run (with gates handy!), saw some lovely leaps,
and at last left them of our own accord, to be in time

for Guilsborough luncheon. Saw Lord Feilding and Col. (W.) Feilding, the latter of whom had a tremendous tumble. Unlucky Mr. Horace Seymour was thrown early in the day, and his horse, running away and leaping a high fence, pitched on his head and broke his neck! Papa in his glory on a gigantic, powerful creature called Shamrock more than 16 hds high, rode over everything, tho' not *as* perfect as on Marmion! Nice talk the while with Tallee, and at Guilsborough saw At. Yaddy and the tinies, they grown but looking rather delicate, but Vay improved in looks. Granny showed me the most piteous heart-broken letter, which she has received from the Queen, who has sent her a miniature photograph of the Prince in a brooch. Letter from John. Pleasant playing and whist in the evening.

ALTHORP, *Friday, February 7th,* 1862.—Tolerably keen frost. Spencer hunting again. I had much chatter with little Mlle Beccadelli, who made a little attempt (which failed) to convert me! I borrowed a religious book of hers to look at, and was a good deal dismayed ; also surprised at the inferiority of the prayers to ours, in point of composition. The little girl said that when, unable to confess to a Priest, she did so alone, to God, she had not the same sense of pardon and peace. Which sounded awful to me. We drove pleasantly in the aft. Papa to play chess with Mrs. Morton. Charlotte and At. Henrietta pounced upon me, and practised many experiments on my hair (now growing thick), ending in turning me out amazingly done up, with it twined back over a rouleau on each side. They say powder days are coming back.

In the papers, Ld. Dufferin's speech moving the Address, beautiful and overpowering, as far of it as related to the Prince. Two fine prints of the Queen and Prince arrived, given by the Queen.

ALTHORP, *Saturday, February 8th,* 1862.—Papa and Althorp and Major Reilly hunted and had a good run in spite of a sharp frost. I had a particularly nice walk with Charlotte, and loved her more and more, for besides being " lovely and pleasant " in her outward self, she is so in her gentle ingenuous thoughts, simplicity and truth. Dear old Tallee came to stay over Sunday. For the evening, we played a freak : appeared Charlotte, the Prss.,[1] At. Henrietta, Tallee and I, all in powdered hair twined back over a high " pelote," with lace handkerchief at top. In which historical attire we danced majestically. Every one of us looked the better, the Prss. perhaps the most decidedly so, and At. Henrietta amazingly well ; but Charlotte looked too lovely and bewitching.

ALTHORP, *Monday, February 10th*, 1862.—Melancholy partings : Tallee, the Princess and her child went, also At. Henrietta. I cuddled much with Tallee and the Prss., read them my bit of poetry " Evening and Morning " (with a translation ! ! !) and the kind Prss. made me write them in her book. Shall I ever see her again, I wonder ? She has such wonderfully deep, true feelings for a foreigner, and a Romanist.

HAGLEY, *Tuesday, February 11th*, 1862.—Papa and I to the Kidderminster Volunteer ball, he in uniform. A guard of honour (rifles) received us : rather blowing.[2] It was a pretty, lively ball.

HAGLEY, *Wednesday, February 12th*, 1862.—Tennyson has written some beautiful lines on the Prince.

HAGLEY, *Saturday, February 22nd*, 1862.—Arthur is gazetted as Page to the Queen.

HAGLEY, *Tuesday, April 1st*, 1862.—Warm rain nearly all day. Congregation 3 ! but then the weather accounts for it. Uncle Stephen seems very well, trolls away just like himself: has been making out a list of all the old churches he has seen in England : 250 in Kent alone ! Club, the girls and At. E. helping. I wrote a long letter to darling Nevy for his Confirmation to-morrow. Papa went away for it. We were an odd party at dinner, Uncle St., Edward, Albert, and I. I sat with Miss W. in the evening.

HAGLEY, *Monday, April 7th*, 1862.—A horrible little iron battery of the Americans has been destroying a

---

[1] Princess Camporeale.　　　　　[2] Appendix A.

beautiful great man-of-war: proving the uselessness of all that one once called *ships*, and looking like the beginning of the end of all " Pride, pomp, and circumstance of glorious war," which will be reduced to mere monstrous mechanism, on the sea.

HAGLEY, *Easter Eve, April 19th*, 1862.—And so ends this quiet Lent, and again it has been granted me not to miss one service since it began. Whenever I lose my strength and health, I shall have at all events happy recollections of all that it has brought me of blessing. Oh dear! what an Angel I ought to be!

HAGLEY, *Easter Monday, April 21st*, 1862.—The Vestry CONSENTED UNANIMOUSLY AND JOYFULLY TO THE CHOIR SURPLICES!!! Which is amazing. A volunteer sham battle went off with éclat: Papa in full red figg on the hunter.

HAGLEY, *Easter Tuesday, April 22nd*, 1862.—We went wild with excitement over the *surpliced future*.

HAGLEY, *Saturday, May 3rd*, 1862.—Arrived the Surplices! we went and gloated over them and the delightful cupboard wherein they are to hang.

HAGLEY, *2nd Sunday aft. Easter, May 4th*, 1862.— The Choir appeared IN SURPLICES!!!!!! coming in procession, the smallest boys first, from the organ-room. O wonderfully pretty it looked! and so suitable and natural to see our beautiful Chancel full of white robes. The 12 little boys behaved with the greatest gravity and discretion, tho' it must have been very shy, the 1st time.

TEDDESLEY, *Thursday, May 8th*, 1862.—Ly. Hatherton has been particularly kind to me, and everybody so much more agreeable than *young men* generally, for the lack of whom host and hostess have been anxiously apologising to me.

LONDON, *Saturday, May 10th*, 1862.—Aftn. went to the Exhibition, treated by Atie. P. with her young couple: so nice. It's too monstrous outside, but striking inside, tho' far indeed from coming up to the glassy, bowery impression left on my mind of the '51 one, which *was* lovely. We did the nave, the French court, the British court of pictures, the Italian court, etc., of course not at all thoroughly, but pleasantly. The pictures especially delightful ; also mem. busts of Tennyson and Cavour, Gibson's Venus, etc. We stayed more than an hour and a half. They went to the Opera, I not, as it has a ballet attached, in which case Papa doesn't like me to go, even when one doesn't stay.

LONDON, *Wednesday, May 14th,* 1862.—N.E. wind. Got up abt 10 ; had a pleasant ride with Agnes and Uncle Henry at 12½, when Rotten Row is at its fullest : we shot [1] many acquaintance. Dull concert at Ly. Harrington's, I mean the music was dull : one was amused somehow, and Meriel and Mrs. Talbot were there, tho' not within speaking distance. Col. Feilding (the *hare*) shook hands with me : his brother, the other Col., has just married Ly. L. Thynne. Party at the Dss. of Northumberland ; the Japanese ambassadors, dreadful monsters, came.

LONDON, *Saturday, May 17th,* 1862.—Amusing squash at Lady Palmerston's, saw Ld. Shaftesbury [2] sporting his new Garter, Ld. and Ly. Carnarvon. Oh dear ! why do I begin going thro' the names ?

LONDON, *4th Sunday aft. Easter, May 18th,* 1862.— Sultry. O how nice Sunday is ! I really do get rid almost entirely of dressums, ballums, fidgetums and seasonums [3] generally. In the morning I went with Miss Syfret to S. Peter's Church, Windmill St., the laying the 1st stone of which by Ld. Derby I remember so well in '60 : it was the day Papa began to get better. Fine solid lofty church, well attended, hearty singing and clever sermon, ending beautifully, on Right and False ideas of Christ : only went too much, I think, into ancient and modern heresies, which bewilder and distress one to little purpose. All Saints' in aft. Aggy and I walked alone with Herbert [4] and a footman ! The beautiful hymn " Abide with me " sung. St. St.,[5] only, alack ! no Papa, who is commissioning. Dear

---

[1] See Appendix A.   [2] The philanthropist.   [3] Appendix A.
[4] The youthful Herbert Gladstone, then eight years old, was evidently not considered a sufficient guardian !
[5] Stratton Street, where her grandmother lived.

Sunday refreshment ! I hope it will " abide with me " through the week.

LONDON, *5th Sunday after Easter, May 25th*, 1862.—Aftn. M. and I got into a hansom to go to All Saints' ; the man was pleased to go all down Piccadilly and round by Park Lane into Oxford St. When we landed at last, who shd we get out in the very eye of but Lord Cowper, who was probably shocked at the sight.[1] Such a crowd that I had to do without a chair.

LONDON, *Tuesday, May 27th*, 1862.—Alas, alas, after a long day of suspense, we heard of John's [2] being beaten by 8 ; which 8 are said to have cost the Liberal side £2,000 ! Who was to stand against such gross bribery ? I spent the day in G. St., going for bkfast, and felt something like the excitement of the day the baby was born. John has made a famous fight, spoken admirably, and covered himself with laurels ; he will get in when next time there is a chance. This day has comfortably settled my hazy politics. The old dear was wise enough not to be sanguine, but of course it was a horrid blow. The numbers were : White, 228 ; Talbot, 220. Gay ball at Ly. Caroline Kerrison's, where, in spite of a new gown, I danced Once ; with Mr. Lefevre.

LONDON, *Friday, May 30th*, 1862.—Went to the H. of Lords with Atie. P. at 5 : heard Ld. Carnarvon in a brilliant sort of speech " pitch into " Uncle W.'s financial policy, and the D. of Newcastle make a dull reply, poor man. I saw him shade his eyes from the light even of the stained windows. I believe he is going blind. Thought the Lords on the whole looked uninteresting old fogies : hardly any quite young man, except the D. of St. Albans and Lord Dufferin—the latter isn't quite young.

LONDON, *Wednesday, June 4th*, 1862.—I went with Uncle and Aunt to the S. Kensington Museum and saw glorious things, that made one proud of one's

---

[1] Long after this it was not considered quite " proper " for young ladies to go in hansoms.
[2] John Talbot had stood for Kidderminster.

country. Two great collections of Sèvres, together
worth £200,000 ! One single moderate-sized bowl
worth £2,000. We saw there the Dow. Duchess of
Sutherland, with her youngest son Lord Ronald,[1] a
handsome, fair, pleasant-mannered boy of 15.

[1] Lord Ronald Gower, afterwards a well-known social figure and
dilettante of art and letters.

Lucy.　　Neville.　　Charles.　　May.　　Spencer.　　Albert.
Alfred.　　　Arthur.　　Meriel.　　Edward.　　Lavinia.　Robert.

THE TWELVE CHILDREN OF THE 4TH LORD LYTTELTON AND HIS FIRST WIFE, MARY GLYNNE.

I—130]

BOOK VII
JUNE 1862—AUGUST 1863

INTRODUCTION TO BOOK VII

THE seventh volume covers little more than a year, beginning in June 1862 and ending in August 1863. It includes no great private event except the diarist's appointment as a Maid-of-Honour to the Queen. She did not actually begin duty till later, but there is a good deal of " Maid-of-Honourums " (as the Glynnese language calls talk on that subject) in the latter part of this volume. She receives many letters of congratulation, which make her feel as if she " were going to be married." And, whether she yet knew of it or not, there are the first signs of that. The Diary opens with a visit to Cambridge with her father, who received an honorary degree. I have heard Sir George Trevelyan, who travelled to Cambridge, as she records, in the same carriage with them, speak of the impression made on him by her charm and beauty, contrasting with the almost uncouth appearance of her father. She gives a lively account of the granting of the degrees, over which the new Chancellor, the Duke of Devonshire, presided. One of the recipients was his son Lord Hartington, whom he of course addressed, to the amusement of the audience, as " Vir illustrissime." This seems to have been her first sight of her future relations. Lord Hartington asked her to dance at one of the Cambridge balls, but, characteristically, " fell through " ; and a few months later she and her father went to stay at Chatsworth, where she felt very shy. There she first met her future husband, but nothing particular is said of him. The next summer he reappears and dances with her at two " breakfasts " at Chiswick[1]; and comes to what she calls a " clever break-

fast " at Downing Street. But there is no sign of any
exceptional interest in him as yet.

The principal public event here recorded is the
marriage of the Prince of Wales, at which Lucy Lyttelton was present. And, through her grandmother, she
has opportunities of knowing at first hand the delightful
impression of beauty, of charm, and of affection made
on her future relations, even before her marriage, by
the Princess of Wales who was afterwards loved by the
whole nation both as Princess and as Queen.

Meanwhile the diarist continues her busy life, whether
in London or at Hagley. She is always glad to get out
of London ; yet she gives pleasant and pleased accounts
of many of the " seventeen balls, eight parties, nine
dinner-parties, eight private concerts, besides breakfasts of different sorts," which were the chief features
of her season in 1863. But Hagley, not London, was
home : there were her beloved little sisters and brothers ;
there the servants were so delighted to see her that
" it goes to my heart." Besides, Hagley was the
country ; and in the country she found other things,
too, not easily to be had in London, which she dearly
loved. She writes on February 7th, 1863, when staying
with her cousins the Watsons at Rockingham Castle :
" Lovely weather. I dressed with window wide open ;
birds all singing in the soft air ; have heard of *pear-
blossoms* ! " So at Hagley in May of the same year :
" Sarina and I, with the little boys, had a charming
walk thro' Wickberry wood and over the obelisk hill.
O dear, dear ! the soft smiling loveliness of everything !
and the springtide of the trees, grass, and garden,
gives a positive exhilaration to one's feelings." " How
old to write of, how new to see ! " as Edward Fitzgerald
said ! But a diarist who never mentions the spring,
though the ever-new feelings can only find such old
words, can only be half alive.

The old routine of lessons with the children, visits
in the parish, private reading, croquet, archery, billiards,
and cards goes on at Hagley as before. The visit to

Cambridge introduces her to bowls, which she plays with " great enjoyment." Another side of her is seen in her note, on Trinity Sunday, 1862, that she received the Holy Communion for the hundredth time. Church matters, of course, occupy a good deal of space. It is curious to notice that as, in previous volumes, she recorded the immense crowds at the Brighton churches, so here we find an entry on a Sunday in London in June 1862 : " Every Church overflows : Charles tried to get a place in three or four vainly this morning." This eldest brother is a source of great pride to her : she quotes Lady Wenlock as calling him " the hand- somest man she had seen for a long time " ; and she records the " immense compliment " of his being elected to the famous " Apostles " Club at Cambridge.

There are a few items of fact which now seem a long way off. She goes in an omnibus for the first time. That, however, is not so remarkable ; for I have known a lady who never went in one till after the War. She mentions a curious pyramidal system of wearing the hair. She notes her father having a tooth out under chloroform and the surprising fact that he felt no pain. She sees a brother, for the first time, go shooting " in horrid knickerbockers." She notes that the Row is crowded between 1 and 2, so that it is a pity the Prince and Princess should ride at that hour. And she records —what I suspect would not be easily paralleled at Eton or any other school to-day—that her brother Neville " has got on famously at Eton with Italian " ; so that when he comes home she reads Tasso with him. Her own studies, beside many religious books, include a certain amount of Italian and French, and the whole of Alison's " Europe " ; while the poets she quotes or mentions include Wordsworth, Coleridge, Cowper, and Worsley's translation of the " Odyssey."

DIARY, JUNE 1862—AUGUST 1863

Begun June 7th, 1862, at Cambridge.
Ended August 23rd, 1863, at Hagley.
Begun aged 20 years and 9 months.
Ended aged 22 years, all but a fortnight.

CAMBRIDGE, *Saturday, June 7th*, 1862.—All my volumes of journal (except the lost Vol. 1) have had marked events in them, and though, by God's great mercy, the happy events are many more than the sad, yet I have seen enough of sorrow to make every fresh beginning of things rather awful to me ; while the peace and enjoyment that remain to me in such full and most undeserved measure make me dread the inevitable " changes and chances of this mortal life." I might be fifty, for the fear I have of change ! But this is bad and faithless of me, for loving-kindness and mercy have followed me all the days of my life ; and to that I will trust with a quiet mind.

I went to G. St. for breakfast, whence I set off for Cambridge with Papa at 10¼. The drive thro' the City to Shoreditch was very interesting to me, and I took in S. Paul's for the 1st time. In Bishopsgate we passed the smoking ruins of a house, with firemen still busy about it. A Mr. Trevylian [1] (how I have murdered his name !) was in the train with us : he has written first-rate comic verses. Came to Magdalene Lodge ; finding it empty, we ate some (congealed) luncheon, and then set off, 1st, to Charles' rooms, where he was not, then all about the lovely " Backs." Visited the Provost of King's, and went to service at King's Chapel, where the organ was glorious, and there was one of the best trebles I have ever heard. We dined with the Latimers at Trinity, meeting Sir E. and Ly.

[1] It was the young George Otto Trevelyan. He took Lord Lyttelton for " a church dignitary of eminence, on account of the great power and goodness of his face."

Head, D. and Dss. of Argyll, Ly. L. Cavendish, Ld. Bristol, and Ld. J. Hervey, etc.   Singing in the evening. Home by 11½ : unlike London ! Papa is always a lion, which is charming.   Letters ; to Elly.

CAMBRIDGE, *Whitsunday, June 8th,* 1862.—Dined at 5, then went with Papa to Trinity, where the multitude of white robes delighted me as I well remember they did before.   Alas ! the behaviour of the wearers was anything but in keeping with their angelic appearance ! Walked abt. the Backs afterwds with Charles, meeting the Argylls, etc.   Conversational eveng ; Messrs. Wade (with a lovely tenor voice), Hudson (an unparalleled fiddler), Hofman, pleasant undergraduates, have been running tame most of the day.   Also the splendid rifle shot, Mr. Ross, came in : a magnificent-looking man.   I shall go mad if all this book means to be greasy.[1]

CAMBRIDGE, *Whit Monday, June* 9, 1862.—Some thunder showers, with hail.   A pleasant day, with plenty of excitement.   Papa and I went to service at King's at 10, after which we had delightful music here, in the shape of Mr. Hudson's marvellous fiddling and Mr. Wade's very beautiful singing.   Luncheon and then !—to the Senate House to see the degrees con-ferred.   We sat a good while first, hearing the inter-mittent storm (good gracious me, what paper, pen and ink !) of cheers, groans, hisses, cat-calls, etc.   One pig-headed individual, who wd keep his cap on, excited a tremendous roar for abt ¼ of an hr, till a dignitary walked down and got him to take it off.   Uncle W. got mingled cheers and hisses, Ld. Derby more cheers than Ld. Palmerston, the proctors unlimited groans, and at one time a chorus of barks.

The Chancellor,[2] when he took his seat, looked very stately, and did his part with gt dignity.   He was well cheered, but not vociferously.   Of the Doctors, all were more or less well received, except wretched Ld. Belper, who got no applause.   But when the list was read out, the 1st name that was cheered was Papa's !

[1] As this page appears.
[2] The Duke of Devonshire, her future father-in-law.

Ld. Brougham's of course the most, and fine and venerable he looked. He is 83. When his degree was conferred the roar of cheers was immense. But Papa got enough to make me nearly burst with pride and excitement. Oh, it was splendid! The Ralphs turned up. At 9 o'clock came off a delightful concert, Titiens singing gloriously. And so ended a proud, satisfactory, red-letter day.

CAMBRIDGE, *Whit Tuesday, June* 10*th*, 1862.—This feels like 3 days rolled into one. We went off to the Senate House abt 10; the clatter was still more uproarious than yesterday. . . .

After, came luncheon in the fine new hall of Caius: I sat next Lord Hartington. Then trundling about the Horticultural Show in Trinity Hall gardens. Then Papa and I squeezed time for service at King's, whence we walked, and I went upstairs, smoothed my hair, and looked for gloves, and came downstairs—the whole thing in 12 minutes! Then an amusing dinner in Magdalene Hall, Ralph Neville making a facetious speech in giving " the Ladies," the Master proposing healths well and shortly. After which we all dressed, and now I am writing by clear morning daylight—4 a.m. —to a chorus of wakening birds.

Oh, one of the most delightful balls I have ever had! I must say that, after London experience, it was charming to be engaged to every dance in no time; and I suppose it isn't human nature not to be pleased. Partners, Messrs. Meller (twice), Hofman, Howard (a friend of Albert's), Roberts (a substitute for Lord Hartington, who engaged me, but fell through), Ld. John Hervey, Gaskell (friend of Charles'), and, for Sir Roger, the Master of Magdalene himself!

LONDON, *Friday, June* 13*th*, 1862.—Read fifty pages of Alison; wrote up lost journal; did German and French. We went to a sort of breakfast held by Mr. Baring at the Crystal Palace, which did look lovely compared with the monotonous Exhibition.[1] Wretched Blondin did his feats on the tight rope (it was not tight at all) at an awful height: we did not know he would. One

---

[1] That of 1862.

is certain he will some day be killed ; and what a
wickedness to tempt Providence to such a degree !
A moment's giddiness, an attack of cramp, a breakage
of the rope, and nothing could save him.   It *was* marvellous : he hung himself head downwards by one
leg ! walked backwards briskly ; stood on his head,
made somersaults, etc.

LONDON, *Saturday, June* 14*th*, 1862.—Ralph and
Seymour Neville turned up soon after bkfast, and
we had gt fun, talking over delightful Cambridge.   Also
At. Coque, the Duke of Argyll, and the Miss Dicksons
(such an odd party !) came to luncheon.   The Duke
said the Queen in a letter to him expressed her intention of never again taking part in court gaieties—
a natural feeling for her now to have, but it is most
clearly one of her many duties to her subjects (and not
a small one) to continue by her example to give the
tone to society, and to give an opportunity to many
who otherwise would not have it of showing their
respect and love.   There is no fear but that she will
do this, as soon as she feels it to be her duty, as perfectly and meekly as she now does it in other respects.

LONDON, *Friday, June* 20*th*, 1862.—At Mrs. Mildmay's,
a bent and withered old man with a star on his brass-
buttoned coat, his left arm, crippled with gout, in a
sling, sat near me.   He dropped his stick, thanked me
when I pickt it up, and went on to comment on the
singing.   All which facts I record because he was Lord
Lansdowne [1] !

LONDON, *Saturday, June* 21*st*, 1862.—We went to
a pretty bkfast at Stoke, with a very clever little Mr.
Puller (who afterwards went mad [2]).   The Duchesse
d'Aumale was there ; looked much pinched and aged.
Party at Ly. Palmerston's, where was the Viceroy of
Egypt, an acute-looking fat man with one eye, and
much less of the animal look than the Japanese, etc.
Speaks beautiful French.   I made gt notes abt the
fantastic hair dressing which is come into fashion :
odd rolls and curls ; and it all seems to have a pyramidal

[1] The third Marquess, known as " the Nestor of the Whigs."   He
died in 1863.   [2] Added later.

I—12

tendency. The French women paint and what they call " enamel " their faces universally, and some powder a little ! with gold dust, I believe. Were introduced to Lord Clyde, who, when Atie. P. called our attention to his lovely star of India, insisted on pulling it off, and got quite red and a little furious, tugging at it.

LONDON, *Monday, June 23rd*, 1862.—Went with Meriel, Mrs. T., Albert, Edwd. and John, to see the beginning of the University match at Lord's. The Cambridge went in first, and, alas ! we were doomed to see Charles bowled out for a " duck " after a few overs. The first time it has happened to him this year, I believe. However, most of the others played well, and the score reached 171. We left the ground abt 3, the boys staying ; and they brought word that wretched Oxford obtained the modest score of 71, so it will probably be a stupid victory in one innings, and Ch. won't have another chance. I read 60 p. of Alison ; did some French.

LONDON, *Thursday, June 26th*, 1862.—A full day ; 1st a delightful clever bkfast, whereat were Bp. of Oxford, Archie Sinclair, Papa, Mr. Palgrave, and others : poetry came uppermost, which enchanted me : Mr. Palgrave has just brought out a beautiful collection of English lyrics, called " The Golden Treasury." Then my 60 p. of Alison. Then we went to the ceremonies at the opening of the new House (Greek St., Soho) of Charity—or rather the removed old one, including the laying of the 1st stone of the Chapel, which Atie. P. did very successfully. Chanting processions, etc. After it, resolutions were proposed by Uncle W., Mr. B. Hope, Bp. of Honolulu, Papa, etc. Uncle W. spoke very well, dear Papa beautifully ; he was almost overcome when describing the poor people, who have known better days, and who come to the House when at the last extreme of distress, and are saved thereby from perhaps loss of life, or of mind, or of virtue. Then we came home to a concert for which the drawing-rooms were lent. After which the house stood on its head getting tidy. Then a pompous little dinner, for the entertainment of the Viceroy of Egypt ; D. and Dss. of

Argyll, Lord Brougham, Lord Sydney, Lord and Ly.
De Tabley, Sir John Lawrence, Col. Murray, and Mr.
Cobden. Finally, Ld. Dudley's lovely and successful
ball; I didn't miss one dance! Partners: Sir C.
Russell, Mr. Lyme Something, Ld. Dufferin, Ld. S.
Kerr—many Worcestershire folk. Happy to-morrow ! [1]
Letter from Miss W.

LONDON, *Saturday, June 28th*, 1862.—A splendid
match between Gentlemen and Players has been going
on at Kennington Oval for the last 3 days ; Gentlemen
with a prospect of winning. Charles got 57 his 2nd
innings in perfectly faultless style, and Papa had the
famous luck to see most of it, in spite of being up to
the ears in commissionums.[2] Also he caught out 2 or
3 beautifully. At. Wenlock has given me a ball-gown !
Letters : to Albert, At. Wenlock, Mrs. Robartes.

LONDON, *Tuesday, July 1st*, 1862.—I made luncheon
my dinner ; tea and cards when I came home, then the
old dear took At. C. and me to a big party at Devonshire
House. I saw one foreigner who actually had white
powder in her hair ! She looked lovely. At. Henrietta
had an approximation to it ; only her powder was
brown, which simply looks dirty.

LONDON, *Friday, July 4th*, 1862.—We went to a very
smart and charming aftn and eveng at the Duc
d'Aumale's ; where the impress of *ancien régime* dignity
—the arms with all their array of noble old French names
round the room, the pictures of the victories of Louis
XIV, the banners and fleurs-de-lis on the wall, filled
one with a thrill of respect and compassion for the
descendants of the hundred kings of France, ousted by
this scrubby Napoleon ; and with pride that our
country is the one which receives them as Royal guests,
all the more because they are fallen. The Prince de
Condé is short and not handsome, but with a very
pleasing countenance ; the little Duc de Guise is a
tiny fellow of 8, pretty and exceedingly fair. There
were 2 comic Fr. plays, which were an immense delight.

---

[1] On which day she went to " Israel in Egypt " at the Crystal
Palace.   [2] Appendix A.

In the eveng dancing began, but we stayed a very short time.

LONDON, *Tuesday, July 8th,* 1862.—I am writing at 5 a.m. Wednesday morng, in the little smoking-room ; looking over the poor old town reposing in the pure light, its spires sharply cut up agst the sky, its clock chimes pealing with peculiar clearness thro' the unwonted silence ; its birds waking up, and in the distance the 1st rumbles only just beginning. If the ball had over-excited, as it had hes.'ed me—this is the sight to calm and purify one !

The ball has been the 1st thoroughly enjoyable : at Devonshire House ; and we didn't miss more than 3 or 4 dances. My partners : Mr. Cameron ; a nice *innominato* Cambridge acquaintance ; Ld. J. Hervey ; Mr. Baker—and finally, for an ideal country dance, Ld. Schomberg Kerr. Never was country dance more delightful ! The valsing was immense fun to look at. I was asked once or twice over and above the times I danced, and altogether this last ball has put me in spirits, and made me feel I go off with éclat ! Now for quieter thoughts, that better suit this placid day-break.

LONDON, *Friday, July 11th,* 1862.—Last London day ! This is a joyful reflection ; and yet, how odd it is ! I believe I never say " the last " of anything without an indefinable " serrement de cœur." It must be the secret feeling of the uncertainty of things—the dread of all that may happen before next time, and above all, the shrinking from that pathetic possibility of Never More.

Read 170 p. of Alison. Had luncheon in St. St., whence kind Mrs. Robartes lifted At. C. and me in her carriage to Lord's for the Eton and Harrow match. We saw the Harrow 1st innings and most of the Eton 2nd. Scores : Eton 1st innings 96. Harrow 1st inn. 56. Eton 2nd inn. 170, with 2 wickets to go down. From which the result may be guessed pretty well ! Old Nevy has just got into the 11 ; he got 6 in the 1st inn. not out. The ground was crowded—lots of fashionable people. Saw Lord Lorne and Lord Archibald Campbell, pretty fair boys on ponies. Dined with

Papa at Ld. George Quin's, wherewith Ends My London Gaieties. Have been to 14 balls, 15 parties, 5 dinners.

HAGLEY, *Saturday, July 12th*, 1862.—Home ! Oh dear, dear, how lovely, how deeply green the precious old place looks ! And it is delicious repose and refreshment coming back. The children all look well : poor little Win, tho', is still headachy, and we are going to take her to Evans. Dear Rectors are established here, to chaperone the tutor (Mr. Richmond [1]) and me. I am too happy sitting in my fresh little room again. Before leaving London I finished Vol. VIII of Alison, reading 50 p. ; quicker than any other vol. I have read. Miss W., Elly, and Newmany all looked well. I feel I have been away ages ! Can't but be so glad I haven't married or anything upsetting ! but have fallen back upon dear old Hagley's loving arms.

HAGLEY, *Saturday, July 19th*, 1862.—Wonderful but probably false report that the whole northern army in America has capitulated. If so, Canada must look out !

HAGLEY, *Monday, July 21st*, 1862.—The Federals have not capitulated, as far as we yet know ; but are in the last extremity, their general (McClellan) bragging to the last, and lying most tremendously. They must be too ruined, thinned and done for, I shd hope, to attack Canada, where there are 2,000 Guards.

WORCESTER, *Tuesday, July 22nd*, 1862.—Came with Papa to Canon Wood's, Worcester, for the Archæological Society's doings. Went to a meeting where the Mayor and Corporation buttered the Archæologists and the Archæsts. (with Papa presiding) buttered the Mayor and Corpn. After every individual had been both butterer and butteree, we set off to do the interesting things in the town, which I was very glad to see, as it's scandalous not to know the lions of one's Cathedral and county town. Mr. Severn Walker and Mr. Parker ciceroned, and we did SS. Andrews and Alban, the Commandery and the Museum. At which last place mem. especially the gloves King Charles I

[1] Mr. D. C. Richmond, afterwards Auditor-General.

gave to Bp. Juxon on the scaffold. After dinner,
lectures in a gt room on the ecclesiology of Worcester
in general by Mr. S. Walker (horribly dull), and of
Pershore Abbey in particular by Mr. Freeman [1]; also
on little historical and antiquital points by Mr. Something. Sleepiness a little assailed me.

HAGLEY, *Friday, August 15th,* 1862.—At. H., children
and I made heroic and partially successful efforts to
take a wasps' nest. The Misses Rogers called on M.
and were gt audience [2] to Baby, who looked her best.
I had a terrific tiff with the Grim One.[3]

HAGLEY, *Tuesday, August 19th,* 1862.—We shot with
the pea rifle till church time. I never fail to hit the
target (at 70 yds.), and grazed the bull's-eye once.

HAGLEY, *Wednesday, August 20th,* 1862.—We shot
with the rifle, which I do enjoy : no bull's-eye to-day,
however.

HAGLEY, *Monday, August 25th,* 1862.—Tiny George
has fairly found his feet, and goes staggering about,
jabbering and laughing triumphantly, with one arm
high above his head, just as if he was hoisting a sail.

HAGLEY, *Wednesday, August 27th,* 1862.—Papa, the
Sp. Lytteltons, and I went to the county bow meeting
held this year at Hewell.[4] It went off very well ; and
it was nice seeing a good deal of Victoria Clive, who
is charming. Also I saw Mrs. and Amelia Claughton,
Ly. Mary Clive with her fair small children (the little
boy a merry dot,[5] his birthday to-day, so his health
was drunk), Bennetts, Sandys, Fosters, Bakers, Wake-
men, etc. We played a portentously long and frightfully perverted game of croquet, which was amusing
nevertheless. The dancing for abt an hr and $\frac{3}{4}$ great
fun, as there was only one valse, one galop, and one
quadrille ; the rest being double lancers, and one
merry country dance. My partners : Messrs. Mordaunt,
Lygon, Leigh and Wakeman. We brought home with

[1] No doubt the historian, E. A. Freeman.
[2] Appendix A.   [3] Her maid.
[4] The house of Lady Windsor, great-grandmother of the present
Earl of Plymouth.   [5] The late Lord Plymouth.

us for 2 nights said **Mr. Leigh,**[1] a young clergyman brother of Lord Leigh.

HAGLEY, 12*th Sunday after Trinity, September 7th,* 1862.—A happy bright Sunday—I could not but think the cloudy weather as we entered church, and the glorious sunshine as we came out, typical of the cloud of sins over one as one goes in, and the joy and light in one's heart as one emerges blessed and purified. O, what a thought that is !

HAGLEY, *Thursday, September 18th,* 1862.—A melancholy day, for the Spencers went. Darling Tallee makes a vacuum in my heart more than most people : many things go to make up my warm love for her, and I miss her dear bendable tall figure, with its indescribable grace, her face, which has a charm to me shining thro' its plainness, but above all, herself : all the anxious, loving, self-condemning humility that comes out in all her talk with one : her reverence and beautiful thoughts. And then she is a little fond of me, which is so nice.

HAGLEY, *Friday, September 19th,* 1862.—Papa has had an enormous tooth out, under choloroform. He didn't feel the smallest pain, tho' it took a quarter of a minute.

HAGLEY, *Saturday, September 20th,* 1862.—Delightful accounts of the amiability and attraction of Prss. Alexandra, of the P. of W's. state of bliss, and the Queen's pleasure in the engagement, have come to Granny from Ly. Caroline Barrington. But there is a difficult future, in spite of its immense advantages, before the 18-yr.-old bride.

HAGLEY, *Tuesday, September 23rd,* 1862.—Played a game of billiards with At. E.

HAGLEY, *Wednesday, September 24th,* 1862.—At about 11 a.m. darling old Charles arrived, having been travelling from Sutherland since 7 on Monday morning, with only one night's rest, and having had 2 or 3 accidents from first to last. But here he is safe and sound, thank God, in a most splendid state of health and vigour, and having killed 12 stags, more than anybody else.

[1] Afterwards Dean of Hereford.

HAGLEY, *Thursday, September 25th*, 1862.—Charles went out shooting, in horrid knickerbockers.

HAGLEY, *Monday, October 6th*, 1862.—Grey, uninteresting autumnal day. After such a glorious moonlit night. I said my Prayers looking out into it, and it seemed to purify and exalt them.

WINDERMERE, *Friday, October 17th*, 1862.—Papa and I left Hagley at 10½, and arrived at Windermere, joining Uncle Stephen at Kendal, at 4½. A gt event for me to see the Lakes ! And my 1st glimpse, I must say, was most beautiful. There was a regular angry lurid sunset over the Old Man, breaking through the heavy clouds, and sending a yellow gleam of light along the neighbouring ridges, as we came puffing up to Windermere. We trapesed [1] a little abt the village, Papa being frantic to get a ferrol on his new stick ; and the stormy weather, though it makes us shake in our shoes, made grand effects in the sky ; and I am in hopes of every sort of light and shade. Meanwhile, a clatter-patter of hail comes dash agst the windows of what Uncle St. calls " Mum Rigg's parlour " from time to time. We had a splendid dinner, and, barring a soupçon of exceedingly bad tobacco in the passages, all is luxury.

CONISTON, *Wednesday, October 22nd*, 1862.—The very wildest howl of wind and pelt of rain, with one or two short bursts of sunshine, till luncheon ; and we sat resignedly in " Mum Atkinson's parlour " with books and letters, giving up all hope of doing the Old Man. But after luncheon, it cleared, and we set off just to go up a little way, and to our joy it kept fine, and we went further and further there, into all the beauties of glen and mountain and, what delighted us most of all, innumerable waterfalls. One was a really great one, and all most lovely and the delicious music of the rushing waters was all round us, everywhere. Tiny threads of water came dancing down the side of all the hills. And oh, the tinting lights, the towering peaks, and the deep valleys ! We got up as high as

---

[1] Appendix A.

the last cascade of any size—abt ⅔ of the way, and then, as it began to rain and the wind became so wild that I was actually blown down, I was pintoed [1] enough to turn back with Uncle Stephen, Papa going on. We came down quickly, hopping across innumerable little streams and torrents, and when we were as far down as the copper mills, the tremendous cloud which had been scowling over the Old Man, contrasting most beautifully with the serenest sky and golden sunset light over the lake and valley below us, came down in one of the violent storms. It caught Papa sitting like Pillicock on the top! which he reached triumphantly. A glorious day of beauty : a joy for ever!

BROUGHAM, *Monday, October 27th,* 1862.—This visit I shall look back upon as historic. There are here certain Spaldings, and the William Broughams, with sons and daughters, with the eldest of whom (drs) I cuddled amazingly after dinner! Lord Brougham [2] took me in, and made me shy and deaf, the latter misfortune generally following upon the former. He has not a sign of failing intelligence : asked kind questions and isn't deaf himself—hardly—which made me feel the stupider.

BROUGHAM, *Wednesday, October 29th,* 1862.—Very lovely day, with a sharp frosty feeling in the air. Cross Fell looked beautiful all day with the purple shadows of the clouds upon it. We spent most of the day seeing the coursing, which was certainly fine on the whole, with the drawbacks of having to walk and stand about in bog, getting cold and clammy feet in consequence, and living in an atmosphere of tobacco. But such of the courses as I saw well made it worth while. The eldest Miss Brougham, poor thing, poured out to me all the griefs of her 9 years' attachment and 1 year's recognized engagement to their clergyman Mr. Edwardes, brother of Ld. Kensington : they are to wait for a better living.

HAWARDEN, *Thursday, October 30th,* 1862.—I am a fool to leave this place with no more notes abt Ld. Brougham, but he is silent and seems out of spirits

---

[1] Appendix A.   [2] The Lord Chancellor of 1830. He was 84.

and we see little of him. Papa thinks him altered, as
he used to be full of fun and conversation.

HAWARDEN, *Friday, October 31st, 1862.*—Drove with
Atie. Pussy to the new walks on which they are employ-
ing 6 poor Lancashire unemployed factory men. Such
an excellent plan ; the poor fellows work with a will,
and get 12*s.* a week, and 2 are to have their wives up.
The walks will be an immense improvement, there
surely never was another park with only one drive
through it ! I followed the marked-out track with the
children. Papa rode to Chester on Uncle's beautiful
horse Firefly. In the house, being trained for service
are 10 factory girls ; I wrote letters home for 2 of
them, nice forthcoming simple creatures. One dictated :
" Please to let me know if trade is any better "—alas !
it gets steadily worse, but there will surely be an end.

HAWARDEN, *All Saints', Saturday, November 1st,*
1862.—Much talk about the cotton famine ; in Preston
what they call the " famine fever " has broken out,
and everywhere thousands of fresh paupers come upon
the parish weekly. Some of the mill-owners do a good
deal, but others, they say, make money by secretly
selling the cotton they have in stock while their hands
are starving for want of work. Next year cotton things
will be frightfully dear. Nobody knows what dreadful
misery the winter will bring, as there doesn't seem a
hope of improvement for months.

HAWARDEN, *Wednesday, November 5th,* 1862.—The
aftn sun has a beautiful trick of shining upon the dear
picture in the dining-room, making it so lovely, that
I am reminded of the lines—

> And yet a spirit too, and bright
> With something of celestial light.[1]

HAWARDEN, *Thursday, November 6th,* 1862.—The
ball was very pretty and first-rate ; but I have come
to the melancholy conclusion that I have become a
little tired of balls !

HAWARDEN, *Friday, November 7th,* 1862.—Alas ! a
riot broke out yesterday in Blackburn—the 1st there

---

[1] Wordsworth wrote : " Something of an angel light."

has been, but not against the Guardians or mill-owners, but about some sentencing of poachers. But one fears the example may spread. There seems miserable close-fisting on the part of the Board, which in one case allowed only 4*s.* to a man and wife and 4 children, who had besides only 6 lbs. of bread and 6 lbs. of meal from the relief committee, and it was reduced to 3*s.* because he got one week's work. The poor wife fainted 2ce in one morng from hunger. And there are many like cases. It is in the papers, but is hardly credible that the Bishop of Gloucester (the youngest on the Bench) is appointed Archbishop of York ! It is an injury to all the Bishops, but a positive insult to the Bishop of Oxford whose curate he was ! As to Church views and general excellence, however, Bp. Thomson is admirable.

HAWARDEN, *Monday, November* 10*th,* 1862.—We wrote many copies for Atie. P. of a plan for setting up a soup kitchen in Blackburn, which is the sort of thing best to be done ; for the papers say if the people are not fed now, before the great cold begins, it will kill them, with fever and atrophy coming upon exhaustion and depression of mind and body.

HAWARDEN, *Friday, November* 14*th,* 1862.—The Relief Committees have a miserable mania for economizing, in order to give more later in the winter : this is horrid, because it is urgently necessary to feed the people now, that they may lay in some stock of strength to resist the bitter weather and the almost inevitable fever, which coming upon half-starved constitutions must be fatal.

HAGLEY, *Wednesday, November* 19*th,* 1862.—Went to the Rectory after church ; found At. E. up to the ears in old and new clothes which have been sent for Lancashire, and which filled the large bedroom.

CHATSWORTH, *Thursday, November* 20*th,* 1862.—A notable day ; I came to Chatsworth chaperoned by At. Y. and Tallee, in default of Papa, who is too busy commissioning, besides he told me he had a romance abt Chatsworth, and wanted to see it in lovely weather,

never having been here since '39. It is most delightful
being again with my Tallee, and we have managed
already a quiet sit and a spell of capping verses! I
can't judge of the house yet, only it seems immeasurable.
We find the Duke of Devonshire, Ly. Louisa, and Ld.
Frederic Cavendish,[1] Ld. and Ly. George Cavendish
and daughter, Ld. and Ly. Fanny Howard and daughters,
Mr. Charles Clifford, Mr. Vyner, etc., all family I fancy.
Round game, at which I won 4s.

CHATSWORTH, *Friday, November 21st*, 1862.—We
walked in the grounds, and saw the glorious conservatory, and the Emperor [2] playing. Ly. C. Grosvenor
came. Ld. Granville was expected, but Ly. Granville
is ill. Oh dear, I have an oppressed feeling, which is
my form of shyness, I suppose. Nice bits of Tallee ;
she read aloud one of Stanley's sermons in the East :
beautiful. Letters from and to Papa.

CHATSWORTH, *Saturday, November 22nd*, 1862.—
Lovely morng, very little frost. As usual the 3rd day
makes a great step in pleasantness ; but be at my ease I
cannot. The poor little nervous Miss Howard (Ly.
Fanny's daughter), who comes meekly up to one as
if for protection, touches me. She has ill health.
We saw the state rooms and the statue gallery, all full
of splendour. Drove behind the p. carriage with Ly.
Louisa and Ly. Constance (not behind !) to beautiful
Haddon Hall : the retriever who came with us caught
a rabbit on an ivy-covered buttress. Tallee drove back
instead of Ly. Constance, and we three capped verses.
The Argylls came, and Ld. Grosvenor is expected.
Tallee read a still more beautiful sermon of Stanley's
preacht before the Prince.

CHATSWORTH, *23rd Sunday after Trinity, November
23rd*, 1862.—Fine bright day. The church (to which
we went in the morng) is something too dreadful :
behind the altar and sitting upon the E. window,
which it entirely hides, is a hideous and purely heathen
monument of two brothers (one a skeleton) supported
on one side by Mars and a suit of armour, on the other
by Minerva and a peer's robes ; the whole surmounted

---

[1] This is the first mention of her future husband.　　[2] A fountain.

by a clumsy trumpeting angel (or Cupid?) What words can describe the worse than Smithfield pens we were jammed into? and in which the care necessary to avoid falling foul of everyone's eye, kicking everyone's hat, and sitting upon everyone's lap, was most oppressive. Oh dear! how can people go Sunday after Sunday to such a place, and think they are worshipping God in the beauty of holiness? Scott has, however, made a plan for a new church.

CHATSWORTH, *Monday, November 24th, 1862.*—Sharp frost. I have not often done a more blowing [1] thing than marching into the breakfast-room this morng at ¼10 and bidding a round of good-byes to all the august guests there assembled! Like many awful things, however, it was soon over, and I was immensely flattered and a little astonished at receiving a kiss from both Ly. Louisa and the Duchess of Argyll!!

HAGLEY, *Monday, November 24th, 1862.*—Mr. Smith (one of the guests) came with us to Derby, where I sat for an hour; got home at 4, and had a snug evng nearly do. to last Monday. The house looks a little scrubby and threadbare!

HAGLEY, *Wednesday, November 26th, 1862.*—I heard Papa whistle (softly and half to himself) for the 1st time since '57.

HAGLEY, *Thursday, November 27th, 1862.*—I rode on the hunter with Winny on the Maid, and Bobby (who is a sad coward, but doesn't sit amiss) on Charger with leading rein. The hunter was exceedingly fresh, but went pleasantly enough, with occasional capers, which I am used to and rather like, till we got to the Brake, and there cantering along the sandy bit of road beyond Widow Smith's, he gave a tremendous kick, the 1st time he has ever done so with me. To my astonishment and humiliation, off I fell, but, thank God, was only rather bruised, falling on my side and arm. We went home by Stukenbridge, but I couldn't canter without a kick, so we trotted and walked. But we set off as usual for the avenue, and accordingly the hunter

[1] Appendix A.

gave another amazing kick, worse than the first, in spite
of which I rejoice to say I kept on : and so we got home
with my nerves a little shaken.

HAGLEY, *Friday, November 28th,* 1862.—Garotting
and ticket-of-leave men are great subjects ; they are
rife enough to make even the principal London streets
unsafe.

HAGLEY, *Advent Sunday, November 30th,* 1862.—
Letter : from Atie. Pussy, who gave many Blackburn
and other Lancashire details : they are collecting to
give the poor people a Christmas dinner. Her kitchen
already feeds 1,000 daily.

HAGLEY, *Wednesday, December 3rd,* 1862.—Bp.
Colenso has written a foolish and shallow little set of
arithmetical doubts about the Pentateuch. Garibaldi's ball has been got out ! The Greeks want to
elect as their king either Prince Alfred or—*Uncle
William !*

HAGLEY, *2nd Sunday in Advent, December 7th,* 1862.—
Uncle B. on the Lancash. distress, for which the collection was made ; viz. £1.

HAWARDEN, *Thursday, December 18th,* 1862.—With
anything but alacrity, Albert and I, minus the dear
young couple, came to Hawarden, where we find Ly.
Louisa and Ld. Frederic Cavendish, Lascelles and
Wilbrahams, Mr. F. Wortley, Hugh and Arthur Gladstone, Ly. L. Cotes, and some others. Stephy, and
Willy, who, poor fellow, has only taken a 3rd in Law
and Modern History ; but hardly expected to do better,
as he had to begin late. I must say, if anything cd
comfort me for leaving home just now, it wd be one of
the very best and most lively balls I ever was at. We
began at 9½, and ended about 2½. My partners Ld. F.
Cavendish, Mr. Astley, oh I cannot remember them, but
I danced everything. Two glorious country dances,
and a reel ! Not that I danced that, except a hop or
two to relieve Atie. P.

HAGLEY, *4th Sunday in Advent, December 21st,* 1862.—
Collections for Lancash. came to abt £16 : the statistics
are still awful, in spite of the enormous sums that have

been sent ; more mills stop every week, the population
is losing wages at the rate of £8,000,000 annually, and
the distress is gradually widening to other classes.

HAGLEY, *Tuesday, December 23rd,* 1862.—And, in
the evening, came off a memorable delight : Papa's
lecture on poetry, with selections from Milton, Byron,
Shelley, Pope, Wordsworth, Cowper, Rogers, Longfellow, Burns, Hemans, Hood, Crabbe, and others.   I
can't go into raptures somehow on paper about it ;
but it was to me enjoyment only next to listening to
mighty music, and I am in a realm of beauty and
harmony which has, Oh me ! too much of heaven
in it to abide long with me in this work-a-day world.
Charles' raving of it to me afterwards, showing all his
deep and high appreciation, was not the least of the
delight. Mr. Claughton, Mr. and Mrs. Turner, Mr.
Stayner, and the Miss Rogerses dine, the latter much
gratified and touched by the beautiful bit of " Human
Life " which Papa read from their uncle's poetry.   Win
greatly delighted in spite of her prosaic nature.   Alas
for M. and John !   Mem. very especially " My Mary."

HAGLEY, *1st Sunday after Epiphany, January 11th,*
1863.—Granny has received from the Queen a copy,
in white morocco, of the Prince's speeches, with an
inscription written by her own hand, and most touching.

HAGLEY, *Monday, January 12th,* 1863.—There is
a real steady increase of work in the N., thank God,
and a notion that the American War may possibly end.

ALTHORP, *Tuesday, February 10th,* 1863.—Delightful
day, which got brighter and warmer every hour, and
ended in a lovely mild starlight night.   We drove with
4 in hand to Weedon, thence with 4 posters to Worm-
leighton.   Pottered abt pleasantly among the cottages
while Althorp and Ld. Suffield tried hunters, and had
excellent luncheon at the agent's.   Mem. the white-
haired wizzy woman of 50, who had a fat 17th baby of
16 months old ! !   The drive home was very charming ;
Miss Spalding and I capped verses most of the way.
The open carriage wasn't a bit cold at $\frac{1}{4}$7.   The D. of
Rutland has had another tremendous fall out hunting.
Papa went to London at 6½ a.m.

LONDON, *Tuesday, March 10th*, 1863.—The great day of the Prince of Wales' marriage to Princess Alexandra of Denmark. I must try and put down a detailed account, for of course this day has been one in a thousand, and it can hardly be that one life-time should include another pageant so great, magnificent, and stately, combined as it is in this case with so much that is true and beautiful and deeply moving. In short, a pageant with inward as well as outward beauty! Agnes and her sisters, Toney Gladstone and I, got excellent places in the nave of S. George's Chapel, after some difficulties on the way. The seats in the nave, when we came in, were not half filled; but by the end of the two hours that we waited, every place was taken. I can't describe the glowing effect of the tiers of bright colour, immensely heightened by the uniformed grandees that kept passing through, the Beefeaters and gold-encrusted trumpeters, and the heralds in their tabards, which are only worn when the Sovereign is present at great State occasions. From time to time gorgeous duchesses, etc., every one in full Court dress (except the train) and diamonds, passed down the nave; but only to look about them, as they had seats in the choir. About 11½ the Archbishop of Canterbury, and all the officiating Bishops and clergy, of whom the Bishop of Oxford and the Dean of Windsor were in robes of the Order of the Garter, passed into the choir by the N. transept door and later all the Knights of the Garter, in their splendid blue velvet robes. But all this was only preparing one! Abt 12½ the Danish Prince and Princesses and suite went up the nave into the choir; and very soon after we heard "God save the Queen," faintly, but quite audibly, played over and over again outside the Chapel, and in the middle of its glorious music, which always overcomes me with its pride and pathos—a burst of cheers. That *went through* me, somehow, most of all. Then there was a silence of expectation, till the band quickly formed at the W. door, and the 1st procession came in, preceded by the drums and trumpets. This was all the Royal family: the Princess of Prussia, leading her little son, Prince William; Princess Louis of Hesse, their husbands, Princesses Helena, Louise and Beatrice, and Princes Arthur and Leopold; Prince Alfred, alas! kept away by his illness, which he had not quite recovered. All looked graceful and Royal indeed! Princess Royal become exactly like the Queen, whom in a manner she represented. She looked a little sad, and was the one who cried most during the Service. Princess Alice looked wonderfully well, though her confinement is to be next month: both the younger ones grown pretty, with their fair bright faces, and the tiny one of all, though small and white, very winning and darling. After these had disappeared into the choir, the Lord Chamberlain, preceded by the heralds, left the Chapel, to bring the bridegroom. And very soon after, the trumpets and drums again sounded joyously, the officers of the Prince's household marched in, all glittering in uniform, and then! as the trumpets filed off into the transepts, and the organ pealed, the Prince of Wales, in the robes of the Order of the Garter, entered the nave; the blue velvet cloak giving height and dignity to his figure; his face a little pale, but bright, gentle, and gracious, in its youth and happiness: his bows right and left full of royal grace, his whole manner beautiful and regal. When this procession had passed, the Lord Chamberlain again went out, and this time the clang of the trumpets was followed by the organ and orchestra thundering out the " Wedding March " in *Athalie*; and the Bride whom all England was greeting, and for whom the prayers of millions were going up; our pride and hope; in all the beauty of her youth, her sweet face bent down, her small head crowned with orange-flower, her step queenly, and her whole look the perfection of maiden grace, entered the nave. Her white train was carried by eight bridesmaids, daughters of the Dukes of Buccleuch and St. Albans, and of Lords Westminster, Elgin, Listowel, Hardwicke, Cawdor, Clarendon, Mount-Edgcumbe and Cowley. 2 of these are in by mistake: which I don't know. And now the Service began, the Archbishop's sonorous voice was so clear, that, having prayer-books, Agnes and I were able to follow it all; and wonderfully striking it was to hear the simple

solemn words, which bless quiet marriages in little
country churches, spoken here in the face of all the
splendour and pomp of England, and addressed to
these two descendants of kings. I know this is a trite
thought, but it is a grand one ; and may one not hope
that in many hearts it awoke the earnest longing prayer
that the King of Kings, thus acknowledged, would
pour down upon them the blessing without which vain
and false indeed would be all this rejoicing and all
our loyal hopes. A beautiful solemn chorale of the
Prince Consort's was sung, Jenny Lind's glorious notes
ringing above all, and the Deus Misereatur chanted.
And the Service ended with the great blessing : " The
Peace of God . . ." Then followed a short pause, while
the joyful bells chimed, and the guns fired from the
Castle. The first was fired immediately after their
hands were joined. And now all in the nave rose, while
the " Mount of Olives " Hallelujah burst from the
orchestra, and the Prince and Princess of Wales, this
time heading the procession, left the choir, followed
by the whole gorgeous array. Both looked less agitated ;
the Princess ventured to raise her eyes, and the beaming,
proud happiness on the Prince's face was a joy to see.
All this was what we in the nave saw ; but ah me !
what it *must* have been to have been in the choir !
All agree in saying that the Prince's manner, in the
trying minutes that he had to wait alone at the altar,
was perfect in its simple, unaffected seriousness. The
solemn and most moving point in all the ceremony
was the presence of the Queen, who took no public
part, but sat in her place (visible to all in the choir)
at the N. of the altar, in her widow's weeds. To her
the Prince looked up as soon as he reached the altar,
and she seemed to bless and pray for them. She bore
up through all, crying only very little, though it must
have filled her with mournful memories and sad yearn-
ings ; for oh, it would have been a day without a
cloud, if *his* presence had been there ! As it was, the
sight of her, around whom all centres, the head and
Queen of it all, in her deep sorrow and loneliness,
cast a heavy shadow over the sunny hope and joy.
May the marriage only be to her a blessed source of

cheering and comfort, that her evening time may be light!

The Bride trembled extremely at first, but was heard giving her troth in a clear childlike voice, with a slightly foreign accent. The Prince's "*I will*" was distinct and emphatic. The Queen knelt, burying her face in her hands, during the concluding blessing. And so—it was over! Oh that our prayers may prevail! that Thou wouldst indeed bless them!

Granny had the honour of being with the Queen.

From 8½ to 3½ in the morning Atie. Pussy, Miss Gladstone, Mrs. Talbot, John, Edward, and I, were struggling through the mighty crowds, seeing the illuminations, in a great van. We cd not get into the City, and so failed to see S. Paul's, which was illuminated, but it proved a failure. We saw the W. end illuminations well, but it wasn't worth the hours of jam and wedge. A great sight, however, for never was such universal and vehement rejoicing : millions of excited people, all wonderfully good humoured and well behaved. The Talbots got home abt 3, walking from Waterloo Bridge, where we came to a hopeless stick, but finally got home by the Strand. What an endless acct! and yet I have not mentioned half, either of facts or feelings. Bright sunny weather till late. Fine night.

HAGLEY, *Saturday, April 11th*, 1863.—I have mastered the Scotch reel, and Charles has fairly learnt to valse.

LONDON, *Friday, April 24th*, 1863.—At. C. picked me up, and we went to S. James at 11, after which we went with the girls and shopped with extraordinary vigour and success : got them and myself hats of the high-crowned fashion, which in its extreme (but ours are moderate) is suggestive of something between a bandit and a Tyrolese.

LONDON, *Monday, April 27th*, 1863.—Still warmer. The lilacs are all out. We went to the Kensington Museum to see the Princess's wedding gifts, which were hardly worth the exertion. Most of the jewels have been taken away, and many things were in very bad taste. Afterwards we went to breakfast at Ld. Grosvenor's : such luxurious splendour their house is full of ; it looked like fairy-land. Saw their eldest children, Lord Belgrave, a fine fellow of ten, very tall, and a little like Cousin Ebbett ! and Lady Elizabeth, a most lovely angel-faced little thing of six, like the Duchess of Argyll. She came softly in in her tiny riding-habit.

LONDON, *Friday, May Day*, 1863. *SS. Philip and James.*—I had the immense treat of going with Mrs. Watson and Miss Boyle to hear F. Kemble read " King Lear," as I did once before, in '56, I think. I cried horribly.

LONDON, *Saturday, May 2nd*, 1863.—Rode with Agnes. As we cantered up Constitution Hill, we saw a young man riding in front of us, who proved to be the Prince of Wales ; only one gentleman with him, and a groom. And near the Marble Arch, a little phaeton with pair of ponies driven by a very pretty young lady, passed us : somebody in deep mourning was with her. The carriage looked like a Royal one ; and we have nearly made up our minds that the young lady was the Princess ; the only objection being that she was not very like her ! Coming back, the Prince of Wales passed us, and made us a beautiful bow. We saw him within the gates of Marlborough House, where they are just established.

Ly. Pam's [1] party very full : I saw Lord Robt. Cecil,[2] who is supposed to have written a keen, clever, and cutting article abt this governt. in the Quarterly some time ago ; " Four Years of a Reforming Administration."

LONDON, *Monday, May 4th*, 1863.—We drove a little, and then ! went to the House of Commons and heard Uncle William's splendid speech in defence of his extraordinary proposal of income-taxing charities. He bore down all before him while he spoke ; defending himself, as none but he can do, by dint of his marvellous eloquence and ingenuity, and by the evident strength and depth of his own convictions, which gave tenfold power to all he said. But I can well believe the opposition, when it calls the scheme " monstrous." The cry against it is tremendous : an enormous deputa-

---

[1] Lady Palmerston. [2] Afterwards Lord Salisbury, the Prime Minister.

tion waited upon him this afternoon, headed by the D. of Cambridge and the 2 Archbishops, the House was nearly to a man against him, and so (though his speech converted some), he withdrew the motion.

We went, somewhat exhausted in mind and body, to Ly. H. Vane's ball after this. I danced with Messrs. Lascelles and Wortley, Lord Cowper, and was engaged to Lord Lennox, when we had to go. But there! I haven't mentioned that the Princess of Wales came quite incog. with 2 ladies, to hear the debate! and had to go before the speech. We saw her lovely, fair, gracious profile very well.

LONDON, *Saturday, May 9th*, 1863.—Agnes and I dined with the P. Gladstones en famille ; while uncle and aunt dined at Marlborough House, and came away raving of the Princess of course!

LONDON, *5th Sunday after Easter, May 10th*, 1863.— Same weather ; finer than yesterday. Whereas in London I generally hear but one sermon in church, to-day I have heard *three*. Papa came as usual, and we all went to Whitehall, where Canon Stanley preached beautifully on the Triumphs of Death. S. James in the aft : the Bishop of London preached on the use of the historic books of the Bible. Thence I went to St. St., where Mrs. Talbot called to see *me*, and I went at 7 with her and Ldy Wharncliffe and daughter (the latter really recovered) to a delightful, hearty, congregational Service at S. Peter's, Windmill St., where they have just set up a new organ. Good sermon by Mr. Kempe on Church music. Papa dropped me at home, and so it fell out that I came in for prayers here, and a *fourth* sermon, a short striking one, Uncle W.'s own, on the Ascension.

LONDON, *Wednesday, May 13th*, 1863.—Bkfast in G. St., whence I went alone in a cab, with nothing but a footman, to Shoolbred's again, for the N. room carpet, which I forgot like an idiot yesterday. Willy was presented in his brand new Deputy Lieutenant's uniform. He, his parents and Agnes, had the honour of going to a wonderfully select ball at Pam's, to meet the Prince and Princess.

LONDON, *Saturday, May* 16*th*, 1863.—Some rain : soft and pleasant. I breakfasted in G. St., and saw old M. set off for the drawing-room, looking her very best, in blue and silver. She was tired to death, having to spend six hours in the performance ; which we happy entrée people [1] achieved in little more than an hour. It bewilders me to think that, at the last drawing-room I was at, the Queen stood there ; the unexampled sunshine of her life yet uneclipsed, and her husband beside her. This one was held by the Princess of Wales, who looked pale and not so lovely as she is generally thought ; but very sweet and winning. Prss. Alice shook hands with me. There were 5 curtseys to be made, as, besides those, there were there Pr. of Wales, and the Cambridges.

LONDON, *Sunday after Ascension, May* 17*th*, 1863.— Thence to Chapel Royal ; I grieve to say that I cannot so abstract myself as to feel like a Christian in church, when I form part of that select circle of the nobility who sit in the Peeresses' boudoir ; and I was nearly as painfully conscious of a pair of dirty gloves as if I had been at a concert. Oh dear ! there are things allowed by our Church which one wd be ashamed of a dissenter or Romanist knowing !

We went thence to St. St. for the evening, and now Papa has walked me home. Not having been once on wheels, I must have walked about 7 miles.

HAGLEY, *Tuesday, May* 26*th*, 1863.—Sarina [2] and I with the little boys had a charming walk thro' Wickberry wood and over the obelisk hill : O dear, dear ! the soft smiling loveliness of everything ! and the springtide of the trees, grass and garden gives a positive exhilaration to one's feelings. This summer, I think, will seem a double one to me.

LONDON, *Tuesday, June* 2*nd*, 1863.—I sat next an exceedingly agreeable Mr. Bourke, who has seen a good deal of America. He said the people were quite as hateful as books describe them. And he told me of one horrible thing : they dare to push their democracy into their very ideas of Heaven ; i.e. they will never

---

[1] The Gladstones, of course, had the entrée.

[2] Sarina James, daughter of 1st Lord Northbourne : afterwards wife of Sir Arthur Godley, created Lord Kilbracken in 1909.

give to the Almighty the title of " King of Kings," or any other which implies sovereign authority, as being contrary to their notions of universal equality ! !

LONDON, *Monday, June 8th*, 1863.—. . . Then with Papa to St. St., to see Arthur [1] in his Court costume for the levée. (Query, is he to hold up the Prince's coat-tails?) I must say he looked bewitching, in his red George II coat faced with gold, his white silk tights and stockings, his red-heeled, buckled shoes, his cocked hat, shoulder-knot of satin ribbon, lace ruffles, and rapier ! He stepped into the pompous Royal coach which came for him with amazing dignity.

LONDON, *Thursday, June 11th*, 1863. *S. Barnabas.*— An amusing ball, unlike the general run, at Miss Coutts's ; there was at first not a partner to be seen ! and when a few did turn up, they wouldn't dance with me. Consequently my two dances were with an *innominato* and Ld. Feilding.

CLIVEDEN, *Saturday, June 13th*, 1863.—Set off (*beyond* blowing [2]) to Cliveden—connected in my mind, for ever I shd think, with old M.'s engagement, and our very shy and very lovely visit here just aftr. There are here the Argylls, Ld. Richard Cavendish, the Wm. Cowpers, Ly. C. Grosvenor, and poor Mr. William Harcourt,[3] who 4 months ago lost his young wife in her 2nd confinement, their first beautiful baby having died the year before. It does make one's heart ache to think of such grief ; and his whole look and manner touch one extremely, the more because he joins in conversation, and *puts on* no affectations of sorrow ; but his face tells it all. The little baby lives. During dinner America was the topic : the Duke and Duchess are Northern ! in their sympathies : as there was no zealous Southerner to give battle, I did not come in for a regular elaborate argument about it, which I long to hear, that I may make *some* head and tail of the subject. Mr. Harcourt said slavery was the cause of the rupture, but abolition was not the object of it.

CLIVEDEN, *2nd Sunday after Trinity, June 14th,*

[1] He was a Page-of-Honour.   [2] Appendix A.
[3] Afterwards Sir William, the statesman.

1863.—Hot with soft rain ; lovely afternoon, but felt thundery. My experience hitherto of peculiarly grand country places (and this *is* grand, though not large) certainly gives me no favourable impression of their *churchums*. Some of the party went to Cookham, and most to S. George's, Windsor, in the aftn ; but Agnes and I were doomed twice to a dreary bare room where service goes on pending the restoration of Hedzor Church : no chanting, a barrel-organ, laborious, long-winded, and truly dreadful hymn-singing, and in the morning no sermon owing to the poor clergyman's being ill. The aftn sermon, however, was good, on Watching and Praying. A. and I walked down to the river afterwards, views peaceful and lovely. Also we capped Sunday verses, and read aloud a good sermon of Jebb's. The Duchess of Argyll's wonderful cleverness is delightful to listen to ; and most gracefully it sits upon her, as she looks up with her shining eyes, and in that low gentle voice comes out with such knowledge of books, events, and politics. Meanwhile the perfect taste, refinement, and luxury of the place almost oppresses me. When one lives in Paradise, how hard it must be to ascend in heart and mind to Heaven !

Oxford, *Monday, June 15th,* 1863.—We came away last of all, and arrived here (at Dr. Stanley's) about 5, on a notable visit, viz. to celebrate Commemoration and the Prince and Princess of Wales' coming—he to receive a D.C.L. degree. These kind people have packed unheard-of numbers into their ingenious little house : the Stanleys of Alderley (minus parents), the Dufferins, and others besides are here. Ly. Dufferin has a gentle, winning countenance and manner, but is not pretty. A large dinner-party, cleverly divided between hall and dining-room. I sat between Ld. Dufferin, who was extremely agreeable, and Mr. Howard,[1] who can talk to any degree about drawing ! In the evening amongst others came the too-famous Mr. Jowett, whose mild intellectual face wd not lead one to suspect him to be one of the tamperers with the Faith, as, however, he *must* be called.

[1] No doubt George Howard, afterwards 9th Earl of Carlisle, a great lover of art,

OXFORD, *Tuesday, June* 16*th*, 1863.—An almost un-broken *soak* of small, soft, penetrating rain, cruelly taking from one's enjoyment, and O *how* one hates one's unavoidable smartness in weather when a short print petticoat and waterproof cloak and hood wd be the only comfortable garments ! Nevertheless great have been to-day's enjoyments. We went 1st to the Deanery to see the lovely rooms prepared for T.R.H.'s, and soon after saw them arrive in *Tom Quad.* I saw them quite beautifully walk up to the Deanery, and for the 1st time realized the loveliness of the Princess, her noble, innocent, and peculiarly dignified expression, her winning grace, and her most beautiful smile. She gave away the prizes standing at the top of one of the flights of steps, under an awning. At about ¼ to 3, Agnes and I found ourselves wedged into a corner of the Ladies' Gallery in the theatre, close to one of the rostrums, and albeit we had nothing particular to sit on, and but little to stand on, we saw and heard famously. And never shall I forget the astounding cheers when the great doors were opened, and our Princess walked up ! As the Prince appeared im-mediately after her train, the cheers ceased only for the whole mass of voices to join in " God save the Queen " with a mighty shout ; and this was the sub-limest thing, in its *intense* effect upon one, that I have ever heard. Afterwards the tremendous cheers began again and again ; till the theatre and everyone in it was ready to burst ; of course there was plenty of noise besides, and more, and more unruly, than at Cambridge, but this is all I care to remember.

OXFORD, *Wednesday, June* 17*th*, 1863.—Very lovely and hot. Darling old Meriel is 23 to-day. Agnes and I spent a most notably sleepless and unquiet night ; the garret where we were put being rather close, the bed bumpy, hard, and too small, and Agnes, as a rule, unable to sleep well with a bedfellow. So we got al-ternately on to the floor full length, tucked up in a chair, listened to the innumerable clocks, and went into a succession of giggles, which helped us through many a weary hour. Finding the floor made me

ache all over, and the chair was little better, I managed about 4 o'clock to lie down across the foot of the bed, and the contrast was so delicious, that an hour of comparative comfort and some sleep followed. And the night ended at last leaving us in an exhausted and stiffened state. We breakfasted very jovially with Stephy, meeting Johnny and Edward. Got prosperously into the theatre, where the reception of their R.H.'s was as uproarious and enthusiastic as yesterday. I didn't stay out the prize recitations, but got escorted home by John. Then came a State banquet at All Souls', to which it was a great honour to be asked, and afterwards we went to the Deanery garden, where the Prince came, and played with immense zest, boyishness, good nature, and some skill, at ball with his equerries and friends, using a croquet ball, and getting his fingers battered many a time, and once his nose ! A select circle of *tufts* were there : Lords Newry, Parker [1] ;
also Ld. Albert Leveson-Gower. Thence we stumped off on foot to see the boat procession, which was a great success, in the lovely weather. High tea, and the Christ Ch. ball. We feasted our eyes on the Princess. I was asked to dance by Lords Hamilton and Adair, Messrs. Parker, Warren, Wood, innom°. [2] Ag. danced with the Prince.

LONDON, *Thursday, June 18th*, 1863.—Lovely hot day. The Prince and Princess came to Dr. Stanley's garden, to see the tent which the latter slept in in the East, and we, the select few on the lawn, of course looked at both to our heart's content. And Atie. P. had the presence of mind to present me to the Princess ! who shook hands with me. My curtseys were beautiful, but O dear ! I *couldn't* make out what she said to me, with her low peculiar utterance and foreign accent. Luckily Agnes interpreted for me. Afterwards we went to see Magdalen, etc., and then saw T.R.H.'s go away, and the town, as one may say, visibly collapse after all the excitement.

[1] Space left for other names not filled in.
[2] I.e. innominato, somebody whose name she did not know.

LONDON, *Friday, June* 19*th*, 1863.—I went to luncheon in St. St., and there was told a wonderful bit of news. Ly. Augusta Bruce has written to Granny to ask whether, on a vacancy occurring, and the Queen being graciously pleased to offer it, there wd be any objection to my accepting the post of Maid-of-Honour ! ! ! ! ! ! ! And after some consultation, an answer was sent, signifying my grateful willingness. The very anticipation is so overpowering that I have had a headache all the aftn and I certainly dread the prospect, viewing my perpetual blunders, and the probable cuts into Hagley holidays and Papa. But ! £400 a year ! I shall be *more than* off his hands, and there is much that " I look the look over " (a case of dropping asleep ! " look forward to " I meant).

LONDON, *Saturday, June* 20*th*, 1863.—I breakfasted in G. St., and we talked a good deal *Maid-of-honourums.*

LONDON, 3*rd Sunday after Trinity, June* 21*st*, 1863.— Maid-of-honourums : a confirmatory letter came from Ly. Augusta.

LONDON, *Monday, June* 22*nd*, 1863.—The Belmores came to luncheon. After which came Granny and At. K., bringing with them the Queen's official offer of the post to me, through the Duchess of Wellington, Mistress of the Robes. So know all men by these presents that I am a Maid-of-Honour. This is a momentous event in my life, and I am quite tired of ruminating and speculating about it.

LONDON, *Wednesday, June* 24*th*, 1863.—*S. John Baptist.*—Six letters of congratulation poured down upon me, which, added to what greets me everywhere in the beau monde, make me feel very much as if I were going to be married.

LONDON, *Thursday, June* 25*th*, 1863.—Hot. The Duchesses of Sutherland and Argyll, the Duke of Argyll, Charles Kean, the Cambridge Public Orator, Dr. Stanley, Papa, etc., came to the clever breakfast. The Exhibition building and what is to be done with it was the prevailing topic : rather a dull one. After bkft, however, Agnes and I had Kean to ourselves, and he was very entertaining with stage anecdotes and experiences. Said nobody would guess what an inclination to *laugh* comes over actors at the most awful moments. As when Garrick was playing King Lear (the last thing I should have thought he ever cd do, by the bye), a butcher in the pit, who had with him a dog which stood with its fore-paws on the seat in front contemplating the stage, took off his wig to cool his head, and having no peg, put it for a moment on the dog's head. As Garrick advanced, preparatory to falling on his knees and uttering the tremendous curse on Goneril, he caught the eye of the bewigged dog; and went into such hysterics of laughing that he had to go off the stage. I received the last quarterly allowance I shall ever receive from Papa's poor pinched pocket, I suppose! And I floundered about in my accounts as usual. At 6 we rode with Willy and saw the Prince riding with Althorp and Col. Keppel. Mr. Baird joined us—I broke my stirrup strap but can luckily manage without: so we put it into Willy's pocket, and went on unheeding.

LONDON, *Friday, June 26th,* 1863.—At 11 we went to the great thing of the season: the Guards' ball, in what was the English picture-gallery of the Exhibition, given to the Prince and Princess. It was all on a royal scale; and I shan't soon forget the beautiful effect, when T.R.H.'s went away, of the procession streaming through the antechambers and down the flag-emblazoned staircase lined with picked Guardsmen; " God save the Queen " going on the while. The Princess looked lovely and as if she enjoyed herself, but pale. I didn't dance " nor didn't expect to." The Royal quadrille was often a lovely sight, being composed of many beauties: Charlotte Spencer, Ly. Adelaide Talbot, Ly. Mary Craven, the Dss. of Manchester, Princess Mary, etc. Lord Dunmore dancing with the Prss. was a sight to see of good looks and perfect manners.

LONDON, *Thursday, July 2nd,* 1863.—A *most* delightful clever breakfast. At the table (1 of 3) where I was sat Papa, Mr. Monckton Milnes, Mr. Herbert of Muckross, Miss Stanley, Count Struzlecki (there is no spelling his name), and a Northern Yankee, Mr. Cyrus

Field. I'm afraid I shd have preferred being disgusted with the latter; but truth compels me to say that he was agreeable, and seemed to be candid and modest—the very last 2 qualities I shd have looked for. Also free from *twang* properly speaking, tho' his accent and pronunciation were curious. He said " poblic," "*On*-questionably," " South Car'lina," and once " no thing " in 2 distinct words. He spoke with contempt of Lincoln to whose inanity he attributed the duration of the war, said that he wished no ex-president cd be re-elected, or given any government office, as according to what it is now, presidents are more occupied in the effort to secure future votes than in their duty to the country. This he implied: and said the whole war might have been crushed in the bud, if President Buchanan had not been thinking of the Southern votes. A nice state of things indeed! The expenses of the war hitherto amount to half our national debt; but he said much of the money spent circulated profitably in the country.

Beautiful select concert at the Aumales' to which Papa and I went, kindly lifted by Lord Harrowby. Mario, Grisi, Alboni and Delle Sedie sang, and Thalberg played; and tho' Grisi's voice is much gone, and Mario's high notes a little strained sometimes, it was glorious. The Duc de Chartres was there with his nice young bride: also the Comte de Paris; it was nice to see the two brothers' evident affection for each other. Ld. Amberley[1] took me to supper; a very small, scrubby-looking youth, but full of intelligence and with pretty manners.

LONDON, *Saturday, July 4th*, 1863.—We got the anxious news that poor old May has got the scarlet fever, in spite of having had it slightly in '56. Her throat is bad, but the telegraph this afternoon said it was a favourable case. The 6 who have had scarlet fever have all had it favourably, and how often altogether anxiety of this sort has ended in relief and thankfulness! God grant it may be so again. We did not hear of the certainty till the aftn. In the morning Papa

[1] Son of Earl Russell, the Prime Minister, and father of the present Earl and Mr. Bertrand Russell.

and I went again to the Oval, and this time saw Charles
get more than 20 runs in most beautiful style ; getting
a lovely cut for 4, first ball, and a square leg hit for
3 the next.

LONDON, *Tuesday, July 7th,* 1863.—We went to a
breakfast given by the Dow. Dss. of Sutherland at
Chiswick, meeting the Prince and Princess. She is
in mourning for some Danish relation, and wore a hat
which didn't quite suit her as it hid her lovely brow.
We had a country dance on the grass : she went down
it with dignity with the Duke of Sutherland. We
were immense audience to the darling little Grosvenor
children. The eldest Sutherland boy, little Ld. Stafford,
isn't pretty and lookd delicate, but his brother (who is
called Ld. Macleod, I believe : his mother's 2nd title)
is a beauty. Mary and Helen came with us. I played
one game of croquet ½ through. In the evening an
exceedingly beautiful ball at Stafford House. I was
asked to dance by Lords Amberley, Fred. Cavendish,
George Lennox, Mr. Lascelles and an *innominato*
with whom I executed what pretended to be a Scotch
reel ! We walked home, Atie P. with Willy, Agnes,
Ld. Adare, and I, like a convict, marched in the middle,
thus guarded. The night was lovely ; and before getting
into bed, about 4, I counted 20 towers and spires in
the serene, opal-like morning atmosphere.

LONDON, *Wednesday, July 8th,* 1863.—I had the
wonderful treat of going to S. James Hall with Miss
Gladstone, to hear Jenny Lind sing in the " Allegro "
and " Penseroso." I suppose her high notes are a
little gone, but the matchless expression and *heart-
feeling* can never go out of her voice, and there is a
ringing purity of tone unlike anything else. Mem.
" Sweet bird," " Hide me from day's garish eye,"
" Let the merry bells," and " May at last my weary
eye." It was a rare perfection to have words, voice,
and airs all so glorious and all glorifying each other.

LONDON, *Thursday, July 9th,* 1863.—To breakfast
came the Comte de Paris, grown manly-looking since
his American campaign ; his manners very noble and
graceful ; his English extremely French. Also came

no less a man than Fechter, who was very agreeable. His face is finer seen in private life than on the stage : a great look of the great Napoleon—full piercing eyes, hooked noʒe, and expressive mouth ; his figure dumpy and fat. Ld. De Grey's little boy, who is frantic with admiration of Fechter, was sent for to see his hero : his parents being here.

LONDON, *6th Sunday after Trinity, July 12th,* 1863.— Very hot. I have at last reached, I really believe, my last London Sunday. Went with Papa and Charles to the John St. Chapel to hear Mr. Brookfield, who preacht. with great fervour, point, and severity on Pharisaism. Saw there old, old Lady De Dunstanville, who still enjoys London gaieties, tho' looking as if a pinch wd crumble her. Also the Mildmays and Mont-gomeries were there. It refreshes one to see people whom one only connects with diamonds and wreaths —in church. Aftn to hear Dr. Goulburn preach very well on behalf of the Whetstone Penitentiary. Charles went back to Cambridge after dinner. The match was drawn. Harrow not going in at all for 2nd innings : wd have had 200 to get, so we shd probably have won. Spencer got 10 runs 2nd innings, and he and Nevy got 6 wickets between them.

I read a short sermon, and began Goulburn's " Study of the Holy Scriptures."

LONDON, *Tuesday, July 14th,* 1863.—We went to a Chiswick bkft, and got a little revived by the bit of country. The D. of Sutherland and other young men played at leap-frog ! and there was croquet, a country dance, and valsing on the grass. A good recherché ball (my last) at Ly. De Grey's : I was asked to dance by Lords George Lennox, Frederic Cavendish, Amberley, and Messrs. Lascelles and Stanley.

LONDON, *Thursday, July 16th,* 1863.—Suddenly on the cold side of cool, without rain or anything to account for it. Last clever breakfast, to which came the Dss. of Sutherland and Ly. Herbert, Dr. Acland, Dean Trench, " Garibaldi's Englishman," Ld. Frederic Caven-dish, and a china dealer. Slavery was talked of. The Duke of Hamilton has died of congestion of the brain

from a fall downstairs.   I went with Atie. P. to Heath's
for a chimney-pot riding hat (the height of the fashion).

A detachment from S. Martin's school came for
tea, games, and little gifts, and enjoyed themselves
hugely ; more delighted with the scamper on the gravel
terrace than our sch. children are with half the park
to play in.   Mary and Maud Herbert came to see.
Gladstones to a tiny dance at the Grosvenors' ; but
I have actually wound up my gaieties, which have
consisted of : 17 balls, 8 parties, 9 dinner parties, 8
private concerts, besides breakfasts of different sorts,
etc.   Letters : to M.

FALCONHURST, *S. James, Saturday, July 25th,* 1863.—
We went for luncheon to the Nasmyths', a delightful
old couple, he the gt sledge-hammer man.   Their house
lovely and full of interesting and beautiful things.
Mem. especially, his observatory—where he showed us
a model of the face of the sun, which he has just discovered to be covered promiscuously by willow-leaf-
shaped things, from whence comes the light, and which
Sir J. Herschel, from observing that they move in-
dependently of each other, is inclined to suspect
may be living creatures.   They are 2,000 miles long
and 90 broad ; if they are beings they must be mighty
dazzling Archangels indeed.

HAWARDEN, *Thursday, July 30th,* 1863.—A horse
ran away with a boy of 16, who was thrown and grievously hurt, midway between the Chester Lodge and
Broughton Church.   Atie. P. flew off to nurse him.

HAWARDEN, *Saturday, August 1st,* 1863.—I got an
arrow into the blue at 60 yards, shooting with Uncle
Henry's prize bow, weight 55.   Could only manage
abt 15 shots, and my arms ache a little.

HAWARDEN, *Monday, August 3rd,* 1863.—Papa went
off to night to sleep 4 hours at Chester, thence to Birmingham for breakfast, thence to the Board of Guardians
at Bromsgrove ! If that isn't energetic doing of duty,
I shd like to know what is.

HAWARDEN, *Wednesday, August 5th,* 1863.—Walked
with Ats P. and C. and the 2 Maries to see the poor
thrown boy at Mancot : he seems recovering.

BOOK VIII
AUGUST 1863—SEPTEMBER 1864

INTRODUCTION TO BOOK VIII

THE eighth volume is much more fully represented here than its predecessors and needs the less Introduction. Its great event is Lady Frederick's engagement and marriage. The last volume gave us her first meetings with Lord Frederick. He does not appear in this till she goes to stay at Chatsworth in December 1863 ; when, on the first night, she records that " at dinner I got into an argument with Lord Frederick Cavendish on the Church which excited and interested me." It seems to have interested him, or, at any rate, not to have interfered with another sort of interest. For things begin to move fast almost at once. He followed her immediately to Hawarden, where he again " discussed Church questions " with her, and where his presence evidently had something to do with her having " the most delightful ball I have ever had " ; and on December 14th she enters in her Diary : " I feel in something of a dream." She wrote at the same time to her sister Mrs. Talbot : " I could not help having my head turned by Lord Frederick seeming rather to like me. He is so very pleasant that this did put me into a state of mind. I know this may be stupid and that it may all come to an end : but Oh dear ! " The sage sister evidently replied that there probably was nothing in it, for the second letter justifies herself and tells Meriel of various marked attentions he had paid her, one of which, very marked in that house, was that, when asked by Mrs. Gladstone to buy some photographs (probably of the great man) for a charity, he had demanded one of Miss Lucy Lyttelton ! She was evidently already in love with him, and almost sure that he was in love with her. But her strong

173

religious faith keeps her calm and peaceful during the
period of uncertainty. On December 31st she enters
in the Diary : " There is much in my heart to make
me thankful, and to give me a sort of awe, in looking
forward ; and if it were not for my trust—a faithful
trust, though so weak and blind—in the Heavenly
Guidance, I should be full of restlessness and excitement.
And as it is, I fear I shall be, sooner or later." So,
when she goes to London in April, " this going away
from home fills me with awe and anxiety. But I can't
write about it. ' Lead Thou me on.' " Mrs. Gladstone
was, of course, in the secret ; and her niece had
not been in Downing Street many hours before she
saw Lord Frederick who came to dinner the very day
she arrived. That was on April 6th ; after that they
met almost every day till he proposed to her at the
Stafford House party in honour of Garibaldi on April
13th. She had a few doubts and fears, but on April
21st she notes : " We are engaged, and my doubts
and fears have all been absorbed in the wonderful
happiness and peace." The marriage took place on
June 7th in Westminster Abbey. It was one of the
happiest man and woman have ever known, during all
the eighteen years it lasted. To the end, whenever
they had a time alone together, it seemed to them
another honeymoon.

The two other things which, after her engagement and
marriage, do most to fill this volume are the coming
of age of her eldest brother, afterwards Lord Cobham,
which she describes in great detail : and her experiences
at Court as a Maid-of-Honour, which she got to enjoy
very much. When she left Osborne in January 1864
she writes : " After the kindest good-byes from everybody, off I went with my heart rather full ; and I don't
think I shall be again heard lamenting that I am a
Maid-of-Honour." When she first got to Windsor
in September 1863 she had written to her sister that
the Household dinner " was not quite so bad as it might
be. To be sure we all spoke below our breaths, but

this was not much worse than Cliveden [1] ; and we had a good deal of murmured conversation, considering." And she is relieved to find that her "scrambled-into dress is correct: black with black gloves but gold ornaments; and green leaves and lilac flowers are allowed." But still she feels like a servant at her first place, that "cold, forlorn sensation" which servants call "feeling strange." But a few months later at Osborne she has already discovered that "the Household is composed of all the nicest people in England." She is particularly delighted with the Queen's Ladies; and says of Lady Churchill that she is "without an exception the most highbred person I ever saw: just like a gazelle: tall and dignified and graceful, with a small, noble head and a kind, simple, unaffected manner."

And she has nothing but praise to write of the Queen and her family. All seem to have been very kind to her, and Princess Louise got into trouble by taking her out riding, instead of a governess, without leave. She had always been much impressed with the smallness of the Queen's sons, as former volumes show. Here she writes of Prince Arthur, now the Duke of Connaught, the last survivor of them: "Prince Arthur is a charming little fellow, full of bright courtesy and pleasant talk, and more of a John Bull than the others. A handsome face but such a tiny mortal for 14 ! "

There is not much else which calls for note. Of small facts which now seem odd perhaps the most curious are that she notes that bonnets are being given up for bridesmaids; and that the process of reducing corpulence, now known as "banting," was invented by a gentleman of that name who wrote a pamphlet on the subject. How many to-day, even of those who "bant," ever heard of Mr. Banting ?

[1] When she had stayed with the Duchess of Sutherland.

HAGLEY, *Monday, August 24th,* 1863. *S. Bartho's Day.*—Prescott with Arthur, Tasso with Nevy, " Childe Harold " with Albert, Yonge with Bob. Old M. came in after church, rather wretched with a cold. I rode with Arthur.

HAGLEY, *Wednesday, August 26th,* 1863.—I received my warrant of appointment, for which superfluity I am to pay £25.

HAGLEY, *Thursday, August 27th,* 1863.—I then rode on the hunter, with Lavinia and Bob, and had the satisfaction of keeping on in spite of a very lively kick.

HAGLEY, *Saturday, August* 29th, 1863.—Have finished Wordsworth's tour in Italy, which gives a thoughtful, temperate, and far-seeing view of the Church of Rome, the possibility and the crying need of its reformation, and (which is the point of the book) the necessity of its reforming itself. Present political excitement and disturbance seem to open up the way.

HAGLEY, *Saturday, September 5th,* 1863.—The eleven of us, with Papa, Newmany, and Miss Merlet, had a most jovial and successful monster expedition to Hereford ; and so I have, to my great delight, added that noble Cathedral, in all the glory of its matchlessly excellent restoration, to my list. Tho' small, the richness and variety of its Norman work, its perfect specimens of E. English, in which were specially beautiful deep mouldings, and many details, as the early Decorated 2-light windows 50 feet high, the lovely tiling, and the splendid screen, make it rank very high in beauty. Alfred much struck with his first Cathedral service : said he liked the Cathedral better even than the dinner, or the uproarious fun in the train.

HAGLEY, *Tuesday, September 8th,* 1863.—A notable

and most upsetting, exciting, and bewildering day. There came a letter from Ly. Ely (which lost a post by going to London), summoning me to Windsor on the 10th to be in waiting till the 14th. Having been told Xmas was the earliest date possible, this interesting communication finds me without " a thing to my back ! " I tore off to Stourbridge with Gielen and At. C. and bought silk, etc., for two black gowns ; must trust to London when I go up for bonnet, flowers, and so on. The wretched Gielen must go blind and mad with work, in spite of many helpers, but ! " la Royne le veult." An unpleasant state of bathing-feel [1] I am in ; still, when the terrific 4 days are over (they *never* will be, I think !), without any hitch or blunder, I *shall* be glad to have made the 1st plunge.

HAGLEY, *Wednesday, September 9th,* 1863.—Mild and fine, but with something of the Novr. look and feel. My bathing-feel " va crescendo." I drove with At. E. and May to Stourbridge, and falling in love with a be-witching linsey, bought it against winter for 33*s.* ; 12 yds.

WINDSOR, *Thursday, September 10th,* 1863.—The much-to-be-remembered day of my first entering upon Maid-of-Honour duties. I left Hagley at 9, *inside out* with bathing-feel, reached London in time for a scramble of indispensable shopping, and thence to Windsor, which looked noble and ethereal, bathed in hazy sunset light, as we came in sight of it. I was shown up to 2 snug little rooms by a comfortable old body, and soon made the acquaintance of Miss Stopford and Miss Kerr, who came to me. They are *both* together here by some mistake ; but it is very pleasant for me. Miss Stopford has won my heart, and I wish she was to be my colleague (Miss Cathcart, a dread being, is to be). They were most kind, comforting me by de-claring my clothes all right. Lady Ely next came in, and took me to Ly. Caroline Barrington, and next I saw Lady Augusta Bruce for a few minutes. All kind and comfortable. I was prepared for finding the dinner and evening silent and stiff ; but it was much better than I expected. Present, Lady Ely, the two above

[1] Appendix A.

named Maids-of-Honour, Lord Caithness, General Seymour, Colonel Liddell, Major Cowell, M. Buff, Major Elphinstone. The Queen dines apart now. The sotto-voce conversation on very Courtly and regal subjects was impressive ! And I confess I was also impressed by the 8 noiseless servants and indeed by all I saw. O the dignity and beauty of the corridor and rooms ! After dinner, Miss S. and Miss C. having disappeared, I was sitting alone with Ly. Ely, when one of the noiseless servants came and said : " Her Majesty desires your Ladyship to bring Miss Lyttelton into the corridor." So kind Ly. Ely put my arm in hers, and I went, trembling. The Queen came forward from the end of the corridor, and gave me her hand with all the grace and gentle dignity of old times. And O what it was to kiss her hand again, for the first time since I saw her at the height of her happiness, without so much as a shadow cast before by the dark sorrow in store for her ! I can't exactly tell what it is in her face which is altered, for she looks well ; but she has gained an expression which there used not to be : her grief has set its stamp there, but so as to refine and ennoble it. Her sweet and kindly smile went to my heart. She asked after Granny, Papa, At. Coque, and " Meriel," saying of the latter, " She has two children, has she not ? " Said more than once that I was like Mamma, but also like Aunt Lavinia. Lady Ely said I was nervous ; the Queen said smiling, " Nervous ! O no ; she will soon get over that," or words to that effect. She then beckoned up the 2 Princesses who were with her ; they both kissed me. Prss. Louise is very pretty—Prss. Helena asked after " Laddle " [1]— Prince Alfred was in the distance (grown rather fat), also pretty Prince Arthur. The interview lasted only a few minutes ; but after it was over, I shd have liked nothing better than rushing off somewhere and having a good cry ; instead of which I had to go back in a very tremulous state to the solemn drawing-room, where we sat round a table the rest of the evening, and were rather dull. I went to bed tired with excitement.

[1] Lady Lyttelton, Lady Frederick's grandmother.

WINDSOR, *Friday, September 11th*, 1863.—Oh dear, I shall sympathize for the rest of my life with poor peggies [1] launched at their first place ! To-day has taught me what it is to " feel strange." I am not naturally shy ; and the actual bathing-feel has pretty nearly gone off, but I am unked and forlorn, in spite of everybody's kindness. Ly. Ely took me to the kennels (mem. 16 puppies), the lovely dairy, and to Frogmore, where the mausoleum, which does so jar upon one's English feelings, is still being worked at. The Queen goes there daily. Ly. Ely told me much that was interesting the while. After breakfast we were in the corridor, when the Queen came in with the children. Prss. Louise brought little darling Prss. Beatrice up to me and I kissed her tiny hand. She is not pretty, but has a dear little intelligent face. The little Princes were at the kennels in the aftn, when Miss Stopford and I passed. They called, and we joined them. Prince Arthur is very handsome, if only he looked more like 13 years old ; but he is wonderfully small. Prince Leopold has a funny, waggish face, with the brightest blue eyes ; he is miserably thin and puny, though they think him stronger : Lady Caroline Barrington told me the doctors hardly expect him to live—poor darling ! Miss Stopford told me much about Prss. Louise, whom she has been with at Osborne. H.R.H. seems to be rather naughty, with a mischievous will of her own; draws beautifully.

Miss S. and I had a pleasant walk, seeing the old porter at the garden gate, and the tombstone to the memory of a magpie he loved. I was afraid the dinner wd be worse than last night, as Miss S. (who begs me to call her Horatia) and Ly. Ely dined with the Queen ; but it was not dreadful ; I had to sweep down the stately interminable corridor all by myself to dinner ; but luckily caught Ly. Caroline. In the evening, Gen. Grey and I, Ly. C. and Gen. Seymour played at whist ! which made the time go pleasantly.

WINDSOR, *Saturday, September 12th*, 1863.—Fine, but rather misty and Novembery. I have got rid of " les

---

[1] I.e. maidservants.

vapeurs " and begin rather to like Court life ! I asked
leave to go to S. George's in the morning (more like a
peggy than ever! " Please'm, may I go out for an
hour ? "). Little I thought on the great marriage day
when I shd next be in the glorious Chapel ! The singing
lovely. Anthem, " O sing joyfully," not very pretty.
Then came my own room. At luncheon were several
Privy Councillors. Ld. Palmerston, his beauty much
impaired by particularly bad slate-coloured false teeth,
the D. of Newcastle, looking ill, Ld. Granville, Sir
George Grey, Sir Andrew Buchanan. Horatia rode
with Prss. Helena and P. Arthur. The Queen went,
unattended, to plant a new oak in the place of Herne's
oak, which has lately fallen. I walked with Ly. Ely
from 5 till ¼ to 7 : she sent a cold chill through me by
saying I shd very likely dine with the Queen to-morrow.
Sir T. Biddulph and Ly. Augusta Bruce dined : Ly.
Biddulph came in the evening. The same party,
transposing Sir Thomas for Gen. Seymour, played
whist. Prss. Louise sent for Horatia, and cried and
sobbed at the thoughts of losing her on Monday, after
their long bit at Osborne together. The same soft
heart and quick affections that Granny found in the
elder ones. Letters : fr. Papa, Atie. P., Meriel. To
Atie. P., At. C. and At. Yaddy. The sentries presented
arms to Ly. Ely and me ! misled by the Queen's little
dog, who was with us, and who doubtless took all the
honour to himself.

WINDSOR, 15th *Sunday after Trinity, September* 13th,
1863.—Serene mild day. Having reached the top of
the tree as to great houses, I find here no exception to
my reflection made at Cliveden, that magnificent
places have shocking Church arrangements. In the
1st place, it is startling to one's feelings to go to a
Sunday service in a chapel bonnetless, as the household
have to do here. No chanting, except in very bad
style to the responses to the Commandments, disagreeable tunes to inferior hymns, sung in a drawl, and
the Morning Service divided in two, which last plan
has, I know, many advantages, but not to a strong
person whom the longest service cannot tire. The
Queen, Prince Alfred, and all the children attended

the first half alone ; and 3 carriages were used during the day.   One wishes (I fear vainly) that something cd lead the Queen to find comfort in that most consoling and peace-giving thing—our Church's Liturgy—that thereby she might be helped and strengthened on her desolate way.   How the words in the Psalm went to one's heart—" He is the Father of the fatherless, and defendeth the cause of the widows."   Well, we must trust our Queen to Him, and His Loving Wisdom.   He has answered many prayers for her !   I walked with Lady Ely again in the garden, and ended, to my refreshment, at S. George's ;   anthem, a spirited, florid one, " When Israel came out of Egypt."   Mr. Ellison preacht in the noon-day half of the Chapel service, on Hades and death.   I was told it was possible I should dine with the Queen, but it was not so.   The evening was lightened by ivory letters.[1]   I think I must have met the pick of the Court for pleasantness and kindness.

HAGLEY, *Monday, September 14th,* 1863.—And so it is over !   I almost feel as if I had spent a fortnight here.   It is peaceful and pleasant indeed to think I have gone through my first waiting and really without a rub.   The Queen was to go to Balmoral this evening, but we were allowed to go early.   Got home in time for dinner.   We did certainly make a noise ! and the evening was a funny contrast to my last four.

HAGLEY, *Wednesday, September 16th,* 1863.—Fine, serene, mild day.   At. Coque, Lavinia, and May set out for " Orchard Neville " (late Baltonsborough) en route for Antony ;   whose name recalls to me one of the very happiest and merriest weeks in my life. I think these girls much enjoy the prospect, but they enjoy things (especially Lava) as grown-up people do, to whom life has a little outgrown its freshness : take events and pleasures, I mean, with sedateness ;   I have never seen them really carried off their legs with excitement, or anything like it.   And this is a little sad at their age.   Poor pussy's [2] head discomforts account for a good deal, no doubt.

---

[1] I.e. I suppose a game played with ivory letters.   [2] Lavinia.

HAGLEY, *Friday, September* 18*th,* 1863.—Busy most of the morning after church in going over the rooms with Elly : we shall be 30 in the house, besides servants, if we live till dread October.   Played at billiards with At. E. and afterwards walked parochially with her. Took a partridge to Mrs. Stringer, who held up her hands in speechless bliss before bursting into gratitude —poor old body.   Met sweet Mary and Annie Herbert in their little white sun-bonnets, out of which they look at one with shining open eyes of a kind peculiar, I think, to tiny maidens under 5.   Said their new sister was to be called Lucy.   " Is baby well ? " " Ess, sankoo."   Also took pudding to the Mrs. Meredith with twins, which have both lived after all.

HAGLEY, *Saturday, September* 19*th,* 1863.—Began " Henry VIII " with Arthur who likes both poetry in general and Shakespeare in particular.

HAGLEY, *Saturday, September* 26*th,* 1863.—Lovely golden day, with a few heavy showers, after a night lit up with a harvest moon that dazzled one to look at.   I saw a little black cloud, just like an armed man, march up to her in a threatening manner, and vanish into nothing on coming within the influence of her pure and steadfast rays.

To dinner came Sir Th. Philips : disturbances, mobs, and riots were talked of ; and Charles and I showed our ring [1] at recollecting something about the Chartist riots in '48 ; especially how we were sent into the Green Park as likely to be a quiet place, and how yells in the distance drove us home in double quick time.   Also there is an impression on both our minds of a bludgeon ; not unnaturally, as Papa was a Special Constable.

HAGLEY, *Thursday, October* 1*st,* 1863.—I translated and finished Guizot's " Charles I," finding myself as much moved at the account of the King's death as I was on reading it in Clarendon 9 or 10 years ago, although I do now see, very unwillingly, the faults of the Royal martyr.

HAGLEY, *Tuesday, October* 13*th,* 1863.—A good deal

[1] Appendix A.

of rain : still mild. Big club day. It's pleasant
to see these girls come back as cheerfully and heartily
to their work after such a holyday. The sort of thing
that used to try me beyond anything ! Cong.[1] 2.
Girls, Miss M., and I took pudding to Mrs. Burford, and
visited the Stringers' new house. Paperums, perron-
awning-ums, step-carpetums, ball-chairums, stableums.

HAGLEY, *Thursday, October 15th*, 1863.—The billiard-
room was transformed into an elegant Louis XV
" salon," with the drawing-room furniture, china, etc.
Gallery emptied and uncarpeted. A little parochial
toddle with May.

HAGLEY, *Monday, October 19th*, 1863.—Most delightfully soft and warm, though cloudy all day. I
went to Birmingham, after oilcloth, satin shoes, blotting-
books, winter jackets for the girls, and a print for Nevy.
The gallery floor begins to assume a lovely light toffee
hue, by dint of rubbing. At. Yaddy came. It's odd
to see her here in autumn, and without her little couple,
who are recruiting at Brighton. She is full of the
departure of the Spencers, who have set off for Egypt
with Tallee, he having not recovered all his strength
after inflammation of the lungs. Thus we lose the
three people we most wanted for the do-ment (Mary
Page's forcible word for doings). Letters : fr Albert
and Bob. I missed Church.

HAGLEY, *Friday, October 23rd*, 1863.—Slight morning
frost, but became very mild : a profoundly still, hazy
day. I walked with At. Y. We were audience[2] to
two splendid triumphal arches in the avenue.

HAGLEY, *Monday, October 26th*, 1863.—Raw yellow
fog. Ld. George and Ric. Quin, Atie. P. and Agnes,
Uncles Stephen and Henry and the 5 boys came. I
stayed in to get rid of the end of my cold. Ld. George[3]
has never been here since before Meriel's birth.

Atie. Pussy is in the dear room, never used till now

---

[1] I.e., congregation at church, exclusive of Hall and Rectory.
[2] Appendix A.
[3] Lord George Quin married Lady Georgiana Spencer, sister of
Sarah, Lady Lyttelton.

since the night when our darling [1] rested there in her arms and then passed to the blessed repose of the Everlasting Arms.

HAGLEY, *Tuesday, October 27th*, 1863.—A red-letter day, adding to the many that shine out at intervals through my life. Not that it was by any means a day of unmixed enjoyment ; on the contrary, I don't think I began really to enjoy myself (such was one's anxiety) till after midnight ! But it was a day of deep thankfulness, and awakened bright hopes for the future. The events that happened to mark dear old Charles' birthday were guns fired early in the morning ; a procession of the school with garlands and flags to the back of the house, where they sung, and an address to Papa was read by Stephens ; wine and cake were given to all the children at the school ; and finally a ball given to all the county (about 500), including the Duc and Duchesse d'Aumale and the Prince de Condé. We received in the hall and the billiard-room : danced in the gallery and drawing-room : supper in the dining-room, tea in the library, Papa's two rooms cloakrooms. There arrived to-day Wenlocks, Braybrookes, Neville Grenvilles, Mrs. Charles Robartes, and, to sleep in the village, Lord John Manners, Ld. John Hervey, Messrs. C. and H. Wynne, Ross (the gt rifle shot), Stopford Selfe and Stewart. Also C. Robartes slept out. At the school was Charles's first speech, my first time of hearing him : his opening sentence was enough to relieve one's fright as to how he wd do it. It was really perfect : simple and to the point, forgetting no one, and just the right length. One word about Papa my wretched head has managed to retain. After saying something of desire to be like him, " not that I can hope to emulate him, for who could ? " The simplicity of this made it so much better than a long compliment. After this had ended with tremendous cheers from all the children, some of us went to church, where the Psalms for the day spoke to one's feelings at the time, as they always do in every marked circumstance of life. The 126th, 127th, and 128th psalms put into

---

[1] Lady Frederick's mother, Lady Lyttelton.

words all that could come into one's heart about Papa,
and left one with a happy trust that the blessings there
spoken of would long be his. " Blessed are all they
that fear the Lord, and walk in His ways."

The monster dinner of 38 people came off at six :
we had to sit round the room at a horseshoe table !
In the middle of it arrived the Wenlocks ; about $9\frac{1}{2}$
the guests began to arrive ; old Meriel helped me to
receive them, and looked so handsome in her lace.   The
Royal people came early, and were established on a
little dais opposite the fireplace in the gallery.   The
Duc was exceedingly gracious and pleasant : in the
first Quadrille he and I danced, Charles with the
Duchesse vis-à-vis ; the Prince de Condé proved to be
very pleasant and conversible too ; talked a good deal
about his dislike of having to go for his " stoodees to
ze continent," and so missing the season ;   and announced that he was quite an Englishman, except as
to politics.   " How should I be elsewise ? "   I couldn't
help thinking his English might have been a little less
unmistakably French, therefore !   Till supper, I was
a little unhappy : the room grew terribly hot and the
crowd certainly *was* [1] ;   but everybody seemed exceedingly jovial.   We went in state to supper at 12 ;   the
Royalties had a round table apart under the middle
window, where was a small platform.   Papa, At.
Yaddy, Granny, Atie. P., and I sat down with them
and I suppose about 200 people squeezed into the room,
the rest remaining in the drawing-room, and as many
as possible in the doorway.   In progress of time, the
Duke mounted the platform and made an excellent
speech proposing Charles's health, very fluent and
graceful, in spite of the strongest French accent ;
and then dear old Charles got up, and stood for some
minutes while everybody cheered him.   He did look
grand, with his face softened by feeling, and a little
paler than usual.   He spoke slowly, especially when
what he said moved them, and there was a manly
modesty about his manner that went straight to one's
heart.   He thanked them all most heartily, and then
dwelt really beautifully on how he felt that he owed

[1] Appendix A.

their kindness entirely to their love for Papa, reserving nothing for himself, and how he knew he cd say nothing stronger than that he hoped to follow his example. Spoke of hoping soon to know them all, and of always remembering their kindness. Oh dear! if I cd but remember it all! It was such real happiness to hear him give expression to such deep and true feeling : I always instinctively felt that he had it in his heart, but his reserve is so great that he has hardly ever spoken out anything of the sort, and now to hear him say he rejoiced to be able " thus publically and emphatically " to express his sense of all Papa's example was to him, and his hope that he should prove himself not altogether unworthy of it, was an overpowering joy to me. . . . I went out of the room with a light heart indeed! but had a blow in missing Papa's speech, which was unexpected, Ld. Dudley giving his health after we had marched out. It was beautiful, all say who heard it. The last guests got away about ¼4, and the happy, successful end of everything rubbed out all the previous anxieties, and I can only repeat that it was a red-letter day.

HAGLEY, *Wednesday, October 28th, 1863. SS. Simon and Jude.*—Old Nevy's birthday; like Charles, he spends it at home for the 1st time since he went to school, 10 years ago. The weather was exactly what one wanted ; bright and pleasant, with gleams of sunshine breaking out. Breakfast was rather promiscuous, between 10 and 11, everybody appeared in high spirits, and delighted with last night's success. Church at 11½, with about 40 people! which was very nice to see, after a ball.

The labourers' dinner, which included all, in and out of the parish, who work for tenants, was at 1. 250 men were the numbers. Capn. Wolrige spoke very well, proposing C.'s health, and presented an excellent address, signed by nearly all the parish : Chs. responded in another excellent little speech, and thanked good old Dilworth for a splendid basket of fruit. Then Uncle Wm. got up to give Papa's health, which he did most beautifully, speaking of the one terrible shadow over all this joyful time ; Papa's answer dwelt upon it for a little while in a way that moved and overcame me indeed ! but I was so glad that her dear name was not left out at such a time as this, when the longing for her presence—for her to be there if only once to smile upon her boy whom she wd have been so proud of —was so deep in one's heart. The one thing wanting : surely meant to draw our thoughts upward where she is, and remind us of the better things, when we might be rejoicing overmuch in all this earthly pride and happiness. Oh, darling Mammie, you may have looked down upon him ! you may have been praying for him with the pure prayer of those who are with Christ !

After this, all went to the park for games, which were very successful, and then came the poor women's tea, most comfortable, amusing, and satisfactory. Great was the delight when Uncle William dandled a twarly [1] Meredith twin, and made it quite good ; also my telling them all they were each to drink 10 cups of tea was reckoned an excellent joke. Kind At. Yaddy and I marched off to the lodge with a jug of tea, 4 pieces of cake, 6 (I think) bits of bread and butter, about 8 slices of meat and 13 lumps of sugar, for Mary Page and Widow Read, who couldn't get to the Arms. Fire balloons and red and blue lights came off at night, and the perron (the hideousness of whose ball-awning was quite made up for by evergreens, flowers, and flags) looked lovely with innumerable little lamps. Our huge horse-shoe dinner went off with éclat, as did the evening spent in the hall and billiard-room, enlivened by At. Y's singing. I gave old Nevy a print, at sight of which he fell on my neck with a burst of affection !

HAGLEY, *Thursday, October 29th, 1863.*—The kind weather, which I do think I shall never abuse again, having done all that could be expected of it, and more, naturally gave way to its feelings to-day, and we had a most astonishing howl of wind and rain nearly all the morning. But nothing happened to-day except a highly successful and delightful dinner at Halesowen, to which went all the gentlemen except Lord Wenlock and Ralph Neville, who stayed at home and squired

---

[1] Appendix A.

I—15

us. They all came home about 11½ in tremendous
spirits, everyone having spoken, except John; Albert
returned thanks for Granny! Uncle W. excelled himself, and was full of praise of Charles' speech (saying
he had the making of a good speaker, which I note
down for the benefit of futurity); Mr. Ross and Ld. J.
Hervey both spoke capitally; in short all was charming.
To-day went away Braybrooks, and Ric., I think.

HAGLEY, *Friday, October 30th*, 1863.—Weather howled
again all night and nearly all day. Addresses have
poured in—50 tenants dined at the Arms, Papa and
Charles Mathews, etc., spoke: M., girls, J., and I came
in for a little while to hear them. Charles wisely took
the facetious line, as it was plain enough the stolid
party wd have been entirely unmoved by any expressions of feeling. As it was, some of them laughed
till they were purple, when he said his knowledge of
farming consisted chiefly in his being aware that
when turnips were good the partridges lay better in
them, and that when fences were well kept, he found
wounded birds in them the sooner, and was less likely
to tumble off when riding at them. The cheers were
famous. A great melting away of guests took place,
none being left but Lady Estcourt.

HAGLEY, *November 1st*, 1863. *All Saints' Day,
22nd Sunday after Trinity.*—This was a day of real peace
after all our happy but exciting and overpowering
week. Dear Sunday comes like a chime of bells over
all the bustle of life, with its " sweet thoughts of peace."
Uncle B. preached on All Saints, Mr. Stayner on being
good. Having a remarkable croak in my voice which
reached its climax a day or two back, I had no class,
and much enjoyed the leisure. At dinner Ly. Estcourt
gave vent to the following singular remark: " If my
mother had been a boy, and if I had been a boy, I shd
have been Lord Lyttelton! " Which led to a great
many mad hypotheses of the same nature.

HAGLEY, *Monday, November 2nd*, 1863.—Alas, alas,
exeunt Granny, At. Coque, and Ly. Estcourt. Granny
has been here 4 months, with a short interval. A
dinner was given to Papa and Ch. by the gentry, which

was as successful as everything else, only poor old
Charles at last made one recollect that it was his 7th
speech on the subject, and hesitated a little ; but ended
well with some pretty words about his love for the place
and neighbourhood. " The retired medical man,"
who has been all along beside himself with enthusiasm,
was there, clapping fervently. On its being suggested
that " the ladies " ought to have some wine, he flew
up to me with a glass of claret, and such were his feelings
that he could utter nothing but " I hope . . ." Mike
Grazebrook was in the chair, and spoke at some
length quite remarkably well and strikingly. Old
John, at a moment's warning, had to propose the Army,
Navy, Yeomanry, and Volunteers, and did it capitally.
As we came home, we found, to our grief, that one of
the fine old avenue elms had been blown down right
across the road, and indeed the wind has been tremendous. Granny's health was drunk, Papa returning
thanks beautifully.

HAGLEY, *Tuesday, November 3rd,* 1863. — Grim
weather. A splendid servants' ball, to which came
Stourbridge tradespeople and Hagley farmers, ended
our week's doings ; and perhaps was the merriest and
most spirited thing of all. The only drawback, but O
dear, it was a great one, was dear old Elly knocking
up this very day, and having to go to bed ; so that
she missed the servants' ball for the 1st time. Charles
had to go down the middle with Gielen, which was very
flat. But great was the fun. I had Herbert ; Lavinia,
Rowe ; May, Robson ; Edward, Shirtliffe ; Alfred,
Jane Brown ; Johnny Mooreman ; Miss Merlet, Stephens !
In Sir Roger it was pretty to see Charles lift up Alfred
that the couples might duck under his little arm.
Before supper, Papa made them all a little speech,
thanking them warmly for all their good feeling and
heartiness. This seems to have delighted them all
extremely : 3 cheers followed and another (" and a
good one too ") for Charles, and then the " Fine Old
English Gentleman," Stephens solo, everybody chorus,
and fiddle obbligato. Papa having incautiously said
he hoped they wd stay as long as it suited them, we
heard they kept it up till 6½ ! and many of our servants

didn't go to bed at all. Great was the enthusiasm for
Papa and Charles, as Newmany told us afterwards,
and altogether it puts another warm bit of gratification
into one's heart.

HAGLEY, *Saturday, November 7th*, 1863.—A great
deal of drizzle, but rather a pleasant mild afternoon.
Abberley the deepest purple. We had a little fright
last night to break into the monotony of life. Hearing mysterious sounds, as of knocking at a shutter,
and steps on the gravel under my window at 11½, I called
up Newmany, and she called up Shirtliffe, and both
called up Jane Brown, who was attired in the most
astonishing huge frilled mob-cap. A footman upstairs was sought for in vain, so the 1st-mentioned
trio of witches [1] prowled down the wooden stairs, and
by dint of 5 or 6 peals at the drawing-room bell, we
elicited a response from William, who appeared dimly
in the distance on Elly's stairs, and protests he had
heard nothing, knew of nothing, and nothing was to
be found. So we all went back to bed again, rather
flat and very cold. This morning I solemnly summoned
William, and soon the cat came out of the bag. " To
tell the truth, Ma'am, I had been out smoking a pipe
of tobacco ! " and he was the tapper at the pantry
window, at 11 he says ; but I maintain at 11½, the doors
being then all locked. I next had a pompous interview with Herbert and begged him to let a man sleep
upstairs, while we are a set of unprotected females ;
and he will restrict William and his pipe to more respectable hours. Peace then resumed her sway.

HAGLEY, *Monday, November 16th*, 1863.—I am reading
Mr. Godley's letters to Mr. Adderley with gt interest :
there is one in '43, treating of the terrible state of
things then—misery of the working classes, and luxury
of the upper—which anticipates, as if no one cd be
surprised at such a result, an outbreak like the Fr.
revolution : and which finds comfort in the Church
movement then beginning to make way, as a counter-
acting and energetic principle opposed to the evils of
the time. And to think that we have weathered the
storm ! It gives one courage to face all the new and

[1] Appendix A.

different dangers which are now around us. " Though I am sometime afraid, yet put I my trust in Thee," are words which true Religion and Loyalty might—and do, I think—take for their motto. There must be mighty prayers shielding our country, and much faith and love leavening it, or there could not be in it such life and earnestness working among all its terrible sin and darkness.

HAGLEY, *Saturday, November 21st,* 1863.—Rained with few intervals all day : about 3.20 there was a hurricane of hail. At. E. turned up at 1 for an inauguration game of billiards on the newly cloth'd table in the hall, in which I made the 1st stroke, while she won the game. Billiards, Quartets, " Romeo and Juliet " with the girls.

Wednesday, November 25th, 1863.—Papers talk about the homeless poor, but nothing effectual is ever done : a poor man died of sheer starvation the other day.

Saturday, November 28th, 1863.—Lovely. Newmany has brought me a bunch of big fragrant violets ; the pear blossoms (misguided creatures) are coming out ; and the other day we shot [1] wild geranium and a harebell in the hedge, not to speak of light green fern. The very words breathe of spring.

WITLEY, *Monday, November 30th,* 1863.—I joined Papa at the station at 4 and came here with him. Find here Ld. Dudley, Mrs. Ward, her two very pretty daughters, Major Anson, and other gentlemen. A weary evening consisting of an hr and $\frac{1}{4}$'s waiting, then a long-drawn-out silent dinner, then sitting up till nearly 12$\frac{1}{2}$, playing at a feeble sort of bowls! Our long drive from Kidderm[st]. was the pleasantest part, Papa and I having much to talk about.

RAILWAY HOTEL, DERBY, *Thursday, December 3rd,* 1863.—A day of adventures. First, such a hurricane of wind in the night as I have never heard, which only subsided a little in the day to rise again in the evening. Results in the park were two trees on Prince's Hill, one huge bough near the church and another in the

---

[1] Appendix A.

avenue, and a fine chestnut in the shrubbery blown down. The morning I spent peacefully enough, entering the names in the club book for next year ; church, letters, etc. At 2½ set off with Gielen and Rowe, bound for Derby where Papa was to meet us at 6.20 and go on with us to Chatsworth. We got to Dudley with nothing more exciting to remark than the unfortunate station shed at Brettel Lane blown down upon its back. But on leaving Dudley my griefs began. First, Gielen bothered me with a disagreeable bit of abigailums [1] ; squabbles between her and Ellen, which led, by the bye, to the latter giving me warning immediately after Prayers this morning. After Gielen had said her unpleasant say, I begged her to hold her tongue (not in those words), and *morne* silence prevailed for some time. Darkness fell, and we stopped dead for more than an hour at some horrible junction on the Dudley side of Burton, while the wind took the opportunity of howling wildly, accompanied by hail which encrusted the windows. The upshot was that we got to Derby at 7.40 instead of 6.20. No Papa ! And there we sat till past 10, waiting for the last London train—which never came in. At that hour into the waiting-room marched a maukin,[2] with a telegram directing me to go to Chesterfield by the 8.15 train ! This delay was caused by the blowing down of the telegraph wires. Nothing now remained to me but to come here, and order dinner and beds. And I was comfortably writing this account of the day's proceedings, when Papa himself turned up, furious with the telegraph ; mutual explanations took place, and now bed, O bed !

CHATSWORTH, *Friday, December 4th*, 1863.—Fine, though grey. We came here, arriving about 12½. Saw nobody till luncheon time. Walked after luncheon very pleasantly to the rabbit-warren, whence the view was lovely, lit up with a sort of sunless brightness. Found a number of gentlemen shooting there. At dinner I got into an argument with Ld. Frederic Cavendish on the Church, which excited and interested me.

---

[1] Talk about servants' affairs.   [2] Appendix A.

I don't think I was wrong, as I did not introduce the topic on purpose; but I wish I had been somebody who cd have convinced him!

Round game. There are here the Duke and Ly. Louisa, Ld. F. and Ld. Edward, Mr. and Ly. Fanny Howard and their 2 daughters, Ld. and Ly. George Cavendish, and their daughter, lately married to Mr. A. Egerton, Ly. Caroline Lascelles and her 3 daughters, of whom Emma [1] is a new Maid-of-Honour like me, with her 1st waiting, however, still to come.

CHATSWORTH, *Saturday, December 5th,* 1863.—Stormy soft wind, with a good deal of small rain, and a beautiful sunset. Such a pleasant day; Papa and I drove with the Duke and Ly. Louisa to Hardwicke where we spent 2 hours going over the wonderful old house: I wished for Tallee with her antiquarian tastes, and I do wish indeed for a head that would remember all the curious things. The drive there and back very enjoyable, in spite of boisterous wind and wet: Ly. L. and I capped verses coming home. Dinner pleasant, my neighbours being Lord Frederic and Mr. Ashby who are both nice.

HAWARDEN, *December 7th,* 1863.—I left beautiful Chatsworth and all its nice kind people, at 9½.

HAWARDEN, *Tuesday, December 8th,* 1863.—Same soft weather, turning to rain after luncheon. It was delicious walking to early church in the spring-like mildness. Breakfasted at the Rectory. Drove in the rain for an hour with Mrs. and Emily Mildmay and Agnes. Ld. Frederic came. Pleasant evening of whist. Mr. Tollemache,[2] though nearly blind and with a terrific stutter, is clever and can be agreeable.

HAWARDEN, *Wednesday, December 9th,* 1863.—A slight touch of frost. Arrived Ly. De Tabley and her 2 daughters, Ly. Louisa and the Miss Pennants, Ly. and Miss Seymour, Ld. Brabazon, Messrs. Tracy, L'Estrange, Stopford, Ross, Finch (the last 3 caught

---

[1] Afterwards Lady Edward Cavendish; mother of the present Duke of Devonshire.

[2] This, I think, must be Mr. Lionel Tollemache, author of "Talks with Mr. Gladstone," and other works.

at Hagley by Atie. Pussy!), and then 2 Robertson Gladstone eldest sons. We had a capital little dance : I was asked by Messrs. Tollemache, L'Estrange, Hugh Gladstone, Ross, Stopford, Lds. F. Cavendish and Brabazon. Such was the number to-night that I went to evening church instead of to dinner ! to save space.

Odd subjects sometimes come uppermost when hardly to be expected : I have been discussing Church questions with Ld. F., and the end not justifying the means with Mr. Tollemache, in re charity balls and bazaars.

HAWARDEN, *Thursday, December* 10*th,* 1863.—The most delightful ball I have ever had, beginning before 10, and ending after three. Asked to dance by Lds. Brabazon and F. Cavendish, Messrs. Tollemache, L'Estrange, Finch, Tracy, Ross, Stopford, Charles Robarts, Hugh Gladstone : and Aggie and I did Sir Roger.

HAGLEY, *Monday, December* 14*th,* 1863.—Lovely and very mild. This day 2 years ago the Prince Consort died. A *Times* leading article takes the opportunity to give the poor Queen another of its numerous lectures about coming out again, as if two years of the most piteous and terrible of all widowhoods was too much to allow for mourning ! At the same time it is only fair to say that the tone was loyal and loving, and full of respect for the Prince's memory.

I feel in something of a dream.

HAGLEY, *Wednesday, December* 16*th,* 1863.—They say it lightened early this morning. I wrote a long letter to M. Did district, where I found distress, owing to a strike among the spade makers. Sum-total I have collected there in the yr, mostly monthly pennies, 18*s.* 11½*d.*

HAGLEY, *Wednesday, December* 23*rd,* 1863.—Lovely and soft. A man writes word to the *Times* that he has seen swallows.

HAGLEY, *Saturday, December* 26*th,* 1863. *St. Stephen's Day.*—I had a famous ride to Kinver Edge with Spencer and Arthur. I rode the Maid, and jumped clean over a gap, successfully. Cong. 3. The girls, Albert, Nevy,

HAWARDEN CASTLE.

[W. Bell Jones, Hawarden.

1—194]

and Spencer and I had the treat of going to Birmingham to hear the " Messiah," which was performed admirably, the solo singers being Sims Reeves, Winn, Mme Rudersdorf, and Julia Elton. It was the 1st time the girls had heard an oratorio, and great was their enjoyment. I do believe one's joy in listening to the Hall.lujah Chorus brings one nearer to Heaven than any other joy which is not directly religious.

HAGLEY, *Thursday, December 31st, 1863.*— . . . Last come my happy visits at Chatsworth and Hawarden. There is much in my heart to make me thoughtful, and to give me a sort of awe, in looking forward ; and if it were not for my trust—a faithful trust, though so weak and blind—in the Heavenly Guidance, I shd be full of restlessness and excitement. And as it is, I fear I shall be, sooner or later. But the Love of God has shone round us all for many years, through the shadows, and all the bright sunshine : to Him I would leave all the coming time, " casting all care upon Him, for He careth for us."

HAGLEY, *Wednesday, January 6th,* 1864. *Epiphany.* —This good-bye to home is most disquieting, and fills me with every sort of anxiety and bewilderment. I dread Osborne very much—indeed I am altogether awed in looking forward ; and *the one thing* only can make me quiet-minded—" So long Thy Hand hath blessed me, sure it still will lead me on."

HAMPTON COURT, *Thursday, January 7th,* 1864.— A commission or two, and then came the comfort and delight of driving to dear George St., going up to the baby's room, and having my 1st sight of her, hearing my old darling's voice calling me and finding her on her sofa in her pretty room, all warm and snug in the firelight : a picture of peace and brightness ! And such a delightful 2 hours of talk as followed : all my excitement and perturbation are stroked down ; Osborne itself puts on a less awful face ; for old Meriel has a calm good judgment and serenity about her that infect me. The baby is a decidedly improved version of George [1] at the same age, the same fair skin, shapely

[1] Mr. Justice Talbot.

little head, and besides tiny taper hands ; but she is a great deal larger and has a prettier mouth. Of all dear couples George and Mary are certainly the dearest. He greeted me with the most beaming smiles and hugged me in his soft arms, knowing me perfectly but not coming out with my name for some time. His talk is ridiculously fluent, as is proper indeed for the eldest of three !—himself not 3, however, till June. He is a regular Talbot, both in looks and ways. I asked him if Xmas was gone. " It's not gone, it's come." On my becoming a horse for him to ride, he immediately became a tiger to jump upon me. When he was consulted as to the baby's name he at once suggested Bison.

HAMPTON COURT, *Friday, January 8th*, 1864.—Frost felt less severe. O such a scramble of shopums as I have gone through ! That kindest of people, At. Yaddy, took me up to London this morning (darling Va with us), and under her auspices I have bought velvet and cloth cloaks, a hat, flowers, a bonnet, boots and shoes, gloves, collars and cuffs, a canezon, a sealskin muff, a linsey petticoat, a set of jet, a buckle, a set of studs, a fan, a new gown, etc., etc.

OSBORNE, *Saturday, January 9th*, 1864.—I left Hampton Court at 9½ and got to London early enough to have another 20 minutes of M., which rejoiced my heart. And at George St. I heard the wonderful news of the Princess of Wales's premature confinement at Frogmore of a " fine boy," [1] yesterday evening at 9 ! A seven-months child ; but so was George III, who certainly throve nevertheless. Astonishing to think of the Prince of Wales with a baby. My journey was successful, the crossing entirely peaceful and unruffled, and a regal conveyance met me at Cowes. To my relief, I was shown straight up to a sunny little room, where I was discussing some chicken, and had just paused to count a quantity of money into which I had changed a cheque, when, to my horror, in walked Princess Louise, and it's a wonder I did not precipitate £37 at her feet. She has an exceedingly pretty manner, like all the others,

---

[1] Afterwards the Duke of Clarence. Died 1892.

compounded of dignity and kindliness.   The Queen and
Princess Helena went to Windsor early ; and this
evening the Queen sent a telegraph saying all was well,
but the poor wee Prince very small, and no wonder.
There were at dinner Miss Bowater (I don't exactly
know in what capacity, but she is an intimate friend of
Prince Leopold—I was glad to see somebody under
40 !), Ly. Caroline, Countess Blucher, and Col. Ponsonby ; and we dined with Princess Louise and Prss.
Hohenlohe.   The dinner was certainly sepulchral,
but the evening much helped by Prss. Louise showing
Miss Bowater and me her photographs, and laughing
and talking gaily.   I was delighted to see photographs
of Princess Royal's trio, of whom Pr. William seems
like her brothers, Prss. Charlotte like her, and Pr.
Albert something *too* ugly.   There was a little playing.

OSBORNE, 1*st Sunday after Epiphany, January* 10*th*,
1864.—A complete thaw, rather damp and chilly.   To
my satisfaction, we all attended the whole service at
Whippingham (except Prss. Hohenlohe) in the morning.
The church is fantastic and of no definable style, but
rather attractive ; music bad.   Mr. Prothero preached
on the Magi.   Nobody went to church again, so I missed
the 2nd service for the 1st time since I recovered from
the fever.   Was glad I brought Arnold's sermons, and
Archb. Leighton with me ; but O dear, it doesn't feel
much like Sunday.   Had tea with Prss. Louise and Pr.
Leopold.   Evening diversified with ivory letters, as at
Windsor.

Monday, January 11*th*, 1864.—Grey and mild.   Miss
Bowater and I rode very pleasantly with Prss. Louise,
I on a nice little horse called Claudio.   I was got up
regardless of expense in a splendid new Wehnerhausen
habit, with the horrid fashionable swallow-tail, and a
chimney-pot ! which was so good as to fly off.   Prss.
Louise spoke of her father more than once, and mentioned one thing which touched one much.   Speaking of
the trees he had planted, he said once to the Queen :
" I shall never see my trees grow up."   " O, why not ? "
said the Queen.   " You wd only be 60 ; that isn't so
very old."   " No," he repeated, " I shall never see

them grow up." And Ly. Caroline said that he always knew, if he had a fever, that he shd never recover from it. I walked in the grounds after luncheon with the Prss., which was a little dull, especially as a new boot pinched me ; and I cd not help pitying all these Royal people who are never allowed to go out of their own domain, Miss B. and I during the ride raving of country-house visiting. " I should like it ! " said the Prss., half hesitatingly. " Ah, that is one thing we are deprived of." Goodness ! life must be rather mono-tonous. Excellent accts again : and the Princess of Wales delights in her baby. Poor tiny infant, how little it guesses of its great future, supposing it is to live !

OSBORNE, *Wednesday, January* 13*th*, 1864.—A little before 5 the Queen returned from Windsor, and what Granny says Miss Skerritt used to call a " general acceleration " seemed to me at once to be observable. Bustling footsteps, doors opening and shutting, the Lady-in-Waiting taking audible possession of the room next mine, unknown men cropping up in the corridor, and all the blazing liveries bursting out. I saw Prss. Helena, but no one else. Household dinner, whereat were Ly. Churchill (the Lady-in-Waiting), Mrs. Bruce, the Biddulphs, M. Holtzmann, and those already in the house, except Countess Blucher. Conversation flowed about the Princess and baby. It is wrapped up in cotton-wool, but thrives and is perfectly formed ; wd have been a very big child if it had waited the proper time. When the Queen arrived there were 7 doctors in the house who had all appeared on the scene just in time to be too late, except Brown, who came in for it all. The name was discussed after dinner ; is to be Albert-Victor, I believe (Albert ought to be God-father !). Both names much too foreign, as one can't but think, in spite of one's love and veneration for the Queen and Prince.

Thursday, January 14*th*, 1864.—Yesterday's weather aggravated. Poor Miss Bowater heard of her cousin's death, and went away in great trouble, thus interrupting the early growth between us of a very promising friend-ship : indeed I miss her much as the only companion among all these elderly people. I walked with Lady Churchill, who is a most winning and attractive person ; quite the most highbred-looking woman I ever saw, and with the kindest and most simple, unaffected manner : tall, dignified, and graceful, with a small noble head ; and her whole look reminding one of a gazelle. Saw Prss. Helena for a moment in Miss B.'s room : she received me very kindly ; interests one from her gentle, thoughtful expression, and lovely smile like the Queen's, on a face otherwise plain. Her manner is like one who has thought and done too much for her age, and been a comforter when others are only thinking of being merry-makers. Spent the aftn in my own room after the announcement of " No orders," till tea, after which kind, nice Countess Blucher took me to her room, where we had pleasant talk till 6¼. She spoke strongly of the improvement that strikes her in the Queen since her terrible loss : increased seriousness and patient earnestness in doing her duties, which are so heavy that the Queen has sometimes said they are too much for any woman ; and who can tell how terribly she must miss the Prince whose advice she used to ask in every detail, great and small ! Why won't people realize the burden and loneliness, and thank God for the strength He has given, instead of fretting at her not doing this and that ! Countess Blucher said that when Princess Hohenlohe heard of the Prince's death, the Countess found her walking up and down the room in real despair and saying, " One of two things must happen to my sister : I know her. She must either die of this, or go out of her mind." Isn't it a direct answer to prayer that instead of this the Queen is well, doing her duty, and resigned so entirely to God's Will that she said herself she wd not wish him back ? The Household dinner consisted of the Dean and Mrs. Wellesley, Ly. Churchill, Col. Ponsonby, M. Holtzmann, and Mrs. Bruce ; and I was interested all thro' dinner talking of languages with M. Holtzmann ; and whist enlivened the evening.

OSBORNE, *Saturday, January* 16*th*, 1864.—Cold wind, but fine. At Parkhurst, the poor women convicts found out it was the Queen and numbers fell on their

knees begging for mercy and pardon, so as quite to
upset those who heard them, and the Queen said she
was sure, if one had managed to fall down at her feet,
she must have forgiven her ! I rode with Prss. Louise,
on Sampson. Prss. Hohenlohe is ill with a feverish cold.
Whist in the evening, with Sir Th. Biddulph, Mr.
Holtzmann, and Col. Ponsonby ; Dr. Jenner dined, and
horrified me with his ugliness which is something suggestive to me of Voltaire.

OSBORNE, *2nd Sunday after Epiphany, January 17th,*
1864.—Poured all the morning. After many vacilla-
tions of the Royal will, the upshot was that the Household went to church on its own account, Ly. Ch. and I
being diddled out of half the service by the Queen's
keeping us to go with her for the latter half. And she
did not go. Mr. Prothero preacht on death. In the
aft., however, the Queen went, and thus I saw her to
speak to for the 1st time. She took my hand and kissed
me so kindly before getting into the carriage. A very
good thanksgiving prayer was read for the Prss. of
Wales and her baby. The Dean preacht, with a beautiful allusion to the little Prince's birth close to his
grandfather's tomb. There came off my great event of
dining with the Queen, which was very much more
pleasure than terror to me. There was much more
conversation than I expected ; the Queen talking and
laughing cheerfully. She and the Dean spoke about
sermons and Presbyterian preachers ; and the Dean
made no bones of making occasional hits at the Scotch
reverends, which the Queen took as a good joke. Then
came a good deal about the poor of the great towns ;
and how I should have liked to have brought the Mission
Women on the tapis ! But brazen as I was, I hadn't
quite that courage. The Queen spoke to me 2 or 3
times very kindly. We stood talking in the dining-
room for a little while afterwards, then the Queen
vanished, and we went to the ladies' room and joined
the others.

OSBORNE, *Wednesday, January 20th,* 1864.—A 2nd
time I have dined with the Queen ; this time I felt a
good deal of trepidation, for in the 1st place I was the

only one who received the order, and after waiting in vain for the Princesses as long as I dared, I had to march down all alone, when to my relief I found Ly. Biddulph sitting in the drawing-room. And she, Pr. Leiningen, and I got on cheerfully till the Queen appeared abt ¼ 9. She goes straight into the dining-room now without entering the dr. room. Well, in the next place, I had 2 speeches hanging over my head, one respecting a tinted photogr. of myself for the Queen : the other, to tell her I was going to-morrow. I sat opposite the Queen, and was much moved and taken out of by her expression of sadness. It was as if she had had to go thro' something which had stirred up the grief : her eyes reminded me of Mme. de Sévigné's description " des yeux qui ont pleurés," and her whole look had a pathetic and patient sadness in it. And it touched one more from her affecting nothing. At first she was rather silent, but she spoke and smiled. And after a time she cheered up again ; but it has put before my very eyes something of the sorrow which hitherto I cd only picture to myself ; and this did go deep into my heart. She accepted the photograph and admired it. And then came her goodbye, and I felt I cd not help pressing her hand as I kissed it ; for what wouldn't I do for her ?

LONDON, *Monday, January 25th,* 1864. — I read Stanley's farewell sermon at Oxford (Ch. Ch.). It grieved and shocked me, in spite of great eloquence, earnestness, and feeling ; for I cannot help seeing that the aims and the standard he puts forward are not distinctively Christian, but more like those of some refined philosophy ; and one asks oneself, where are the old paths ? the Bible rules, the humble obedience, above all, the following of the simple but Perfect Pattern ? These " dangerous days " are full of teaching that wanders from all these, and bewilders one with false liberality and confused belief. God keep us to the strait and narrow Way !

LONDON, *Friday, January 29th,* 1864.—We dined at Ld. Russell's, which was very pleasant. There were there Dickens & Landseer ; neither very pleasant to look at, though one saw wit and genius in Dickens' odd eyes. Ld. Amberley took me in : seems clever and acute, but like so many men nowadays takes one's breath away by unchurchlike, not to say unbiblical, opinions, as for instance, that all mankind are born innocent and without the germs of sin ; and something very like " truth is what every man troweth."

HAGLEY, *Monday, February 1st,* 1864.—Made a tremendous scrimmage and rout among my clothes against the arrival of my new abigail ; a nice-looking, quiet-mannered body called Morgan, foreign only inasmuch as she is Welsh ; I have had enough of French (Ducelliez), Swiss (Henriette), and German (Gielen) experience ! The papers are full of the most horrible calamity ever heard of : the burning of 2,000 people, chiefly women and children, wedged together in a great church at Chili, where a great festivity was being held in honour of the " Immaculate Conception." The place was crammed with oil lamps and draperies and burnt so fiercely that all was over in a quarter of an hour. The two chief doors were blocked up with bodies, so wedged that hardly any could be dragged out by main force. Whole families have died together. The wretched priests secured the door of the sacristy for the saving of holy sofas, images, etc., and then escaped themselves.

HAGLEY, *Friday, February 5th,* 1864.—Frost, and the 1st snow worth mentioning lay on the ground ; real enough to be galoshed against. Parliament opened yesterday : again by Royal Commission. One can't blame the Queen for shrinking from doing it this one year more : even with the Prince by her side, her nervousness used to be nearly overpowering ; and she must have broken the ice by going through some less trying State duty first. This year, too, of course the speech had to take a Danish line about the wretched duchies, whereas the Queen's private sympathies must be German. But alas ! there is an official announcement in to-day's *Times* that she still feels unequal to any State ceremonials, and the Prince and Princess of Wales are to hold levees and drawing-rooms. I fear there will be great grumbling and discontent at this ; and Oh the difficulty of the Prince of Wales' position !

HAGLEY, *Thursday, February 11th*, 1864.—I went with Lavinia to Stakenbridge, where we gave broth to the Wm. Smiths, pudding to Mrs. Billingham, and an egg to Betty Poole. I have been reading the chapter on Self-denial to the little boys (in " The Birthday "), and to-day there was a bit about not giving in charity of what costs us nothing. They soon understood what was meant, and thereupon we went in to luncheon. I put some broth into a can, and told Alfred I shd like him and Newmany to take it into the village. " O," says Alfred, " but I want to go and slide ! " " Now then," said I ; no more ; to remind him of what we had been reading. " O, I forgot ! " said the little fellow in a moment, getting quite red ; and he went as willingly as possible.

Finding, to my delight, that I have £70 at My Bankers', I spent most of the morning sending off cheques in different directions, to my infinite pride.

HAGLEY, *Thursday, February 25th*, 1864.—There is violent excitement at the Privy Council having passed a judgment in favour of Wilson and Williams, 2 writers in the " Essays and Reviews," whom the Bp. of Salisbury and another indicted before it. Some think the decision of terrible consequence, and likely to compromise the Church, but Papa and others take the more reasonable line of viewing it as what it is—a mere legal acquittal of men whose opinions the Church has disavowed and protested against as strongly as she is capable of doing. And the Judgment carefully disclaims any intention of expressing approval of the horrid book. The " counts " were unwisely chosen, and not to be legally considered as proved against them.

HAGLEY, *Friday, February 26th*, 1864.—Went on trying to thaw. I did district. I received a most disquieting letter from Ly. Jocelyn, announcing the Queen's wish that I shd take the 1st half of an absent M. of H.'s waiting, begg. on Mar. 17, unless it is very inconvenient. I wrote word that it was very inconvenient, and await the result in a state of nervous

tension. I shd be there for Holy Week and Easter Day !
Horrid thought ! A Southern American called Harrington gave a very interesting lecture on the secession and
its causes, and made Southerners of us all. Though he
has been a slaveholder himself, he wd not defend the
institution of slavery, and said he believed the war wd
do good in leading to gradual emancipation. In his
state (S. Carolina) they don't allow husband and wife
to be separated. He spoke with great bitterness of the
Yankees.

HAGLEY, *Wednesday, March 2nd*, 1864.—Papa went
to Worcester for 2 nights, which fact is the prelude to
one of our many small but unpleasant catastrophes :
his letter of dismissal to Miss Merlet whose " rapports "
between us and the girls are very objectionable, and
whose tone of mind and conversation is flippant and
sarcastic.

HAGLEY, *Thursday, March 3rd*, 1864.—Miss M. got
the letter, we presume ; but she gave no sign of surprise,
indignation, or wounded feeling, and was particularly
affable at luncheon. Such a relief !

HAGLEY, *Monday, March 7th*, 1864.—Miss M. looks
unutterable things, but says nothing.

HAGLEY, *Wednesday, March 9th*, 1864.—Uncle Stephen
went to Oxford yesterday, to vote in favour of Jowett's
Greek Professorship having its salary raised, as has
been done with all the others. His heresies not affecting
his Greek teaching, this seems only fair ; but multitudes
of furious clergy, frightened by the Privy Council judgment, posted up to oppose the measure, and it was
negatived by a majority of 72 out of nearly 900. All
Jowett's admirers, and all undecided and neutral men,
will now think of him as a martyr. Of all pities, to
pin such a grievance on him as this, when he confessedly
throws his whole heart into his professorship and is
now only paid £40. It does seem spiteful and blind.
Surely truth can prevail against error though a heretic
receives a sufficient salary for teaching Greek !

HAGLEY, *Saturday, March 12th*, 1864.—Lovely sunny
fresh day, full of the sweet promise of spring : a thing

which has a power, unknown to summer, of " filling one's heart with joy and gladness."

HAGLEY, *March 14th*, 1864.—Did myself good by going out shooting with Charles, the dogs, and the little boys. But the result was small : 3 rabbits only falling victims, and those after I had set off churchwards.

HAGLEY, *Thursday, March 17th*, 1864.—Such a bright serene day, with warm sun and the early songs of birds all round one, that the E. wind could not make it disagreeable. I sat on the octagon bench after church, thoroughly enjoying the dawn of spring. Cong. 1.

LONDON, *Friday, March 18th*, 1864.—Found Atie P. out, and heard that she is more overwhelmed with hard work than ever, as she attends certain meetings at London House where the Bp. assembles ladies to associate them in different acts of charity : an admirable thing, but Atie. P. has undertaken to visit a hospital in S. George's in the E., besides 3 other things. And how is she to do that, and all her own innumerable kind deeds, and her season and societyums, and be deep in politics, and be everything to Uncle W.—all at once ? She looks terribly fagged already. So does he, having been badgered in the House in re his excellent Government Annuities speech.

LONDON, *Saturday, March 19th*, 1864.—Sibyl Grant's wedding day : I was to have been bridesmaid, but feared I shd be late for the drawing-room. To the which I went, in a magnificent made out get-up of lilac train over white net, and in a Royal carriage. Made acquaintance with my colleague Miss Cathcart, a pretty, attractive person whom I think I shall get on with. The Princess looked very well, though thin : and the Prince immensely improved in looks and expression. Prss. Helena was there. I saw my 1st Court acquaintances, in the shape of Col. Liddell, Gen. Grey, and Ly. Ely. The latter not on duty as she had a daughter to present. Miss Cathcart and I being in waiting, failing 2 absent ones, stood on the steps of the Throne, just behind the fat backs of the Dss. of Cambridge and Prss. Mary ; and I was amused beyond measure at looking at the stream of old and young with their great variety of clumsy curtseys. At best, I came to the conclusion that people look rather like fools ; and at worst ! . . . Catherine Phillimore, whom her mother presented, looked better than any other young lady ; and went through the ordeal gracefully and with no apparent self-consciousness or affectation. The other people whom I knew were Ly. C. Lascelles and her daughter Beatrice, Ly. Meath, Mrs. Malcolm, Helen Baring, Ly. Clifden (looking ill and unhappy), Ly. Holmesdale, Mrs. Welby (late Victoria Wortley), Ly. A. Stanley, also a bride ; the Archbp. of Canterbury.

HAGLEY, *Monday, April 4th*, 1864.—Nevy and I had a splendid ride on to Kinver Edge and thence through Wolverley to Summerhill, where we called on Amelia Anson who looked very well. Claughtons out. A 3-barred fence obstructing the way on the top of the Edge, I put the hunter at it. He chose to take it standing, and alack ! off I rolled, dexterously falling pretty gently on my side on soft ground. Thus, mercifully, no harm resulted ; but I expect to feel well pummelled to-morrow. Perhaps, had I been *3 pummelled* at the time I shd have stuck on ! but I won't stoop to that. We had grand gallops and only just got home in time for dinner.

LONDON, *Wednesday, April 6th*, 1864.—Got here only just in time to scramble into a pink silk gown for a dinner and party. At dinner were Sir Robert and Ly. Emily Peel, Mr.[1] and Ly. Laura Palmer, Ld. Frederic Cavendish, Mr. Stansfield, Herbert the painter, Baron Rothschild.

LONDON, *Thursday, April 7th*, 1864.—London feels oppressive and almost hot after Hagley : streets already a good deal blocked. The *Saturday Review* the other day had a disagreeable sort of threatening article about the Queen's maintaining her retirement ; and this (as is supposed) has led to her putting into the *Times* a statement of her determination to continue to delegate to others the matters of mere ceremonial, at the same time that she will never shrink from anything that may

[1] Afterwards Lord Selborne and Lord Chancellor.

be beneficial to the people, of whose loyal affection she speaks warmly. She also says that the quantity of business that falls upon her in her loneliness and desolation has tried her health. Now all this should never have been allowed, as it is undignified for the Queen to defend herself in the *Times* against a wretched article in the *Saturday Review*; but the expressions are most touching and pathetic, and I for one cd never bear to blame her. The country knows nothing of the Queen's peculiar desolation. It behoves us better to pray for her and to have pity, than to goad her, when she is devoting herself to duty and works of mercy, into Court gaieties. Aggie and I had the treat of going to hear the Budget, which took 3 hours, and was very interesting on the whole. A splendid surplus of 30,000,[1] accordingly the income tax comes down from 7*d.* to 6*d.* and the sugar duties are greatly lowered.

LONDON, *Friday, April 8th*, 1864.—All the papers smile upon the Budget, even the *Standard* saying nothing more snubbing than that it was a réchauffé of one of Dizzy's 2 years back! Uncle W., speaking of certain plays moving one to tears, said that there was something that made him feel ready to cry in his Budget! viz. the description he gave of the gigantic power and prosperity of England. This I can well fancy. Drove with Agnes to call on wonderful old Miss Robertson, in her 89th year, able to walk briskly, and hear well, and bent upon coming the night Garibaldi dines here to squint at him from behind the door. For Garibaldi is in England, which fact makes everyone stand on their heads; and I suppose all young ladies will shortly appear in red shirts, which, to my disgust, have come into fashion.

LONDON, *Saturday, April 9th*, 1864.—Atie. P. whisked off to the H. of Charity, then to be photographed; and after luncheon, to which came Ld. Frederic and Ld. Richard Cavendish, and Uncle Henry, she went with Ld. F. and me to see a fine fresco of Moses showing the Tables of the Law, which Herbert is painting in one of the chambers of the Houses of Parliament. I conjecture humbly that its faults are, some monotony of

---

[1] *Sic*; but presumably a mistake for £3,000,000.

expression and attitude, and something feeble in the
drapery ; but the grouping and colouring are beautiful,
I think ; also Moses' face, and the soft hot light and
shade wonderful. I went to tea at the Stanleys of
Alderley ; pleasant enough. Very pleasant party at
Ld. Palmerston's.

LONDON, *Monday, April 11th,* 1864.—We spent a
notable aftn in a window of the Privy Council Office ;
Atie. P., Agnes, and I, with Ld. Frederic and Mr.
Palgrave, waiting to see Garibaldi pass, on his way to
Stafford House, which takes him in. We waited, and
so did the great crowd that had assembled, till 6½, when
at last, some time after a long procession of Working
Men's Clubs and societies, with banners, had passed,
the great man appeared in a carriage-and-six, wearing
a blue-and-red cloak and wideawake. I suppose such
a scene as has greeted him has never before been known,
and never could be but in England. All the working
people, of their own free will and enthusiasm, turned
out in his honour ; nobody directed or controlled them
(very few policemen), and to be sure it is grand to feel
and see the perfect trust that may be placed in the
mighty free action of Englishmen and their sympathy
with what is high-minded and disinterested. They
poured and flocked round the carriage, shaking hands,
waving hats and handkerchiefs ; and he was accompanied all up the street by unbroken cheers. We were
tolerably knocked up, even I ; yet I with Mary and
Helen went after dinner to the Bishop of London's, to
hear a woman read (not particularly well) passages
(mostly beautiful) from Shakespeare, Tennyson, etc.
The W.E.G.'s afterwds to Stafford House to meet
Garibaldi ; poor Aggie to bed.

LONDON, *Tuesday, April 12th,* 1864.—I bkfasted in
Geo. St., whence, to my delight, I was summoned by
Atie. P., an invitation to a Chiswick luncheon given to
Garibaldi having been sent to me. So I saw the great
man close ; and was immensely struck by his simple
dignity of manner during the trying process of being
introduced to different people by the Dow. Dss. of
Sutherland. One saw his mind was too great and

humble for shyness. I had a very happy afternoon. Ld. Frederic (who was at Chiswick) came to high tea with us, and thence with us to the Adelphi, where " Leah " was acted.

Wednesday, April 13th, 1864.—W.E.G.'s dined at Stafford House, to meet Garibaldi : We went there in the evening. And it was to be a never-to-be-forgotten evening to me.

WINDSOR, *Thursday, April 14th,* 1864.—Ld. Frederic came to breakfast. After luncheon Ly. Louisa came to see me. I strive to lean entirely on the Loving Hand which has led me all my life long until now, and has ordered this for me. But I seem frightened, in spite of the strange happiness. God make it right for me ! God guide me in my decision ! I am so foolish and bewildered. It is a thought full of peace that I am surrounded with many prayers. I came here, where all feels dreamlike to me. Darling Meriel came to Carlton Terrace, saw Ly. Louisa, and took me to the station.

WINDSOR, *Friday, April 15th,* 1864.—The quiet monotonous day, outwardly so like my 1st days of waiting, had this wonderful undertone running through it, and I am in a new life. If I could only feel more comprehensibly : see more clearly ! But I trust to God's Love for that. I wrote to my little Bob, and to Papa and Atie. P. Walked and drove with Miss Cathcart. Ly. Jocelyn is Ly.-in-Waiting. The Queen has got neuralgia in her face, and has accordingly put off the reception that was to have been to-morrow. The Duke and Duchess of Argyll came to dinner. At bedtime the dear kind little Duchess took me to her room, and kissed me, and said how good he was. O that I may deserve it all !

WINDSOR, *Saturday, April 16th,* 1864.—My darling old boys came to tea in my room ; I having begged of Sir Thomas Biddulph unlimited eggs, etc., for them. Old Spencer was at S. George's. The little bit of home talk was very snug and refreshing, in spite of the serre-ment-de-cœur it gave me. I longed to tell them some-

thing of my wonderful secret ; but I could only hug
them very much. I took them for a peep at the corridor ;
they were in mortal dread of being caught by " Her
Sacred Majesty " ; but no such thing happened.

WINDSOR, *3rd Sunday in Easter, April* 17*th*, 1864.—
To-day my doubts and fears (which have been many)
began to melt away.

WINDSOR, *Monday, April* 18*th*, 1864.—Soon after 4,
we went to London with the Princesses (Ly. Caroline,
Ld. Caithness, and Mr. West also in attendance) to a
Philharmonic concert at Hanover Square : music out
of Shakespeare principally, and partly in honour of
his tercentenary. It was very good and delightful ;
and I confess I enjoyed considerably the luxuries of
Royal travelling and Royal places at the concert.

LONDON, *Wednesday, April* 20*th*, 1864.—Same glorious
weather. I carry away with me from Windsor such a
vision of stately, smiling towers basking in pure sunshine,
and nature blossoming and budding all round. And
there is just such a springtide beginning in my heart.

The Queen went to Osborne abt 4 : Ly. Caroline,
Ly. Augusta and I, off duty, came to London. I dined
with old Meriel, O so snugly ; and had the nicest of
talks with her, and with Mrs. Talbot. Garibaldi dinner
and party here. The Duke of Devonshire, Ly. Louisa,
Ld. Frederic, and Ld. Edward were here. Such a
happy evening.

LONDON, *Thursday, April* 21*st*, 1864.—A bright,
serene day of inward and outward sunshine. We are
engaged, and my doubts and fears have been all absorbed in the wonderful happiness and peace. " Full
measure, pressed down, and shaken together, and
running over, doth He give into my bosom."

I have got my 1st present : he brought it me this
afternoon : a locket with diamonds and pearls, to have
his hair in it. He dined here : as did my old Meriel. . . .
I wrote to *all* my darling boys : even to my little fellows
at Hagley.

LONDON, *Friday, April* 22*nd*, 1864.—I had a long
talk, a *Sunday* one, with him ; and he told me all his

opinions that he thought I shd not agree with him about. I don't—but he has built his house on the Rock ; and I can't but trust him ! He dined with us, and we went to see " Henry IV " at Drury Lane, which was very delightful. The Dss. of Argyll came this morning ; and I believe now everybody knows it. Ly. Chesham sent me a beautiful ring. He brought me the locket with his hair in it, and I wore it to-night, hanging it to darling Mamma's little pearl chain. It felt to me as if I was telling her about it.

LONDON, *Saturday, April 23rd*, 1864.—He came to breakfast with Lady Louisa ; after which he stayed with me till nearly one, again talking on serious subjects. He gave me the deepest feeling of happiness I have yet felt, in saying he should like to go with Papa and me to the Holy Communion to-morrow.

LONDON, *4th Sunday in Easter, April 24th*, 1864.— Papa and he came after breakfast, and I went with them to Tennyson's Chapel,[1] where we received the Holy Communion together. May God's blessing of peace then granted us abide with us evermore ! It was so wonderfully happy praying for him then, and feeling he was praying for me. If only our whole lives may be so sanctified ! After the service we went to Devonshire House, where even the being taken to the Duke's study didn't much frighten me ! He kissed me very kindly. I also saw Ly. Fanny and Margaret Howard, Ld. Hartington, Ld. Edward ; and Ly. Louisa gave me a photogr. of the Duke, and one of Lady Burlington,[2] who must have had a look of Mamma. At 4½ I went with him and Ly. Louisa to Ly. Caroline Lascelles's, where I saw her daughter May, Lord and Ly. Chesham, and Ly. George Cavendish, who were all most kind.

OSBORNE, *Monday, April 25th*, 1864. *S. Mark.*— He came to breakfast, and we had a nice talk before he saw me off. It was horrid going away ; but as I came into the lovely blossoming country, full of spring

[1] Was this at Archbishop Tenison's School in Leicester Square ?
[2] Mother of Lord Frederick. She died before her husband succeeded to the Dukedom.

greenness and the singing of birds, the sunshine around
seemed to answer to the sunshine in my own heart;
and I think the fortnight here will have a brightness
of its own. I just saw Ly. Jocelyn and Emily Cathcart
on the landing-place. Mrs. Bruce met me very kindly
on arriving. I wrote my first letter to Fred: O how
strange that looks! He won't expect it; for I told
him he shd write first; but I thought he wd be feeling
rather grim to-morrow. Mrs. Bruce and I dined with
the Queen, the Princesses, and Prince Alfred; Prince
Leopold and Prss. Beatrice appearing in honour of
Prss. Alice's birthday. The Queen was as kind as
possible to me: saying as she kissed me, " I must
congratulate you, but I must scold you a little too!"
She shot [1] my locket! Asked who he was like, and talked
some time to me after dinner.

OSBORNE, *Tuesday, April 26th*, 1864.—Same brightness, but E. wind. I wrote 8 answers to congratulations:
all " thank you " in different forms. And I received
my first letter from him: such a dear one! grave and
simple, like himself. It makes it all very real to me.
What paper is it written upon but a Privy Council
Office sheet, reminding me of the Garibaldi entry day?

OSBORNE, *Friday, April 29th*, 1864.—Drove with the
Queen, Prss. Helena, and Pr. Leopold to Ryde: 4 horses,
equerry, 2 out-riders, and all very imposing; but my
Court bathing-feel [2] has left me for good and all! Poor
little Prince Leopold was full of talk and cheerfulness,
but his small thin face grew pinched with cold; and
I wished I cd take him into my arms and cover him
warmly up. The Queen asked if F. wd come and see
me at Windsor: I had no notion it wd be allowed:
O how nice it wd be! We played demure whist in the
evening; and I made 1 hideous blunder.

OSBORNE, *Monday, May 2nd*, 1864.—The first day
of really soft, balmy wind. A day with a great hole
in it, for there came no letter from F., owing no doubt
to the tiresome Sunday post. Mrs. Bruce, Gen. Grey,
and I had a delightful drive to Carisbrooke Castle amid
bright early verdure and blossoming fruit trees. Spring

[1] Appendix A.   [2] Appendix A.

was never so much to me as it is now, when there is such an answering springtide in my heart.

OSBORNE, *Tuesday, May 3rd,* 1864.—Among my congratulations this morning came, to my great astonishment, a love-lorn farewell in verse from a poor little man called P., who I had no notion cared about me ! I laughed till I nearly cried over it, and couldn't resist sending it to Fred, as a model for his further letters.

Wednesday, May 4th, 1864.—Grey and raining out of doors ; but what a " golden day " ! The Queen being so kind as to hold a Privy Council to-day, Ld. Granville brought Fred (who is his private secretary : have I ever said so ?) with him. And we had all the afternoon to ourselves, in the ugly little ladies' room, which will never look ugly to me again.

O precious hours ! O golden prime !

The Queen and Princess Helena both saw him. I was let off a Royal walk and drive. He came to the Household dinner, after which Mrs. Bruce, Ld. Granville, a German maukin,[1] and I were marched off to the Queen's drawing-room. But we got back in time to say good-night : he sleeps at Cowes, and comes here to breakfast. He brought me loads of kind letters to Papa, from dear Hagley neighbours, etc. Likewise a diamond betrothal ring.

OSBORNE, *Ascension Day, May 5th,* 1864.—Heavy soft showers. F. came to breakfast ; then we had another little talk ; then he came to church with Mrs. Bruce and me : then again we had " sweet converse " till he had to go off with the messenger at 1½. Oh, ardent, overflowing lovingkindness is round us ! giving us these two days' happiness over and above, when already we were so very happy ! Life felt a little flat after he had vanished.

OSBORNE, *Saturday, May 7th,* 1864.—Lovely spring weather. I have remembered that this is the 1st time for years that I have watched spring blossoming into summer, having always been in London. It is very nice that this wonderful year will have all this bright beauty

[1] Appendix A.

connected with it. My letter came all right, enclosing certain verses that he repeated to me the other day : sad ones, but full of beautiful thought. They bring his voice to my ears. I sat out of doors part of the time with Prss. Helena, part of the time reading " Dynevor Terrace." Mrs. Bruce and I went to the Queen in the evening. I am much distressed about poor Prss. Helena who is cruelly overworked, the Queen having no notion how her mind and body are strained, and indeed having no one to take her place.

OSBORNE, *Sunday after Ascension, May 8th,* 1864.— We had matins in the Council-room, an interval, and then Mrs. Bruce and I went to church for the Litany and sermon. We were late, and missed the chief part of the Litany ; and this was all my church-going, for there was no getting a chaperon in the aftn rain. Prss. Helena sent for me to play battledore and shuttlecock and we walked abt the house together. I read Trench on the Parables, but feel rather heathenish. We dined with the Queen. F. wrote a dear letter.

WINDSOR, *Monday, May 9th,* 1864.—Heavy rain in the morning : no sun all day. I left Osborne with all the " serrement de cœur " that such a good-bye to a place full of associations can give. I daresay I shall never see it again. And I have had peaceful days here, amid the greenness and sunshine, and singing of birds : " golden hours," too, those two days that he was with me, and his dear letters to be treasured all my life. I like Royal travelling exceedingly ! The crossing was pleasant though rather cold. Most of the time I spent capping verses with the Princesses and poor little Prince Leopold, who made great play with " To be or not to be." How the arrival at Windsor did bring to my mind my days of—doing what he asked me at Stafford House to do ! I was greeted by such a dear letter ; also a very charming one from old Nevy. The sight of Miss Cathcart ! who's who and what's what [1] ! She had to rig me out for the evening, one of my boxes hanging fire. Ly. Biddulph dined, and

[1] Appendix A.

chaffed me very unmercifully, but I didn't mind one bit. Dear Ly. Caroline congratulated me.

WINDSOR, *Tuesday, May* 10*th*, 1864.—I went off to London by the 9.10 train ; got Miss Sewell's " Preparation for the Holy Communion " for Princess Helena on my way to Carlton Terrace, and got there about 10½. Talked trousseau-ums and saw my wedding presents (wonderful sound !). I must make a list of them elsewhere, they will take up too much room in my journal. But I will mention the prettiest, completest little writing-table in the world from my old Meriel, and a pretty inkstand (quite his own choice) from Nevy. These will come very near my heart. My Fred turned up before long and we had " sweet converse." Also multifarious shoppums : I chose an onyx signet-ring for him, to come on Saty ; and gave him to-day a crystal locket with a scratchy bit of my hair in it, with which he was certainly pleased. Ly. Louisa came after luncheon, and took us both in the carriage to Mimpriss's, where, after gt cogitation, we chose lockets for the bridesmaids, six with small pearl crosses, six with small turquoise ditto. I paid Granny a little visit ; then to M. (he also coming there), and came back here for dinner.

LONDON, *Wednesday, May* 11*th*, 1864.—We all came up to London for the Queen's 2nd Court : a very small one, but very striking and imposing. It was held at Buckingham Palace. People may carp and sneer at the poor Queen for keeping on her mourning, but everyone must have thought her dress to-day most suitable and becoming. The gown was trimmed deeply on the skirt with crape, but was cut square, with white up to the throat ; long hanging sleeves. Her cap was Marie Stuart, showing her hair turned back, and with a row of pearls round the border ; broad white lappets reaching to the feet ; and she wore the Garter ribbon with a diamond brooch on the shoulder, a star, and a great pearl necklace in many rows. Altogether she looked just as a widowed Queen holding a State ceremonial ought to look. And it was beautiful to see her manner and her dear smile. The Princess of Wales looked terribly thin and pale, in deep black ; must be wretched at the reverses of the Danes, who have just lost Düppel. I had the honour of seeing the tiny Prince,[1] the Queen sending for us to her room, where he was visiting her. A nice thriving-looking plump baby, with bright blue eyes, delicate features and pointed chin ; a nose that will be aquiline, I shd think, and a likeness to both parents. A very intelligent way of looking at one. He cried a good deal, poor fellow, being sleepy. At the reception, the D. of Argyll came and shook hands with me, saying very kindly, " I am so glad to have you for a cousin." After it, I had a snug visit in my room at B. Palace from At. C. and the girls. At. C. brought me a lovely little ring with a pearl cross. Then to Carlton Terrace, where I found Fred ; then pleasant talk with him ; a visit from C. Ebbett ; back to B. Palace for dinner with Prss. Helena, Ly. Carolina, and Emily. Then a grand concert, held by the Prince and Prss. of Wales. This was a dream of delight, though the music wasn't all good ! I sat with Papa for the 1st part, shooting[2] F. before very long coming ínto the room, looking very nice in uniform, and peering about for me in vain for a long time. But at last I caught his eye ; and it was so very pleasant to see his dear face light up when that happened ! He got up to me after the 1st part. We ran through a tremendous tilt of congratulations. Saw At. Y. Was very, very happy. Slept at Buckingham Palace, attending on Princess Helena.

WINDSOR, *Thursday, May 12th,* 1864.—Very fine and warm. I am glad to have slept here[3] once. Have managed a good deal of Court experience since my apptmt. Breakfasted with Prss. Helena and Co. and then got leave to go to Carlton Terrace. F. came as before ! A little tiresome trying on ; and Ld. Geo. Quin came his own self with a pretty little clock for me under his arm. After luncheon, F. and I went (with Atie. P. and Ly. Louisa) to be photographed together by Mr. Window. I fear we shall look like

---

[1] Prince Albert Victor, afterwards Duke of Clarence.
[2] Appendix A.
[3] I.e. Buckingham Palace.

fools. Then back to C.H.T.[1]; then I plunged into a Royal carriage, joined Prss. and Co. at Paddington, and had my last regal journey. Am tired! but very happy.

WINDSOR, *Friday, May* 13*th*, 1864.—Very fine and warm. My old boys Spencer and Arthur[2] came to see me; Nevy, not being well, could not, alas! I had only a little time with them, but it was very nice. I went to St. George's: wonder whether or when I shall go to church there again. Saw Mrs. Wellesley afterwards for a minute. Wrote, wrote, wrote. My Fred sent me a dear little scratch, though we only parted yesterday at 4¼. And he has got one from me. I don't know when we shall next write to each other. The Prss. of Wales came at 1½ and we received her at the door. After luncheon the Queen sent for me to say good-bye, and I hope I shall never forget what passed. She came towards me with a beautiful Indian shawl and a jewel-case in her hands: kissed me, and gave them to me with many kind words about her regret that I was going, and her good wishes for me. She kissed me again and again, saying she thought and felt the more for me because I had no mother. The ornament she gave me was a beautiful amethyst locket bordered with pearls; on it a little diamond cross.[3] Speaking of the cross, she said, "It is an emblem of what I have to bear day after day," and added something which I cannot bear to put down here in words, but which sunk deep into my heart. I thanked her as well as I was able; kissed her dear hand many times, and began to cry! how could one help it? I didn't wish to help it; but went up to my room, and had it out. Then came good-byes to the Princesses, with whom was the Prss. of Wales playing a duet with Prss. Helena. All spoke kindly and said good-bye; and O dear! good-byes are sad matters.

. . . Now I have come home from a great family dinner and party at Devonshire House, to which I went with Papa: Gladstones and Talbots, and Grauntecoque[4] also coming. (N.B.—I must mention somewhere that

---

[1] Carlton House Terrace, the Gladstones' house.   [2] Then at Eton·
[3] Alas! stolen many years after [Note in original].
[4] I.e. "Granny" and "Aunt Coque," who lived together.

Uncle W. has kicked up a gt dust by declaring in the House in favour of universal suffrage ! ! ! out-Brighting Bright. F., I grieve to say, is delighted.) This sounds very formidable ; but, except a few qualms, I didn't find it so. Everybody was very kind ; and perhaps I don't mind anything when Fred is with me.

HAGLEY, *Saturday, May 14th,* 1864.—We had high tea at ¼5, F. coming ; and soon after 6, he and I, Atie. P. and Papa left London, and now I am writing in my own dear little room at home. Elly, Newmany, and Shirtliffe greeted us ; and I have been to see my little boys in bed. I can't write much to-night : all feels strange and altered to me, and my heart is rather heavy. F. and I stood at the dear library window, looking out into the soft dewy night, sweet with chestnut blossom ; and it did me good to stand there with him, saying next to nothing.

HAGLEY, *Whitsunday, May 15th,* 1864.—A day of great peace and brightness. Oh, such a lovely, radiant morning ! a thing in itself to return thanks for, so much it added of happiness. We received the Holy Communion together in my own dear church. Afterwards sat on octagon bench ; quite silent, but how happy ! Then came the Rectors to see him ; and after luncheon we sat with her on the lawn. I had my class in the morning : O dear ! had to tell them it was the last time ; but I made short work of it, for fear of crying.

HAGLEY, *Whit Monday, May 16th,* 1864.—At ¼5, F. and I went a glorious ride on to Kinver Edge (v. p. 196 [1] : I little thought then of who shd ride with me there to-day !) We came to the hurdle whereat I tumbled off, and F. wouldn't let me try again, which indeed I rather " funked." The view from the top was more lovely than I have ever seen it : we stopped a good while looking at it, F. so much pleased ! Were not home till 7½ : luckily dinner was at 8. We sat together very happily afterwards.

HAGLEY, *Wednesday, May 18th,* 1864.—Very sultry : no view. After church I went (upon Charger) with F. to see old Mrs. Billingham ; thence thro' Wychbury

---

[1] See the entry for April 4th.

wood, all blue with hyacinths, down into the Stourbridge road by Sparry's hill.   I went to see poor,. poor
Sophy Price, and was shocked and upset at the change
in her, and her terrible sufferings.   Repeated to her
the words, " Come unto Me," etc., and cheered her a
little ; but felt deeply how little able I shd be to bear
such a cross, and how I am walking in sunshine amid
so much sorrow and darkness.   We sat on the lawn
afterwards, and in the afternoon on the grass in Whistle-
wail ; and " sweet converse " lightened my heart again :
but it is right it shd now and then be overshadowed.
Fred read aloud to me, with fervour and feeling enough
to counteract the slight disadvantage of his funny
inability to pronounce either " r " or " th," Uncle
Wm.'s startling speech in favour of extended suffrage ;
also his (F.'s) own speech at Leeds last year, which
delighted me more by its cleverness and eloquence than
it scandalized me by its radicalism !   Some time after
dinner with our heads out of window ; then whist.   At.
C. came.   At an American anti-slavery bit in his speech,
he trembled with excitement.

HAGLEY, *Friday, May* 20*th*, 1864.—Fine and a little
cooled by the storm.   I began the day before prayers
with letters : went with Fred at 10 to see old Mary
Page, Charlotte Rogers, and Mrs. Reid (only taking him
in to see old Mary).   Mrs. Reid said she " wished she
cd flog the mon off ! "   Then church ; then we had a
delightful last ride by Clent to Fairleigh Coppice and
home round Clent Hill and thro' the middle of the park.
Daphne gave me a riding-whip.   I did district for the
last time, driving there with At. E. and the little boys.
Evening service, and sermon by Uncle Billy for Ember
evn.   O when shall I be in my dear, dear little church
again !   Elly called me to her room afterwards to give
me a Bible and Prayer Book in one from all the under
servants.   This quite finished me.   But I can't write
about this last day at home.   The last time I shall
sleep in this little room !   God's love and blessing rest
upon all, and follow me.   I thank Him for all my
happy years.   My heart is full.

LONDON, *Trinity Sunday, May* 22*nd*, 1864.—After
luncheon came Fred, who had been to hear Maurice,

and told me some beautiful bits of his sermon. And I read him the " Xtian Year " for the day, and some other verses, and played him some hymn tunes, which he liked enough to show me he has music in him.[1]

LONDON, *Tuesday, May 24th*, 1864.—Bright and fine. The Queen's birthday was kept for the first time since the Prince's death : plenty of illuminations. My Fred came about 1, and took me to luncheon at Devonshire House, which I was glad of in spite of being rather shy, as it got me over some more first steps of acquaintance. I am hardly shy at all with Ly. Louisa now ; my chief awe centres round Lord Hartington, who is very kind to me, however. At luncheon were Mrs. Coke, Emma and May Lascelles. Afterwards F. and I went to Garrard's and got a pretty crystal locket with an emerald cross on it, for Atie. P. to have our hair in. At Dev. House, Papa turned up and gave me a beautiful large gold cross, in which I shall have his dear hair and Mamma's. At 5¼, F. and I, with Willy and Agnes for chaperons ! rode in Rotten Row ; and I thought of our last ride at Hagley. I was on a charming little horse of Ly. L.'s called Snap.

LONDON, *Thursday, May 26th*, 1864.—Did a shy thing in the evening : dined all by myself at Devn. House, meeting only the Duke, Ly. Louisa, F., and Ld. Edward. They were kind and nice, setting me at my ease ; but I cd not quite say I was at my ease ! though very happy after dinner with my Fred holding my hand. Lord E. very taking and pleasant. Came home in a ducal brougham, and read the *Guardian* till 11¼.

LONDON, *Friday, May 27th*, 1864.—F. came soon after 11, after I had undergone a little course of trousseau worrits, and we had a snug little sit together to compose me. At times the bewilderment of all the unknown new clothes, and the vague state of mind I get into as to where they will all go to, and what new place I myself am going to, make my poor addled head spin ; but through it all, the sunshine is bright over the future ! The days go slowly by, and the wonderful new life still feels very distant.

[1] A romantic delusion ! [added later].

LONDON, *Monday, May 30th,* 1864.—Bright lovely morning, with lights and shades. Our departure[1] was comical: some hitch in fly-orders resulted in a necessity for some couple or other to go to the station in the donkey-cart! It was decided that F. and I were the least likely to mind taking an hour going the 4½ miles; so we drove off in triumph, I conducting and the Mesds. Talbot looking on in convulsions of laughter. It was a little trying being a gazing-stock to the beauty and fashion of Edenbridge as we hirpled through.

LONDON, *2nd Sunday after Trinity, June 5th,* 1864.— Beautiful warm day, and O such a refreshing and peaceful one! In the Holy Communion I tried to lay down all this past life of mine at the foot of the Cross, and I trust that all the sins and neglects are forgiven, and that the never-failing blessing will be outpoured upon the future. And this hushed and calmed all my anxieties. It was at the Temple, whither I walked with At. C., joining Papa and Lavinia, and coming back with Papa, which was very nice. I had told Fred not to come: I wanted to be with Papa: but his not being with me did not signify, for he received the Holy Communion; and that draws us together in the most blessed way. Papa and I found him in St. St., and we went with him to luncheon at Dev. House. Afterwards such a nice talk; he told me much of the sermon of Maurice's he had heard. Papa brought me his cross, with these words engraved inside. On the transverse, my new name, which I can't yet write; then: "From her loving Father, June 7th, 1864. In Memory and in Hope." And he gave Fred a Communion book, in which he wrote the last verse of the "Christian Year" on Marriage.

CHISWICK, *Tuesday, June 7th,* 1864.—Our wedding day. I cannot write about it. I can only look backwards with loving regret, and forward with bright but trembling hope. We were married in Westminster Abbey, by Uncle Billy, and came here[2] about 4 o'clock, into peaceful summer loveliness and the singing of birds.

---

[1] From Falconhurst, where they had been staying with the Talbots.
[2] The Duke of Devonshire's house at Chiswick in which both Fox and Canning died. It is now the property of the Municipality.

CHISWICK, *Thursday, June 9th, 1864.*—I have received
my first letters with my pretty new name, from Atie.
P., M., Agnes, and At. C.   We have begun " Westward
Ho ! " and Carlyle's " Fr. Revolution " ; also I spouted
to Fred the " Allegro " and the " Penseroso," and
other bits of poetry ; and I don't find him entirely unworthy.

CHISWICK, *Friday, June 10th, 1864.*—The rain has
only beautified and brightened the delightful weather.
We sat out, spouted " In Memoriam " ; and he, to me,
Canning's " Letter from Lord Russell to Lord Cavendish,"
which was after F.'s own heart, with its liberty and
patriotism-ums.   Also Carlyle.   Walked in the Horticultural Gardens after luncheon.   Wrote, and talked,
and were very peaceful.

BOLTON, *Saturday, June 11th, 1864.*—Left pretty
Chiswick, which has been perfect for these first few
days, and drove back to London.   We went first to
Devonshire House, where we saw the Duke, Lou and
Eddy (I may as well smash the ice at once !), and then
to St. St., where we saw Grauntcoque, Atie. P., Papa
and Meriel, and 1 found the seeing them rather strange
and upsetting : feeling that it wasn't me.   Also was
taken out of at none of them but Papa looking very
bright.   M.'s dots have got the whooping-cough.   We
stayed about ½ an hour, and then went off ; and arrived
here about 8.   Drove under a tiny triumphal arch, with
" Welcome to Bolton " on it.   I felt more wonderful
and bewildered than ever ! but Oh the green, still
loveliness of the place in the evening light, with the
sound of the running river in one's ears.   And then,
there is Fred to make my very bewilderment a sort of
happiness.   Really tired I was.

BOLTON, *Monday, June 13th, 1864.*—Delightfully
fine on the whole.   We went a nice little saunter to
the wooden bridge before luncheon.   Mr. and Mrs.
Robinson called, which brought over me a fresh attack
of who's who and what's what [1] : especially when Mrs.
R. was glad " Lady Frederick " saw the place to advantage !   After luncheon we set off to go to Simon's

[1] Appendix A.

Seat, I riding a fat dun pony, F. walking. It was the first time I was ever on a moor and very grand and striking it was ; contrasting too with the lovely, luxuriant wood, still blue with hyacinths, from which we emerged upon it. Got home a little before 7½. Snug evening. At nearly the top of Simon's Seat we were caught in the fragment of a thunderstorm, which was rather grand. Sheltered in one of the luncheon huts, which I shall remember, methinks, if we come here, as we hope to do, for the August shooting. Can it be me I am writing about ?

BOLTON, *Tuesday, June 14th,* 1864.—Grey, misty day ! but among these hills even such an atmosphere has some grand effects. We have at last tackled to at some books F. chose for the honeymoon : rather an odd trio ! Carlyle's " Fr. Revolution," Butler's " Analogy," and " Westward Ho ! " Had a nice little brisk walk before luncheon : afterwards drove very pleasantly to Barden Tower, plunged on foot down a little deep gorge near it to see a waterfall, and old Fred gave me a little lecture on ferns which grew thick all about it. Then on to Broad Park moor, and round by Halton Heights. Often it rained, but we didn't take much notice.

BOLTON, *Friday, June 17th,* 1864.—F. told me about his American life, and how he killed 2 buffaloes, which made me proud of him !

BOLTON, *Saturday, June 18th,* 1864.—A very delightful, long, happy day. We set off in an open fly and pair soon after 10½, and drove up the valley past Borden and Grass Wood, to Elmsey Crag, and then to Gordale. This was new to Fred as well as to me, and how we enjoyed the glorious things together ! Lovely glorifying weather. From Gordale we walked to Malham, where we had a charming luncheon at the little inn, and then walked to Malham Cove. The long drive home very nice : we have done abt 36 miles. It is wonderful how the returning each time into this dear peaceful valley brings to me already a happy homelike feeling. Yet I have only been here one week. I think it can only be because I am beginning to find that wherever

I am with Fred, there home comes to me. Such a thought of bright repose it is.

BOLTON, *Tuesday, June 21st*, 1864.—And so ends our honeymoon.

It is a bewildering, but by no means unhappy thought, that we shall probably be here again for the grouse shooting in 7 or 8 weeks ! We arrived at Devn. House soon after 6. To dinner came Grauntcoque and then J. G. T.'s,[1] then afterwards Atie. P. and Agnes. Which was very nice. The Duke, sons and daughters, and Ld. Richard also dined. When all my own people had gone, and I found myself left in this big house with Cavendishes, I underwent my first actual feeling of home-sickness. A very gentle one, and soon absorbed in the new, deep feeling which is growing downward, downward into my heart. Found certain tardy presents. We have fine big rooms looking over the park.

BRUSSELS, *Thursday, June 23rd*, 1864.—We breakfasted at 7, and set off directly afterwards ; I first going to Lou in bed to say good-bye. We shall be lucky if we are not posting back again for the election in a fortnight or less ! We crossed to Calais, the sea rather rough, and the boat rolling a good deal : I was perfectly well, but poor old Fred, after sitting meek and silent beside me, getting whiter and whiter, succumbed once about $\frac{1}{4}$ of an hour before the boat came in. The landing, the railway, the people, and all the look of things carried me back wonderfully to our delightful Paris trip in 1860 : little I thought then of all this state of things ! We had a charming luncheon at Calais. Got here about 7 : all new to both Fred and me. We have an affable courier called Holffman, who ordered us a sublime fly and pair at the station, and for dinner we two had soup, fish, beef, cutlets, chicken, salad, ice ! ! ! ! Steps must be taken to cut down these princely ideas.

COLOGNE, *Friday, June 24th*, 1864. *S. John Baptist.* —We have been over the glorious Cathedral, and have streamed a little about the town, making one feeble effort to get an ice at a café which was too insufferable with smoke and too low altogether for us to stop in it.

---

[1] I.e. the J. G. Talbots, her sister and brother-in-law.

I am great audience to the wonderful, clear, bright atmosphere, and all the manners and customs. We have bought two cases of eau-de-Cologne, which I trust will turn out the genuine thing.

MAYENCE, 5th Sunday after Trinity, June 26th, 1864. —We wrote letters, and went through a " crise " of dissolution anxiety on the strength of a paper announcement that the Conservatives meet on Tuesday. The Duke is to telegraph next Friday to F., if necessary.

That I should have come to wish the Conservatives at the bottom of the Baltic ! Having written letters and read the aft. Psalms and Lessons, it cleared delightfully and we had a nice tramp about the town and public gardens, and into the wonderful, rich, peculiar Cathedral, which struck us immensely. Looking into another church, we found service going on in German, and the crowded congregation responding loudly in Litany fashion ; a thing I did not know was usual in R. C. services, at which the cong. generally only assists. After dinner F. read aloud Trench's 2 fine 1st sermons on " the subjection of the creature to Vanity."

RIGI, Wednesday, June 29th, 1864. S. Peter.—I can't say much about it ; but it is true, I do believe, as F. said to me, when I said I dreaded my usual fate of being to some degree disappointed, that the great glories of nature cannot disappoint one. They seem to come too near Heaven. And so I found it as I looked from the top of the Rigi. The hotel quite at the top with its swarms of cockneys, table d'hôte, and scrubby allowance of washing apparatus, brought one to earth with a bump. We came upstairs after the table d'hôte, and laughed till we ached at some charming snobs who sat opposite to us at dinner. So cold, we sat in cloaks.

RIGI, Thursday, June 30th, 1864.—We got up soon after 3, and went to the highest point to see the sunrise. The morning was somewhat misty and the sun had to surmount a bank or two of cloud, so that this was not the greatest thing we saw to-day ; still it was very lovely to see the giant peaks brightening one after the other, and those in the W. catching the faint pink reflection. All had a look to me of standing around, waiting for the light. We nearly died of the cold. Had breakfast, and set off walking down the mountain about 6 ; and this soon warmed one. And now we were steeped in glorious sights. The day grew clear and serene, and only white fleecy clouds floated among the snowy mountain-tops. The climax was a certain view we had when a little way down we sat on the grass for a good while. We drank it in at our leisure ; and it went deeper into my heart than anything has yet done. Such a communing with God's glorious works is a mysterious sort of worship, or something very akin to it ; for " He in His strength setteth fast the mountains, and is girded about with power." All the descent was beautiful, but this' was the crown, for the day went off, and the deep, soft blue of the atmosphere became grey ; and the Jung Frau and her neighbours vanished, and Pilatus put on his invariable cap of clouds. But I have seen enough ! and moreover am a little tired.

ENGELBERG, *Friday, July 1st*, 1864.—We had meant to leave Lucerne at 5.15 and go by the passes of Furca and Grimsel to Mayenwand, but soon after four the voice of dear Holffmann was heard at the door, announcing that the weather wouldn't do ; and as it was hideous to think of going such an expedition in pouring rain, we gave it up : and after yesterday's proceedings did not break our hearts at having 3 hours more in bed. By breakfast time, complication upon complication arose upon us. In the 1st place, behold Morgan upset by her travels and pronounced by the quizzical little doctor unfit to move till Monday ; in the next place, Fred at last getting hold of a *Times* only 2 days old, discovers that the motion of vote of want of confidence isn't to come off till Monday, which leaves us pretty safe till this day week, and makes it necessary for us to re-cast all the arrangements for next week ; in the 3rd place we had let slip the early steamboats, and it seemed impossible to get away from Lucerne so as to fit in a church-going place for Sunday. Under these cheerful circumstances, I sat composedly down to write to At. C., while old Fred, whose head never fails, evolved ideal plans by slow degrees out of Murray and Bradshaw. The upshot is, that we leave Morgan to get well under the auspices of Holffmann and the doctor, and come here alone with 2 bags, i.e., Engelberg. We drove from Stanz, all up a most glorious valley, towered over by mighty mountains. No rooms in the inn but 2 tiny unpainted garrets at the top of the house, which we are now occupying, F. conjuring up horrible visions of fleas, and imagining scores running over his legs already.

MEYRINGEN, *Saturday, July 2nd*, 1864.—A perfect, serene, summer day, with such hot sun, that we are as red as turkey-cocks this evening. We left Engelberg (n.b. unbitten by a single flea) at 6½ and went by the Joch Pass to Meyringen, resting for about 2 hours at a little chalet inn, which, though on the descent from the mountain, is 6,000 feet above the sea. We reached it about 12. I set off from Engelberg riding a pony, which carried me wonderfully up a tremendous mountain-side, of which I only got off at the steepest bit. We got once into clouds, but emerged from them into more and more glorious beauty. Coming to a glacier-stream, my pony thought proper to lie down in it and roll with me! and soon after this we came to such deep patches of snow that I walked the rest of the way. We were often up to our knees, ascending considerably all the time, and I am not a little proud of my first great mountain-climb. It is such pleasure among these glorious Alps never to be disappointed. After our longest pull through snow, I was enough tired by the exertion, and thirsty withal, actually to enjoy and be refreshed by some of F.'s nasty kirchwasser mixed with snow! Changing of boots (which were soaked), washing of feet, an excellent little dinner of soup, cutlets, omelette, bread and butter and ice-cold water, and a nice sit on the grass letting the beauty of the mountains sink into my heart, cured me of all tire. From the inn to Meyringen (Hôtel Sauvage) I rode most of the way. To-night we have anointed our sun-burnt phizzes with milk and lemon. We are in a fix, a bag with clean things from Lucerne not having turned up.

THUN, *Tuesday, July 5th*, 1864. . . . Then by fly and steamboat through Interlaken to Thun, where it was a little refreshing after 4 days' maidlessness, makeshifts, and packing for oneself, to find Holffmann and Morgan ;

also a magnificent suite of rooms, and a landlord in an ecstasy of bows, who introduced me to the pretty verandah, saying it was at the disposal of my Excellency ! ! ! Last not least, delightful letters from Atie. P., Lou, Lavinia, At. Emy, M., and one from Mrs. Bruce, inviting F. and me to luncheon at Windsor " de part la Reine," on Saturday, June 26 !

MARTIGNY, *Thursday, July 7th*, 1864.—The day month since our marriage. A month of ever-deepening happiness, just now of a peculiar brightness and absence of care : a sort of rocking on bright waves before launching out upon new seas—which I know is never to come again ; but as long as this wonderful sunshine is poured round me—I mean the great, new sunshine of our love for each other—all the coming waves must look bright to me ; as the past ones have the golden radiance of memory upon them. Only may all such light and joy lead us nearer to God.

We rode and walked in lovely weather to Camballas ; there, having leisure, sat in the flowery long grass, and read " Westward Ho ! " and had milk and bread and butter ; then a most lovely drive down the deep rich valley des Ormondes to Aigle in the valley of the Rhone. Here we walked up a moderately high, but nearly perpendicular hill, and enjoyed a sight of Lake Leman and some noble mountain-tops ; then had dinner, and went on by railway to Martigny ; having to-day therefore walked, ridden, driven, and railwayed. Got into a bus at Martigny crammed with English folk, but they don't seem to overrun this hotel. Why does one hate and despise nearly all one's fellow-countrymen abroad ?

CHAMOUNIX, *Saturday, July 9th*, 1864.—Spouted to Fred some bits of Coleridge's " Hymn in the Vale of Chamounix," which he liked. We have no telegram to-day, and have some faint hope.

CHAMOUNIX, *7th Sunday after Trinity, July 10th*, 1864.—Behold ! a telegram from the Duke, with the news that there will be no dissolution, Government having a majority of 18. This evening F. has spouted to me Layard's admirable defence of Ld. Russell's policy, which one wd think must have influenced votes.

I am come to a pretty pass, when I find myself crowing over the Whig victory !

STRESA, *Wednesday, July 20th*, 1864.—This hotel (des Îles Borromées) is in keeping with everything else here, by being unlike anything I have yet come across ; deliciously cool, with its stone floors, high rooms, and spotless cleanliness : hardly so much as a whiff of tobacco to be met with !   We sat blinking at the lovely blue lake, blue mountains, blue sky, for some time on the balcony.   At 5½, we went in an open boat, shaded by an awning, to the Borromeo Palace, and round the other island.   The most delightful afternoon of luxurious enjoyment !   The palace and terraces, the glorious tropic flowers and trees, and the all-surrounding loveliness of the view from the island, was like a Fairy-land dream.   I have not seen my old Fred so enchanted before.   Then we rowed about, watching the golden sunset light up all the hazy mountains, sky, and water with tender light.   I am getting hideously mawkish and sentimental ; so will change the subject, and end with the fact which is the real culminating point of all our delight in this perfect place :

No Fleas !

LONDON, *Friday, July 29th*, 1864.—Devonshire House is a little wonderful to arrive at !   Greatly we appreciated cream, chops that *were* mutton, toast, brown bread !

HAGLEY, *Saturday, July 30th*, 1864.—Bewildering, bustling morning, combining packums, shoppums, letterums, and interviews with my 2 new brothers, and with the Mesdames Talbot, who turned up unbeknown as I was sitting exhausted in my petticoat waiting to be robed in smart array for going home.   For so you still are, and so in one sense you ever will be, through whatever changed eyes I see you, dear, dear old Hagley !   We arrived about 7, and were greeted by a village reception, as M. was.   Cheers, flags, and triumphal arches and an address read by Stephens.   It all went deep into me—all the familiar sights and faces overpowering me too—and when we got out upon the old perron, I was trembling all over.   Then my Fred made a little speech, thanking them so well and heartily. I held his hand all the while.

HAGLEY, *Thursday, August 4th,* 1864.—Dinner party of Rogerses, Walriges, Mr. Stayner, Mr. Gambier Parry : too mad Papa hooking me in to dinner, Albert presiding at the head of the table, Granny making the " moving bow " to me, and Fred doing the agreeable to Mrs. Walrige ! I put on my dear Queen's necklace and *Cavendish's*[1] beautiful bracelet ; and a lovely trousseau gown ; but I felt I looked just like Lucy Lyttelton, nevertheless.

HAGLEY, *Friday, August 5th,* 1864.—I had a capital ride with Lavinia and Bob. Butler, Carlyle, and Glynnese Glossary[2] with Fred ! Said Fred is getting on buckish and familiar terms with M., to my delight.

HOLKER, *Monday, August 8th,* 1864.—Another of the great days of which I seem lately to have had so many : my 1st arrival at Fred's own old home, Holker. There was some heart-pinch in leaving old Hagley thus, in the middle of the summer holy-days, and driving away, all the dear faces watching us off from the perron, and Newmany from the nursery window. But I could not be sad ! and the words that ran in my head when I stood in the new home explain why : " Thy people shall be my people." My home is where my Fred is. We arrived at Cark about 5 ; and near where a new school is being built, a knot of men took the horses out and drew us fast up to the house, cheering. I could enjoy this, as it was for F. and not for me ; I cd see it went very much to his heart. He made me stand up with him in the carriage when we stopped at the house door, and holding my hand, said, " My friends, I thank you for yr hearty welcome of my wife home to Holker." How they cheered ! The Duke and Lou met us in the hall, and the Duke kissed me. We had tea in the conservatory, and afterwards walked up Bigland Scar whence the view delighted me beyond anything I ex-

[1] She underlines this : presumably because it is the first time she calls her formidable brother-in-law, Lord Hartington, by his family name. He began life as Lord Cavendish.

[2] For which see Appendix A.

pected. We sat there, and I drunk it in, wondering when all wd be familiar to me! The evening made me a little shy and bewildered.

HOLKER, *Tuesday, August 9th,* 1864.—The 1st day I have spent without Fred, who went off at 9 with the Duke on Furness railway business, and was not back till nearly 8. I did miss him very much! but it was almost worth the break [1] of seeing him come back. And I made great strides in sisterly intimacy with dear Lou who took me before luncheon round the park, and afterwards driving to Old Park, Holker Bank and Beale, and on the sands. I have blundered the names, I fear. Also she took me to a consumptive son of Mrs. Abbotson. She took me about the house, and I made acquaintance with Fred's old room, her sitting-room, the Duke's, etc., and looked at the pictures of them all done when they were children; the little boy who died must have been a darling. I tidied some of my possessions, which talk to me of Hagley; filling my writing-box. At tea in Lou's snug room at 6, began first to shake off some of my strangeness: she is very nice. Was horror-struck at being late for dinner!

BOLTON, *Friday, August 12th,* 1864.—Fine warm day; grey but not hazy. It is delightful to me seeing this place again: I remember some of the moors by name. Father-in-law, brother-in-law, and husband all went off for the 1st day's grouse shooting. After writing to M., sitting a little in the garden, and receiving with Lou a visit from the Robinsons, she and I drove in the pony-carriage to Brass Castle and had luncheon with the shooters, prostrate grouse at our feet. Very nice. We dawdled a little among the blossoming ling before coming home; then went up the terrace; tea and talk, and I read *Edinburgh Review.* About 7½ home they came, my Fred having shot the most birds, viz. 35½ brace: Cavendish looked dejected, having only killed 20 brace.

BOLTON, *Friday, August 19th,* 1864.—All the fat world are dieting themselves with wonderful thinning effect after a plan recommended in a pamphlet by Mr. Banting, whose name is already shining in the firmament of fame.

---

[1] Appendix A.

BOLTON, 14*th Sunday after Trinity, August* 28*th,* 1864.
—Church only in the morning, as we lost our way and
so prolonged the aftn. walk. Mr. Robinson preached
excellently on the 10 lepers. We walked on to Hazlewood and Bolton Park. F. and I had a dear little sit
after the walk, talking, and reading the evening 2nd
Lesson and Psalms, and a little " Christian Year."
Before luncheon I read him Tennyson's new poem,
" Enoch Arden," which we both liked extremely : I
think I shd put it next to " Guinevere." Letter to Atie.
Pussy. I have just read a book which Newman has
written in answer to a very feeble and spiteful attack
on him by Kingsley. The title is " Apologia pro vita
suâ," and it is an account of his religious opinions and
what led him to Rome. I was often beyond my depth ;
but I think I see something of the principle which
influenced him, viz. that Unity is more to be valued
than pure doctrine ; and he got into a dilemma between
Rome on the one hand and scepticism on the other.
He is as little controversial as is possible and defends
none of the great errors, except indirectly. It is
written very fairly and modestly ; and in his beautiful
clear style.

BOLTON, *Wednesday, August* 31*st,* 1864.—No going
to luncheon again, but another thorough duty-doing
in the way of visits : Fairfield and Beamsley Hall were
the gentry, and both have had the treat of receiving
Fred's and my elegant cards which delight my heart.
Freddy shot well to-day : 17½ br. The poor people
we saw were charming : I bought some lemon drops
and barley sugar in one cottage, and we were regaled
with oatcake and milk, so that a good deal of the time
was spent in eating. I announced that I cd not bake
oatcake. " Ay, ye're nobbut a young wife." All the
neighbourhood seems to have heard of Fred's wonderful
bag the 1st dogging day : 35½ brace. They say his
marriage has done him good ! One old woman bade
Lou and me tell " Markis he mun dance in a peck,"
as his younger brother has married first ! Mr. Lionel
Ashley came, and made my hair stand on end at dinner
by announcing that he had just heard for the 1st time
of Keble and the " Xtian Year " ! ! !

BOOK IX
SEPTEMBER 1864—MAY 1866

INTRODUCTION TO BOOK IX

THE ninth volume is the record of the first two years of Lady Frederick's marriage. I suppose most girls when they marry find themselves at first in a strange country. Certainly Lady Frederick did, at least in some respects : for no two families could be less alike than the eager, talkative Lytteltons and the cautious, silent Cavendishes. The diary shows her great shyness with her father-in-law whom she suspects of wishing her " at the bottom of the Baltic " when she spends a day alone with him. He was one of the kindest and most modest of men and by no means one of the least able, but the natural Cavendish temperament had combined with ducal dignity to make him also one of the shyest. A duke was a Duke in those days, however simple his nature might be, and could not escape being treated, even by his family and friends, as a kind of being apart from the rest of the world. There was a sadder reason, too, for this Duke's shyness. His children had been motherless even in their childhood. Before his eldest son was seven years old he had lost his adored wife, and he was a widower in heart as well as in law for all the fifty years he had yet to live. He could never bear to have his birthday mentioned, because it was the day on which his wife had died. He spent that day in seclusion with his memories and affections for his only company. And, as year followed year, he never forgot other days which belonged to her, such as the day on which he first saw her. One would have supposed that a man with such rare intensity of affection as this would have easily understood and loved a daughter-in-law who had the same passionate affection for her own dear ones, especially for his son, and kept days and memories with the same tenacious loyalty. But the silent shyness of the father-in-law and the eager, voluble, not always tactful, enthusiasm of the daughter-in-law divided them more than their common gift of love and loyalty could unite them. She sometimes hoped they were getting easier, writing, for instance, to Mrs. Talbot in April, 1866 :

" My tête-à-tête meals with my father-in-law, which I looked forward to with frightful trepidation (tête-à-tête-ums beyond ¹), did me real good ; they went off so well. I feel sure now that he is at his ease with me ; and that makes all the difference in the world. I have got over a good deal of shyness, I trust, for good and all." But the shyness was never got rid of : or at least came back. There was great kindness on the one side, and great, even loving, respect on the other : but intimacy there never was.

Something of the same sort separated her from her magnificent and alarming brother-in-law, Lord Hartington, who indeed had far fewer points of likeness with her than his father. But she never was so afraid of him, I think, as of the Duke ; and to the end of his life she never hesitated to bombard him with appeals for charities, besides frequently sending him remonstrances on matters of political difference ; receiving cheques in answer to the first, and, what is more, letters of explanation in reply to the second. With her husband's other brother, Lord Edward, and his only sister, Lady Louisa, she was on the most affectionate and intimate terms from the first. Their marriages are among the greatest private events of this volume. Nothing brings out more both the affectionateness of her nature and its incapacity to bridge the gulf between her and her husband's father than a letter she wrote to her sister Meriel at the time of her sister-in-law's engagement. After speaking of the joy of it, she goes on : " I cried for a long while, thinking of the poor Duke.

¹ Appendix A.

Take in he has never been separated from Lou except for a day or two at a time since his wife died. . . . If I could only kiss him and call him something it would be a help."

About Lady Frederick's happiness with her husband there never was a moment's doubt. She writes on April 6th, 1865 :

" This day last year I went up to London, my heart full of excitement and uncertainty ; and met Fred at dinner in Carlton House Terrace. Don't I remember how he took me in when he should have taken Lady Laura Palmer, and how my appetite walked off ! Oh, how happy now is the feeling of changeless trust and repose in each other's love ! This happiness makes me awestruck and half frightened by its very greatness."

The only blank page in her book of happiness, a page never destined to be filled, was that no child came to crown the marriage. This was a great and growing grief ; but it belonged to the generosity of her nature that, as all who saw her in those years and the years that followed recall, she welcomed the children of Lady Louisa and Lady Edward with eager affection and never showed the smallest touch of jealousy at the happiness she was not to share. If her husband had lived he was to have succeeded to Holker on the Duke's death ; and of course if he had had children they would ultimately, as things turned out, have succeeded to the Dukedom. But she loved all her nephews and nieces, her husband's as well as her own ; and certainly not least the children who took the place which her own would have taken : indeed, she early won and always kept all their hearts. Nor did she ever show, I am told, the slightest feeling at the loss of what, even without children, would naturally have been her husband's and so hers. When her father stayed at Holker a few months after her marriage she and he " sat long looking down over the sea on the further Cap Side : radiant summer sunshine bathing everything in beauty and the overarching firmament smiling upon us." And he said to her as they sat, " Well, this is a goodly heritage, isn't it ? " It was : but it never came to her ; and though she visited it at least once every year till near her death, no one ever saw a sign of her thinking that she ought to have been there not as guest but as mistress.

The home she had as her own was in London.   When in the country the Frederick Cavendishes lived at the Duke's houses, Chatsworth, Holker, Bolton, and Hardwicke ; in London they had their own house, No. 21 Carlton House Terrace, close to the Gladstones, who lived at No. 11.   Much of this volume is occupied, as are innumerable letters to Lady Louisa, with the business of furnishing and getting into this house, which remained Lady Frederick's home till within a few years of her death.   There is much talk of economy, and one notes that they had matting instead of a carpet in their bedroom, which does not sound luxurious.   Yet somehow the " monster bills," as she calls them, for furniture, linen, and other domestic apparatus come to over £3,000 which seems a good deal for those cheap days.   Anyhow, there they settled and there they lived their London life ; especially the political part of it, which was ever more closely linked with that of the Gladstones.   Frederick Cavendish came into Parliament in 1865, unopposed, for the West Riding of Yorkshire, and from thenceforth till his death politics took up most of his life.   His wife, of course, found herself getting " desperately political " too ; but thinks that need not necessarily make her " an *odious* woman." She still calls her husband " wicked Radical Fred," but she naturally grows more and more Liberal herself, and is inclined to grumble at her eldest brother's clinging to Conservatism.   She goes continually to the House of Commons : especially, of course, when her husband speaks. He moved the Address in 1866, and she received a great many congratulations on his success, those which pleased her most coming from Hartington : "Wasn't it nice of him," she writes to Lady Louisa, "when he must have had his head full (of the secret of his new appointment to the War Office) to come straight up to the Ladies' Gallery to say how good he thought it ?" Lord Frederick was, in sober truth, never much of a speaker ; but there was character, sense, and knowledge in what he said : and he soon won respect, though he never aroused enthusiasm.

Life in London was divided between politics, society, and good works. Lady Frederick now began the regular visits to workhouses and hospitals and the attendance at the committees of various charities which she carried on for so many years with devoted energy, enthusiasm, and self-denial. In the country, too, she and her sisters-in-law gave much of their time to cottage visits. For the rest, there was continual riding both in London and the country ; and we hear also of hunting and skating as well as of a great deal of shooting. She constantly records the head of game killed, particularly if her "Fred" had killed most. Meanwhile she and he got through a great deal of reading. Carlyle, Mill, Fawcett, Bishop Butler, Hume, Lingard, Guizot, Merivale, Milton, Scott, Jane Austen, are among the authors mentioned, beside a great many devotional works.

Of public events there are the deaths of Lincoln and Palmerston ; the first signs of the shadow of Ireland which was to darken her whole life ; cholera abroad and cattle disease at home. Of social habits now obsolete and forgotten, perhaps the most curious are concerned with clothes. We hear that Lady Louisa and Lady Edward "have each got fine black velvet gowns with trains a yard and more behind them." And Lady Frederick is "triumphant at starting the under servants minus crinoline during their work !" It is also rather strange to-day to read that Gladstone persuaded the House of Commons to adjourn its Committees because of the public fast appointed to be observed in the Diocese of London on account of the cattle disease ; and that the surprise was, not that the House adjourned, but that it was not unanimous about doing so.

POSTSCRIPT

As to that silence of the Cavendishes, to which I have just been alluding, and the extreme lengths to which they could carry it, a story is told by Sir Algernon West in his *Recollections* (I. 272) which did not come to my notice till after this Introduction was in type. He relates that the 5th Duke of Devonshire and his brother (afterwards first Earl of Burlington and great-grandfather of Lord Frederick) were travelling to Yorkshire and " were shown into a three-bedded room. The curtains of one of the four-posters were drawn. Each brother in turn looked in, and went to bed. Towards the close of the next day's posting one brother said to the other : ' Did you see what was in that bed last night ? ' ' Yes, brother,' was the only reply. They had both seen a corpse."

But it must not be supposed that this hereditary brevity and dryness of speech in any way implied hardness of heart. It was quite the contrary, at any rate in the generation known to Lady Frederick. She will presently show us all the three brothers, including Hartington, the most " Cavendish " of them all, breaking down into tears at their sister's wedding.

DIARY, SEPTEMBER 1864—MAY 1866

HOLKER, *September 7th*, 1864.—The beginning of this book is a solemn thing to me ; for how little I can tell or conjecture how much I may be altered, and how much may have happened, before the end ! Of course it was always a sealed thing to me, but, on the threshold of a new and untried life, the veil over the future seems closer than ever. But I cannot now feel oppressed, as I did at first, in thinking of all that was new. For, as I have often said and thought, my past, my present, and my future, are all bathed in sunshine, which but for my own faults and weaknesses would be entirely unclouded.

HOLKER, *September 10th*, 1864.—Whist in the evening : I am getting some gleams of light about its refinements, to my satisfaction.

HOLKER, *September 12th*, 1864.—F. and I, Lou and Eddy, had a lovely ride " round by Bigland," whence the view over the. Lake mountains was beautiful, in the soft light, with purple shadows. Switzerland has not a bit spoilt these hills for me ; they stand majestically on the horizon, instead of rising up sheer above one, as abroad ; and perhaps this makes one invest them with height and dignity. I rode Snap of happy Rotten Row memory. We got upon the sands at Roudsea, and had blissful gallops.

HOLKER, *September 13th*, 1864.—Soon after 12 went to Ulverston with the Duke and Lou, for the laying of the 1st stone (which he did) of an aisle to be tacked on to a most mean and scrubby church. The service was painfully intermingled with civilities and a rush after the trowel and mallet ; it was jarring, to say the least of it, to have prayers, civilities, sermon, blessing

" God save the Queen," a speech from the incumbent,
vociferous cheers and laughter from the crowd, in the
church, and a speech returning thanks dragged out of
the Duke by the said cheers, all one on the top of the
other. Then came luncheon, where I liked my neigh-
bour, Archdeacon Evans. And so home again before
4. Went into the village with Lou, and liked the
people we saw. Then arrived the Edward Howards,
and I was scandalized by these undutiful nephews
calling their uncle *Peter*! Lively whist.

HOLKER, *September* 21*st*, 1864.—Had a glowing
letter of happiness from Rosalind Stanley,[1] who is to
be married on the 4th, and who announces her sister
Kate's engagement to Lord Amberley.[2] F. and I have
had much fun over this state of things; for both the
swains have formerly a little made up to me, and Ly.
Stanley tried hard to hook Fred for one or other of the
damsels! Let us hope matters will turn out better
as they are.

HOLKER, *September* 21*st*, 1864.—We all went to Furness Abbey, which carried me back to my delightful
Lake tour with Papa and Uncle Stephen in '62, when I
little thought under what circumstances I should see it
again! Thence, after a sumptuous luncheon, to lionize
the iron and steel works (the latter F. is concerned with),
the new dock, etc., of Barrow, which owing to the iron,
has increased in population from 200 to   [3] in about
10 years; and is a spic-and-span, bustling place looking
embodied Go Ahead.

HOLKER, *October* 2*nd*, 1864.—I received the Holy
Communion for the first time in my new home, and
felt drawn closer to it. Had happy Sunday reading
and talking together; showed my Fred a beautiful
prayer by Jeremy Taylor for married people to say
for each other. A day of much happiness indeed—
blessings both of earth and heaven are outpoured upon
me.

[1] Wife of the 9th Earl of Carlisle.
[2] Son of the Prime Minister, Earl Russell, and father of the present
Earl Russell and of Mr. Bertrand Russell.
[3] Figure not inserted.

HARDWICK, *October 4th*, 1864.—Fred and I came here alone, under the ducal circumstances of a special train, twenty-two servants, 6 horse-boxes, and two carriages. I recollected the wonderful old house and its approach very well, having been taken to see it with Papa last memorable winter from Chatsworth : little thinking ! How much more than a year ago it seems ! A fine golden sunset showed the place to great advantage, and it looked most imposing on the top of its hill, with the grand old oak trees scattered about. Our evening tête-à-tête was a happy revival of honeymoon ! the 22 servants, horses, dogs, and carriages having vanished utterly from sight. F. began spouting Mill " On Liberty." I began " The Vicar of Wakefield " ; (left it off).

HARDWICK, *October 5th*, 1864.—We did a good deal of reading : Butler on Personal Identity (a subject that I cannot help feeling instinctively it is ludicrous to argue about), and on Virtue ; a long pull at Mill " On Liberty," which shakes and bewilders nearly all my opinions, leaving me with my head in a bag ; and a little bit of Carlyle ; interposing between the 2 latter studies was a good rapid stump down the hill and about the park which did me good. The Duke and Lou came for dinner.

HARDWICK, *October 8th*, 1864.—Not one glimpse of sun all day. Nevertheless, I was able to take in the beauty of the forest scenery we saw to-day, at the same time that one longed for chequered lights to fall among the trees. We drove in the open carriage and four to Narton, and there mounted, and rode through Welbeck, Clumber (where the poor Duke of Newcastle is lingering, though no one thought he could live from week to week in the spring), and Thoresby ; and I saw at last what I have always imagined as an ideal forest, enormous trees with room to spread wide their arms, and their trunks not smothered in brushwood, but springing from a carpet of bracken ; a sight which gives one a pleasure akin to that of seeing the pillars in an empty cathedral nave, clear all the way up. I took the greatest delight of all in a splendid beech avenue, in which the glorious trees overarched like a cathedral roof. We rode for more than 4 hours, then re-embarked in the carriage at Warsop (after some hitches and losings of our way), to the great delight of all the inhabitants, who almost to a man, woman, and child, assembled to see us off.

HARDWICK, *October 9th*, 1864.—Fred read to me a powerful and earnest sermon of Liddon's on the Whole Counsel of God, which dwelt a good deal on the terrible subject of Future Punishment, which, though one before which Angels would veil their faces, is just now discussed even in newspapers, many questioning the Eternity of punishment. I became much overwhelmed and aghast with dwelling upon it ; but a solemn comfort has come to me with the desire to trust entirely to the Love of God, and to be content to know nothing clearly now. Of one thing we are certain : that He *is* Love and Light ; and that we are all weakness and blindness ; but shall know as we are known hereafter.

HARDWICK, *October 12th*, 1864.—I was beaten once at croquet, after which a game of breathless interest, closely contested, ended in my favour.

LONDON, *October 13th*, 1864.—Did not leave Hardwick till 4.40 ; reached London before 10.30. I think Devonshire House will always bring back to me my rather awful visits to it before our marriage.

LONDON, *October 14th*, 1864.—A day of care and responsibility ! We had a solemn interview with Mr. Currey, an excellent fat factotum of the Duke's, who has been sniffing after houses ; and the result was that Fred and I made a tour of inspection. Only 2 houses seem at all desirable ; one in Curzon Street, small and with some disadvantages ; the other a beautiful brannew one nearly opposite the Gladstone one in Carlton House Terrace. This is somewhat too large, and only to be bought ; and is therefore very expensive. . . .

We finished Mill who has certainly filled my mind with new notions. How far they will become convictions, I'm sure I don't know.

LONDON, *October 15th*, 1864.—I inspected the Curzon

HARDWICK HALL.

[C. B. Keene, Derby.

Street House with Mrs. Hislop, one of the 7 ducal house-keepers ; and Fred had another Currian interview. The melancholy result is the condemnation of both houses, Curzon Street as not being up to the mark, C. H. T. as being above it.

HARDWICK, *October 19th*, 1864.—I did what I little thought to do again at all—least of all as a sham charity—helped to sell at a bazaar. It was at Chesterfield, in aid of funds for the hospital. Though I think such a thing a miserable make-shift, whereby people's grudging help towards a good object is obtained by dint of giving them in return a foolish, frivolous, wasteful, and generally tuft-hunting, day's jollification ; yet of course I don't think it distinctly wrong, and would not put up my back, beyond having a few little kicks about it in private ; and I sold to help Lou. Everybody was full of bustle, good nature and energy, the room crammed, and everything likely to turn out successful. It was opened with a splash by Cavendish's making a speech. Fred and Eddy didn't come, my poor old Fred being very rheumatic, and Eddy disinclined. The Duke and Cavendish went back early ; we stayed till 3½ and I felt somewhat done up. We came away in style (open carriage and 4), almost smothered in fairings. I got a doll for little Mary, and 3 sets of poor children's clothes, methinks for Hagley.

HARDWICK, *October 21st*, 1864.—A nice little tramp again, with F. and Lou, in the garden and park. I rather scampered home to be in time for what makes this a red-letter day for me : the arrival of my old Meriel with John and Mrs. Talbot. M. is not looking well, but she *is*.[1] Mrs. Talbot was here for her honeymoon : it must seem dreamlike to her, and haunted by the echoes of happiness. What should we go to, the Duke, Lou, F., and I, but a ball at Chesterfield ! My last ball having been the Hawarden one, made this feel curious. I rather hoped not to dance, but no such thing ; and it didn't break my heart to have my Fred for vis-à-vis. I wore some of the Duke's diamonds on my head and round my neck for the first time.

[1] Appendix A.

CHATSWORTH, *October 26th*, 1864.—We all left Hardwick together ; Ld. Richard alone not coming here.
I needn't describe my curious feelings on coming to this
stately place as my Fred's wife. It was when I was
here the first time with Aunt Yaddy that the thought
first struck him, and I think it was while I was here
last year that I began really to like him. And now
how happy I am ! Our room is an Indian-papered one,
looking east up the hill. We dined in the Stag parlour,
where I well remember arriving at tea-time both years
in a considerable accès of stiffness and shyness.

CHATSWORTH, *October 27th*, 1864.—My first separation from my Fred, who went up to London (with the
Duke and John) for 1 night for a Furness railway
meeting. He has only been gone 6 hours and yet I
miss him grievously !

CHATSWORTH, *October 28th*, 1864.—Read Fawcett,
and began " Martin Chuzzlewit " for the 2nd time.
Capped verses after dinner, almost up to the time that,
hearing certain sounds, I peeped out of the tea-room,
and saw my Fred marching up the hall, about 10¼.
It's ridiculous how long I seem to have been without
him ! Dear old Nevy 19 to-day.

CHATSWORTH, *October 29th*, 1864.—We began discussing a wonderful catalogue of the pictures which I
am to undertake.

CHATSWORTH, *November 4th*, 1864.—Catalogue, Butler, Fawcett, Carlyle, letters ; a walk with all the womankind. Mr. Frank Smith, Frank and Beatrice [1] Lascelles
came. Beatrice looks very ill. Sir Joseph and Lady
Paxton dined.

CHATSWORTH, *November 8th*, 1864.—I looked through
a precious book full of Rubens, Vandyck, and Rem-
brandt sketches and copied a nice big horse's head.
Instead of Butler, Fred finished to me a very thoughtful,
earnest, and, I think, excellent lecture by the Bishop of
London, given before a scientific institution at Edinburgh, on Science and Theology, which I had begun to
myself. I believe no one doubts the Bishop to be a

[1] Afterwards wife of Archbishop Temple.

profoundly religious man, and so his words on such a
subject have great weight; I hope I am not wrong or
rash in finding much comfort in them, as to all the
present difficulties and alarms. I think I can feel
strong faith that God will ever reveal the Truth to
those that love it, and seek humbly either in His Works
or His Word; and that what seems perplexing and
contradictory ought not to be put aside, but carefully
looked into, in the hope—the certainty—that " what
He does, we may not know now, but we shall know
hereafter." And if people will only keep vividly in
mind the consciousness of their own imperfect knowledge, I think no apparent contradictions need much
move them. If only one could hope that all enquiries
would be made in an honest and good heart, and that
people would keep their footing on the Rock ! But this
is the terrible danger, that men will abuse the reason
given them to guide them, making it an infallible rule.
Whereas it can at best only accompany us a little way,
and then leave us with a Higher Guide, to pierce into
infinite things.

CHATSWORTH, *November* 10th, 1864.—Misfortunes never
come alone ; having grown cold with a slow walk, I
thought proper to have a run down one of the gravel
walks, and catching my foot in my crinoline, came down
plump, and broke both my knees !

CHATSWORTH, *November* 16th, 1864.—A sad day for
me, and a very long one. My Fred went away for
three nights, and though I know that isn't really endless,
yet it feels like a great separation, as, except for one
night, we have not yet been away from each other.
But I must learn, I suppose, not to miss him so grievously ! He has gone to preside at a Female Education
meeting at Bradford, and at a Mechanic's Institute at
Halifax.

CHATSWORTH, *November* 17th, 1864.—The time crawls ;
to that degree that I dated a letter the 18th to-day,
thinking 2 nights must have passed ! Nevertheless
this day was much brightened by my Fred's dear
letter, the 1st I've had since our marriage, and by the
report of his *Female* speech in the Leeds Mercury. It

must have been an excellent one ; to the point, original, not too long, and with his own self shining through it.

CHATSWORTH, *November 19th*, 1864.—My sunshine has come back to me ! Freddy turned up about 1½, a little glad, I do believe, to see me again ; and I had a delightful walk with him (mostly in the rain) and happy, happy sits in our room. Oh, I don't deserve all that is given me. A dear letter came this morning from him.

CHATSWORTH, *November 26th*, 1864.—It is actually all but settled that we shall have the beautiful house in Carlton H. Terrace ! !

CHATSWORTH, *December 1st*, 1864.—The Duke and Duchess of Sutherland and a pug came. I cuddled rather with Lady Blanche, who is very nice.

CHATSWORTH, *December 2nd*, 1864.—The C. H. T. house is ours !

CHATSWORTH, *December 4th*, 1864.—This day last year Papa and I arrived at Chatsworth, and I had my memorable Church argument with " Ld. Frederick Cavendish " at dinner !

CHATSWORTH, *December 9th*, 1864.—Another lovely, radiant morning, the sun quite burning one's face through the window. Fred rode with the Duke and Ld. George to Hartington. Ly. G. and Susan went. Cavendish came. Some of us went to the kennels, where are a bewildering number of violent black dogs.

LONDON, *December 13th*, 1864.—Such a busy day as I have seldom had. We had Ld. Richard to breakfast, and after that, an interview with the beloved Currey. Thence to our splendid mansion, No. 21 Carlton House Terrace, where we met my old Meriel and Mrs. Talbot, and Trollope, the builder-and-furnisher's man. And we have settled the whole painting of the house, chosen all the papers, and the principal grates, and discussed many other points. All I think most successful.

HAGLEY, *December 15th*, 1864.—One of the *Times'* peculiarly ill-judged lectures to the Queen, which might have been spared her, considering the many little ways in which this year she has lessened her retirement. And it makes one ashamed of one's country to hear the attacks made upon her, striving as she does in her terrible bereavement and loneliness, to do all the necessary duties, while she never misses an opportunity of showing thoughtful kindness and sympathy for the joys and sorrows of others. And lately she has taken more part in society, tho' it is most painful to her. Under these circumstances, it shows good feeling indeed to reproach her on the anniversary of her widowhood!

HAGLEY, *December 16th,* 1864.—I had a nice walk with Edward Talbot,[1] who strikes one immensely with his thoughtful, powerful mind, coupled with such heartfelt, earnest reverence and deep feeling. I think he must turn out great. He has at length decided on taking Orders, though full of self-distrust as to his fitness to cope with the dangers and controversies of the day. But, if faith and love and humility are any safeguards to a man, he has them, only he lacks hopefulness.

HAGLEY, *December 20th,* 1864.—Mr. Brookfield spouted in the barn " The Merchant of Venice " and the story of Lefevre with great success.

HAGLEY, *December 22nd,* 1864.—I wrote to Cavendish!!! on a small begging errand of Mrs. Otley's. Played billiards with Aunt E. and beat her.

HAGLEY, *December 25th,* 1864.—Cavendish answered my letter, to my infinite pride and satisfaction.

HAGLEY, *December 26th,* 1864.—Albert played in the service for the day. We kept Christmas in the technical sense ; viz., general holyday and monster dinner of all the creatures—counting Fred, we make up the dozen, but oh for Meriel and John! Uproarious fun and games, ending in famous chorus singing and " God save the Queen." Next Christmas, alas! we shall probably be without dear old Nevy, whose Rifle Brigade commission may come any day.

HOLKER, *January 2nd,* 1865.—The Pope has put forth an Encyclical letter denouncing and condemning

[1] Afterwards Bishop of Rochester, Southwark, and Winchester.

all possible inquiry and thought, to a degree that it is supposed will make all intelligent Roman Catholics stand aghast.

HOLKER, *January 16th, 1865.*—F. went hare hunting on foot : a most Holkerish proceeding !

HOLKER, *January 19th, 1865.*—In the afternoon Lav., Lou, and I went to see Aggy, Hannah, and Betty (their surnames *will* not stay in my head !) ; dear old bodies. There has been a good deal of fever about, but it is going off. Poor Brailsford, the keeper, has lost his only child with some brain complaint. Lou gave to 3 old ladies a charming shawl apiece, which she has crocheted.

HOLKER, *January 23rd, 1865.*—Discussion is going on pro and con the admitting of dissenting children to a Church school by means of a " Conscience clause," which is to provide that if it is desired by the parents, they may be excluded from the religious teaching. I am in a wood about it, Papa being con, Freddy pro.

HOLKER, *January 27th, 1865.*—Unable to stand looking at the skating any longer without feeling of envy, I put on the articles, and staggered and floundered about with great enjoyment, squired unweariedly by Compton,[1] who shared with me many a fall. F. and Co. shot. The dear little boys [2] came about 5, had tea with Newmany in our room, appeared at dinner, and behaved with great aplomb.

HOLKER, *January 28th, 1865.*—Ice the order of the day again. I advanced to the stage of clumsy, spasmodic self-propelling, diversified by tumbles, and supported by a stick. F. had to foot-hunt, to my grief. He has a horrid cold. He saw the last 5 minutes of my exploits. Lou and I have begun Ld. Derby's new translation of the Iliad, in blank verse ; it is very nervous, easy, and dignified. Little boys tumbled about with and without skates, and swore friendship with Compton. A young man of three-and-twenty has just died of drink, his grandfather and all his

---

[1] Afterwards 3rd Lord Chesham. She had described him on the 24th as " an ugly but civil nice boy of 14."

[2] Her brothers Edward and Alfred.

paternal uncles having done the same. It is frightfully common about here.

HOLKER, *January 30th*, 1865.—Little boys (and Compton) plunged into the snow before luncheon ; played at hide-and-seek afterwards. I did some French and Latin with them, to my great enjoyment, reviving old-maid recollections. Also read to them the beginning to Kingsley's mad book " The Water Babies " : the only comprehensible part ; the rest being an entangled jumble of allegory, fairy-tale, and natural history—very dream-like and crazy. I have begun a course of English History, and am reading Lingard's first vol. ; Iliad, Carlyle, Butler.

HOLKER, *February 3rd*, 1865.—Began to read the same period in Hume that I have in Lingard : that is, I only read the memoir of Hume to-day : it was flesh-creepy to discern the soullessness and irreligion of the man, and his ghastly cheerfulness and indifference up to his dying moment.

LONDON, *February 17th*, 1865.—We dined at Lord Russell's ; it amused me immensely to go to dinner with Fred ! It was pleasant. Met Sir Edwin Landseer, Ld. Lyons, Mr. Barrett Browning,[1] Cap. Egerton, the Stanleys of Alderley.

LONDON, *February 19th*, 1865.—We went to hear the famous Mr. Maurice in the morning. He preached most beautifully on Triumphant Hope ; with a manner full of love and fervour. If one had not known of his startling, peculiar opinions, I think one would have seen nothing in his sermon but what any Christian might agree with. But alas ! there is terrible difficulty and dispute all round one now, and one is unconsciously on one's guard and in a state of distrust.

LONDON, *February 20th*, 1865.—Lou, F., and I did a deal of furniture inspection, not deciding yet upon much. Also we showed off the house to the Duke who was much pleased with it. F. and I dined very pleasantly at Ld. Granville's, meeting the Argylls, the

[1] Probably the poet Robert Browning, not his son Barrett who was only a boy at this time.

Bruces, Messrs. M. Arnold, Leveson, H. Cowper, Ld. Lyons, and Sir D. Dundas.

LATIMER, *February* 24*th,* 1865.—Went headlong in a hansom to Euston Square from Hyde Park Corner in 17 minutes ; and here we are, in a very pretty house, with Gladstones, Emma and B. Lascelles, Miss Campbell (a sister of Mrs. Wyndham), Messrs. Evelyn Ashley, Cowper, Hugh Smith ; and the Bishop of Oxford, who has come to hold Confirmations.

LATIMER, *February* 25*th,* 1865.—Bright clear morning, indescribably pleasant after the London dirty dinge and slop. Most of the womankind went to the " Waterside Church," where the Bishop held a Confirmation of about 80 several of whom were elderly people. Now, though my own Confirmation is a sacred and precious memory to me, almost beyond anything else, and though Spencer's and Lavinia's was full of deep interest, I can't say I ever saw, till to-day, a Confirmation really impressively and strikingly done. But the Bishop of Oxford has always excelled in this respect (having done, I should think, more good at Eton than can be measured by his Confirmations there), and this was most solemn and moving.

LONDON, *February* 27*th,* 1865.—This is a day to be remembered. I attended the Bishop of London's inaugural meeting of the " Ladies' Diocesan Association," which he set on foot last year, and in which ladies join to do useful and charitable work of many different kinds in the diocese. I became a member ; the Bishop giving me a little book, as token of admittance. I hope to undertake small things ; one is to be what they call a " supplemental lady " for the Parochial Mission Women Institution (that is, one whom some one Lady Superintendent may refer to for help on special occasions) ; the other, to visit S. Martin's Workhouse once a week. I have an awestruck feeling at joining people who have devoted themselves to good, and can only pray that the great blessedness of work for the poor may be mine, and that I may be helped.

LONDON, *March* 3*rd,* 1865.—A little " doment "

with a French play at Ld. Granville's, who had got the Wales's : the Prince astonishingly fat, the Princess looking lovely, tho' she is to be confined this summer.

LONDON, *March 8th*, 1865.—F. deposited me in George St. for luncheon, and thence I drove with Mrs. Talbot and Miss Laura Oldfield to St. Anne's, Limehouse, where we attended one of the " Mothers' Meetings " of the Parochial Mission there ; and I was introduced to Miss Lilby, the Lady Superintendent who is to have me to apply to ; to the Mission woman, Mrs. Bush ; to the clergyman (a missionary), who ended the meeting with reading, explaining, and prayers ; after hearing much about the work which is being done, and talking a little to some of the poor women, of whom there were about 25, we went to the London Hospital to see a girl of 23 who is there recovering from a tremendous operation : and who before going to the Hospital had been working as 2nd mission woman with such marvellous zeal and overflowing love for the work, that she went about amongst the people early and late, in spite of continual violent pain. And now in her weakness her one longing desire is to go back again ; her whole heart yearning after the poor things among whom she went. And all with such simplicity ; evidently she had no idea she was doing anything great.

LONDON, *March 10th*, 1865.—I went to London House, where I put down my name for St. Martin's Workhouse, and as supplemental lady to the St. Anne's Mission, Limehouse. Mr. Rousel mentioned a terrible case of a struggling curate, so poor at best that he could not have a fire in his house, or eat meat, for days together ; and now with his large family in the scarlet fever. Meriel Bathurst (who came for the first time), my Meriel, Mrs. Talbot, Agnes, and I agreed to send him a hamper among us ; and M. and I got the things after luncheon ; viz. tea, arrowroot, tapioca, sago, grapes, concentrated beef tea, currant jelly, ½ a dozen of port wine, and a bottle of brandy. The 2 latter items we found it rather blowing [1] to order. . . .

We dined at Ly. Cowper's, and had to go afterwards

[1] Appendix A.

to a ball at Marlborough House, where the Princess of Wales looked lovely. I saw my dear Princess Helena, but not to speak to, also Princess Louise and many Court friends. I wore all the diamonds on my head for the 1st time. Headdresses are becoming remarkable. The young Lady Wharncliffe had her hair in a frizzled mop ; and many were tending in the same direction.

LONDON, *March* 11*th*, 1865.—F. went to Barker's to sniff after broughams, as we purpose setting up one. . . .
Major Anson and Fred had a furious N. and S.[1] discussion ; F. got the best of it !

LONDON, *March* 12*th*, 1865.—I paid my first workhouse visit with the Gladstones. Went to the sick-ward, and made acquaintance with several poor old goodies. The look of the ward certainly takes away all romantic notions of ministration ; everything most uncomely and meagre, and some of the poor old folk repulsive enough ; but two were wonderful instances of strong love of God and faith in Him making suffering and weariness light burdens.

LONDON, *March* 13*th*, 1865.—Fred had the Furness Railwayums. I missed church, thro' an in-and-out of circumstances, which resulted in my entertaining at 5 o'clock tea the odd combination of Fanny Carew and her boy Reggie, and Althorp ! and going afterwards to the H. of C. to hear a debate on the defences of Canada, which seemed to be of the poorest ; and there is a notion that the American War must shortly end (the South being exhausted, and having just lost Charleston and Wilmington) and that then both parties will unite against us. I don't believe it unless we do something abominable.

LONDON, *March* 14*th*, 1865.—F. after his railways, with the Duke. (N.B. The Duke called me Lucy yesterday to my face for the first time !)

LONDON, *March* 16*th*, 1865.—To the House, where after an hour and a quarter of dreadful dulness I heard Cavendish speak on Army Estimates. He seemed a little nervous, but grew more fluent as he went on, and

---

[1] I.e. North and South : the American War.

gave one the notion of his being very well " up " in his facts.

LONDON, *March 17th,* 1865.—I went to London House, with a brigade of Associated Ladies. Charlotte Spencer came for the first time and was immediately pounced upon by the P.M.W. Lady Manageress to be a Supplemental Lady. Miss Twining, who has the *workhouseums,* shut herself up with Auntie P. and others, and burst forth into schemes for improving pauper sick arrangements. We had a delightful rebound [1] of our Curate-hamper : viz. of the wine and arrowroot.

LONDON, *March 20th,* 1865.—Fred went to hear the judgment in the case of Bishop Gray's deprivation of Bishop Colenso, which the latter protests against. The judgment pronounces Bishop Gray's sentence null and void, and brings to light the oddest and most bewildering facts : viz. that the colonial Bishops (except in Crown Colonies) are not in legal possession of their sees, the Queen having arbitrarily granted them patents little knowing that it was necessary to get the approval of the Colonial governments ! So both Bishops find themselves in a literally false position, and have no powers or rights whatever, except what belong to them as consecrated men. It is a good thing such anomalies have been brought to light. We dined at home. Read Merivale and Milton.

LONDON, *March 21st,* 1865.—We did the pleasantest job, viz., ordering the prettiest, most comfortable brougham in the world, to be our " very own " : a thing I am baby enough to like immensely, when a carriage is in question. Likewise chose breakfast, tea, and coffee services of a lovely description : and some particularly charming bedroom crockery for my room. An exceedingly smart dinner at Mr. Oswald's ; we met Sidneys, Spencers, Castlerosses, Prince and Princess Edward of Saxe-Weimar, Ly. Ely and daughter, Ld. Claud Hamilton, etc. I sat next to Dr. Quin, who kept me bursting $\frac{1}{2}$ through dinner. We discovered that a ball was to follow but shrunk off, I being in velvet, and F. gloveless ! and I was glad indeed, viewing [1] Lent.

[1] Appendix A.

LONDON, *March 23rd,* 1865.—Saw Sibyl Ryder and her husband, and the J.G.T.'s, which was a great break. Sibyl is expecting a baby : I trust she will get well through it, but she used to be very delicate. (It went off.) *That* wonderful, joyful hope has hitherto been withheld from me : this makes a little cloud in my " great heaven of blue."

LONDON, *March 26th,* 1865.—We went to St. Martin's in the morning ; and as the service was very respectably conducted and the sermon good, we have decided, it being our future parish church, to take sittings in it for ourselves and servants. It seems right to go to one's parish church, unless the objections to it were very grave indeed ; and I think we are right. The singing was very nice, though only by Charity children. I wish I didn't so much depend upon externals, for I feel that the frightful glaring kaleidoscope of an E. window without a single reminder of Christianity in it *will* be a real trial.

LONDON, *March 29th,* 1865.—F. read me in the evening a clever speech of Uncle W. supporting a motion of Mr. Dillwyn's that the state of the Irish Church is unsatisfactory. It isn't because I'm becoming a Radical that I think, according to my lights, that it ought to be disestablished. My very faith in the Church makes me sure that its continuance is in no need of being insured by being forced down the exasperated throats of Romanists numbering $\frac{7}{10}$ths of the population. The Scotch Church is in a nobler position. Not that I have an inkling what ought to be done with the endowments.

LONDON, *March 30th,* 1865.—We went and did the deed of taking seats for ourselves and servants at St. Martin's ; and were considerably disgusted by the drive-a-good-bargain fashion in which the official did it ; certainly putting before one the odiousness of the pew system in most lively colours.

HAGLEY, *April 5th,* 1865.—Actually did my poor Stakenbridge after luncheon, driving thither without Aunt E. and May. People very nice and dear and cordial at the sight of me. " And how's Mr. Scavendish ? I *should* say, *Lord* Scavendish," said old Mrs. Poole.

HAGLEY, *April* 10*th*, 1865.—It is a great trouble to me having to travel these 2 first days of Holy Week, but we couldn't rightly help it on many accounts. We left dear Hagley at 8, the little fellows (whom I shan't see again until they're schoolboys, alas !) scampering headlong down the avenue clinging on to the carriage. By a blunder of Head's, we had to delay crossing from Holyhead till night, spending the time from 2 till 11½ at Holyhead. Luckily it was the brightest, most unclouded afternoon, and we walked, and sat and talked and read pleasantly enough. Embarked at 12, three and a half hours before the boat started. A mild, still night, bathed in wonderful moonlight ; and the passage was as smooth as a pond. We got berths and slept pretty successfully. *April* 11*th*.—Landed before 8, managed to squeeze in breakfast at Dublin, railwayed to Cahir, and thence posted 12 miles. The descent to Lismore seemed to me marvellously beautiful and like a fairy-tale : the hills covered with budding woods, the deep glen, the winding river, the glorious castle standing on its steep hill. Lou and Eddy met us some little way off ; he nearly independent of sticks. Nobody else here but the Duke. The view from the north windows still more lovely and stately. One looks sheer down the precipitous bank into the Black water which is [1] ; and the castle is beautiful inside and out. *April* 12*th*.—Lou and I fished or rather toddled up the river, throwing lines with no result, encouraged by a dear enthusiastic Paddy and enjoying the delightful day.

F. and I had happy reads of my " Thoughts for Holy Week," etc., and the quiet is *very* nice, though nothing else would have made me like this for just this week. There was service, but, *instead* of the Communion Service, a Mr. Brown preached a *dreadful* sermon.

LISMORE, *April* 15*th*, 1865.—Horrid accounts of the poverty of the people : some families live on *five shillings a week*.

---

[1] Appendix A.

LISMORE, *April 17th*, 1865.—I ought to have mentioned some weeks ago the bad bit of news that Lady Herbert has gone over to the Church of Rome ; announcing it at last after more than a year of sham. Neville knows Lord Pembroke a little, and thinks him clever, and likely to be firm ; but he is hardly 15. Richmond has just been taken by the Federals, and the war is supposed to be ended. It will have done the great deed, and solved the mighty problem—of the abolition of slavery ; so thinks Fred ; and so an infinite good will have come out of indescribable suffering and bloodshed. Lou and I paid a long visit, immensely appreciated, to the Convent, where a band of very merry, brisk Paddy nuns received us with 3 cheers (Glynnese).[1]

LISMORE, *April 20th*, 1865.—After luncheon the rest of us boated to Glencairn, Eddy and Hal rowing up the river, Lou and I down. Wonderfully few casualties occurred, and it was charming. Divers neighbours dined, including old Dr. Fogarty, the R. C. priest, who spat on the carpet.

LISMORE, *April 21st*, 1865.—The anniversary of our engagement. My Fred gave me a darling little signet ring to mark it with. I spent a good deal of time thinking over my last 21st of April : F. coming to the clever breakfast, but not sitting by me, and looking a little white and odd : a certain old Dean who was a long while before he would make himself scarce : our finding ourselves alone in the bare little conservatory —then everything happy and wonderful ! Papa coming in with his dear bright smile, and Auntie P. and Uncle William ; Lou coming to see me with Fred ; luncheon in St. St. and all the excitement and crying there ; happy, happy bits with Fred afterwards and his giving me my precious locket ; his dining with us, and the day ending as if with sunrise instead of sunset. But I am still happier now, in my *settled* sunshine !

LISMORE, *April 22nd*, 1865.—Lovely and very warm. Many oak trees are in leaf ; and O the sweet smell of laurel blossom and gorse ! To-day we passed a bank so covered with primroses that we smelt them driving

[1] Appendix A.

by. I have been much derided for comparing them,
when one sees them clustered together, to fairy pats of
butter ; but I declare it is a very good notion. We had
a delightful row down the river, as far as Strancally,
going ashore for luncheon on a little clear plot of
ground, under overhanging woods near Dromana. We
all rowed at one time or another ; the Duke and all ;
and I am growing a little complacent over my feathering,
albeit divers crabs were the result. Drove home most
of the way, distributing remains of provisions to the
different little tatterdemalions on the road. Household
cares are beginning with us : Ross and some of the
servants are in the mansion, but it is frightfully behind
hand and won't be ready for us for three weeks, probably, instead of by next Thursday. But our chief
trouble is much more serious, a bad story has come
out about the young Gladstone footman we had engaged,
and we have had to decide on getting rid of him directly.

LISMORE, *April* 24*th*.—Lou and I paid visits, which
were immensely appreciated, to a part of the town
called Botany, and to the National Schools. Nearly
all the female inhabitants of Botany turned out in
front of their houses, and fervently blessed Lou as we
passed. At the school I was greatly delighted with
the girls' reading, which was far better than the best
at Hagley ; the brogue rather bewitches me ; and
some little ragged dots of six did huge justice to " The
Ant and the Grasshopper " in English verse.

We spent some of the afternoon in again sanguinely
flogging the river (in vain) for salmon.

LISMORE, *April* 25*th*, 1865.—Lou, Eddy, Hal, and
Claude tried to fish soon after breakfast ; about 12
I went to join her, and falling in with the Duke, walked
tête-à-tête with him down the river-side ; whereat I
found my shyness at him rather revive ! We then
went all three to the Convent, being joined on the road,
to our despair ! by Father Fogarty, who would come
in with us. It was wonderfully good of the Duke to
undergo what of all things he hates most : a long
series of making talk, and receiving butter of the most
fulsome description ; in which the old priest certainly

excels. The poor nuns were rather bores too, but enchanted at our visit. We saw their school. They were urgent for F. and me " to reshide at Lismore " —sanguine ! After luncheon Lou and I bumped in the car to call at Glenatorr. Oh the loveliness of the country ! But more from its outburst of spring greenness than any special beauty of its own. I am sentimental at going. Finished " The Clever Woman " ; a sad failure of a book, and mostly very dull.

CHESTER, *April 26th*, 1865.—Left Lismore soon after 9 ; posted to Fermoy, which was charming ; railwayed to Dublin, where we dined. Were shocked and aghast beyond measure, Fred especially, at the terrible news of the murder of President Lincoln, placarded in the streets. For him one can hardly mourn ; for it is a glorious thing to die at the climax of victory (and this the fall of Richmond brought to him), and with almost his last words those of peace and goodwill. All his conduct showed a noble forgiveness and desire of brotherhood ; and there seems no one capable of carrying out the great work of reuniting the country. Least of all the wretched man who perforce succeeds him : Andrew Johnson, " a mean white," who, on his election to the vice-presidency the other day, made an incoherent drunken speech, and who may very likely think of nothing but blood and vengeance and defiance of Europe. The murder was on Good Friday evening at the Theatre (!), and the murderer leaped on to the stage afterwards, brandishing a knife, and escaped. Almost at the same time Seward, the Secretary of State, was stabbed as he lay ill in bed, and is not expected to live ; and his son badly wounded.

LONDON, *May 1st*, 1865.—I saw two Jacks-in-the-green, which I thought were nearly obsolete. . . .

Lou and I went to the H. of Commons and heard Sir George Grey move, and Dizzy second, both in very good, suitable speeches, a resolution of sympathy with the United States. Then to the House of Lords, where Lord Russell was inaudible and Lord Derby spoke coldly and grudgingly ; it was rather disgraceful ; and in the House of Commons, it was horrid to hear so little cheering on the Conservative side. Seward is likely to recover. Johnson has made remarkable and powerful but dangerous and vindictive speeches.

LONDON, *May 3rd*, 1865.—F. and I called on Mrs. Milbank, who is to be my Prime Minister in the getting up of the horrid Yorkshire quadrille. Lord Richard came. We went (and I chaperoned Lou! at which I died[1]) to a concert at Auntie P's. Carry Lawley was there, just out, and very good-looking. F. shrunk off early to his Cosmopolitan club! Shows me we are getting a humdrum old prosaic couple. Letters : to little boys; from Mrs. Otley scolding me for becoming Northern. But I know more about it than she does.

LONDON, *May 4th*, 1865.—I read with a good deal of interest a speech of " Bob Lowe's " against Mr. Baines' Reform Bill which is for a £6 franchise. Mr. Lowe made me agree with him, which is sad, as wicked Radical Fred is all for the £6 franchise. But if Uncle William, as is expected, makes a good rattling speech on the other side, I shall probably go comfortably round. I foresee that I shall get desperately political; but I don't think that must *necessarily* make me an odious woman! I shall try and not let it at all events. Went with Lou to the Royal Academy; where were many pretty children, and cottage interiors; two excellent pictures of the Bishops of London and Oxford, by Sant and Richmond, and other good things. Pre-Raphaeliteism seems, like homeopathy, to be becoming less a school apart and more infused into schools than it was. Not but what there are still some tinny, papier-mâché, gaudy skies, solid green seas, ugly red-haired, pink-faced women in all colours of the rainbow, and cotton velvet grass ; and also some soft sketchy pictures aiming at the other extreme, which I can't but prefer, even *in* their extremes.

LONDON, *May 5th*, 1865.—The Bishop of London preached well; his little children are so brought up in the midst of work for the poor, that one of the tiny girls was heard saying : " When I am six, I shall have a ward to visit ! "

---

[1] Appendix A.

LONDON, *May 8th*, 1865.—One of the great days of our life : the day of taking possession of our own new home.   We spent a good deal of the day here, unpacking and arranging ; but we only go into our rooms upstairs and the study to-day.   I spent some time with M. in the afternoon ; then we dressed here, dined at Dev. House, and returned here at about half past 10. Tea came up in the lovely tea-pots and cups we chose, and was our first meal.   Our rooms are too pretty. This is likely to be the last of many wonderful bewildering days that I've had since my marriage : my life has now so settled into quiet every-day brightness, that its strangeness has long worn off.   But this building of our own nest is wonderful and notable !

LONDON, *May 9th*, 1865.—Our first family prayers ; all the servants attending.   My Fred read a beautiful prayer of his own.   We chose the 3rd Col. and the 2 first verses of the 4th to read, and for the other prayers, the confession ; a thanksgiving and a benedictory prayer out of the " Liturgia Domestica," the Lord's Prayer, and 2 others.

LONDON, *May 10th*, 1865.—I am triumphant at starting the underservants minus crinoline during their work !   Did shopping for the drawing-rooms with Lou ; but only decided on two blue-velveted tables at Howards.   Afterwards to Stratton St. in Our Brougham, which turned out to-day and *is* [1] !   F. dined at some Railway Benevolent thing ; I at No. 11,[2] where the old well-known manners prevailed : no particular moment for going in to dinner ; Auntie P. in bed and asleep instead of dining, and appearing late bedecked for a ball : the party was Willy, Agnes, Kate Gladstone, and me.   *Home.*   That it hardly feels yet !

LONDON, *May 12th*, 1865.—The Duchess of Argyll was getting signatures to an address of condolence to be sent to Mrs. Lincoln.   Lou and I signed it. . . . The papers are pretty full of Constance Kent's confession of the Road murder, which she has made through the influence of Mr. Wagner, of Brighton, while in a sisterhood there ; but entirely by her own free will.   The

---

[1] Appendix A.   [2] The Gladstones' house.

Times accounts for a girl of sixteen stifling, stabbing and cutting the throat of her little half-brother of 4, for no better motive than that of spiting her step-mother, on the ground that all girls between twelve and twenty are hard-hearted ! !

LONDON, *May* 16*th*, 1865.—My cold still makes a haggard object of me, the more because I have grown thin. I took divers potations of sal-volatile, which is a new remedy. Did my house-books for the first time ! They came to a heavy total, but I trust that is only the start.

LONDON, *May* 17*th*, 1865.—Some pleasant weather : laburnum, chestnut, and may-blossom look lovely. I am beginning upon troubles I was experienced enough to foresee when I was preparing myself for a new chapter of household cares : viz., failures. The kitchen-maid turns out sick and incapable ; the upperhousemaid pert, fine, and lazy. Woe is me ! . . .

We went to Lady Waldegrave's and Lady de Grey's ; where we were well squashed, but somewhat amused. I find, old wife as I am, novelty and fun in going out with my husband ! Was very smart in trailing white satin.

LONDON, *May* 18*th*, 1865.—I awoke with a sense of household cares such as I used sometimes to have at dear old Hagley, but they melted a good deal away on my conversing with Ross and the peccant but candid Eliza. The next thing is the Drawing-room whereat Aunt Fanny presented me on my marriage. I went in gorgeous array of white lace (my wedding lace) and white moiré train, with my beautiful diamond tiara on my head, and felt every inch a married woman. Princess Helena held the Drawing-room for the Queen, who has held 5 " Courts " this year, but is a little perverse (I must use the word) in refusing to hold Drawing-rooms, which are much less exertion. Carry Lawley [1] and Mary Wortley [2] were brought out : Carry is very handsome, towering above her jenny-wren of a mother.

LONDON, *May* 19*th*, 1865.—I went to St. James' at 11 ;

[1] Daughter of Lord Wenlock.
[2] Afterwards wife of the 2nd Earl of Lovelace. The two girls were cousins of each other and of Lady Frederick.

enjoy the privilege of walking unchaperoned in the morning. Visits, visits in the afternoon : I don't see when they will end. Everybody out. Saw Meriel who is on her legs and very well : the baby went his 1st walk to-day, into the Abbey ! which all the four have been to see *first thing*. The excitement came off of the Duke and Lou dining with us : it was very nice and wonderful.

LONDON, *May 20th*, 1865.—Very warm and lovely. I made a rout-out of *groutle* [1] and *hydra*.[1] We walked to Fisher's in the Strand to get a writing-paper box for Fred. Had a flying visit from Aunt Coquitty.[2] Papa and F. went in red and gold to the Levée. Afterwards I drove to Mrs. Milbank's and some card deeds : tried to go to All Saints', but was too late ; saw Meriel who was dressed and downstairs, and looking very nice and well ; had tea and bonbons at Adéle's.

We dined at Lord Wharncliffe's, meeting the Wenlocks and Carry, Colonel and Lady Louisa Feilding, Captain Egerton, Lord Claud Hamilton (a pleasant, simple-mannered, good-looking little youth), the Burys, Cissy Wortley, etc. Afterwards to Apsley House, which I never was in before, and which struck me very much.

LONDON, *May 21st*, 1865.—Workhouse, where I sung " All shall be well," " Nearer to Thee," and " Thy Will be done." One poor dying woman entreated me to send her a few biscuits, the only thing she could fancy eating ; so I did a little Sunday shopping for the 1st time in my life.

LONDON, *May 22nd*, 1865.—Dear old Charles dined with us : a proposal has been made to put him up for the county against Messrs. Knight and Lygon, but, though there is much reason to prophesy that he will become Liberal, he is still very Conservative, and also unwilling to come in so soon. His decision pends a little, and depends on what would be asked of him. Papa dined too, so we were a snug quartette. Stately royal concert, to which we went in gorgeous array.

[1] Appendix A.
[2] I.e. her aunt, Miss Lyttelton (" Aunt Coque "), and her cousin, Miss Kitty Pole Carew, who were much together.

There is great prospect of Willy standing as a Liberal for Chester, but it is a pity, for he is exceedingly unwilling, and has shown some signs of being at heart Conservative! But Time will show.

LONDON, *May 23rd*, 1865.—We dined at home, entertaining the W.E.G.'s, which was a great treat. He was in great force; and didn't I enjoy hearing him in his swing of brilliant talk, and drawing out my Fred's energetic opinions! All the political talk nowadays is of extended franchise; and F. is rather full of an astonishing brand-new plan of Hare's [1] of allowing a quota of two thousand votes, pollable *all over* the country which shall qualify a candidate for any seat for which he may stand. Uncle W. thought his plan somewhat of a dream.

LONDON, *May 24th*, 1865.—Very delightful and lovely with freshened air. Queen's birthday, kept with guns, bells, illuminations, and holyday as of old. George Street in the morning : M. was to be churched to-day. Auntie P. flew across to see us, her clothes tumbling about her; sat down on the floor, and poured out Willy's electionums, which are exciting her as she *can* be excited. The girls came to luncheon with us, and with me to Waterloo House for Sunday jackets like old times! We drove to Richmond, and dined at the Star and Garter with Mr. C. Clifford, meeting Mr. and Mrs. Leo Ellis, Mr. and Lady Augusta Bromley, Mr. and Mrs. Millais (the great pre-Raphaelite), Mr. and Lady E. St. Aubyn, and the Delameres. The evening very lovely and the view; but I was rather bored.

LONDON, *May 27th*, 1865.—Wound up with Lady Pam's [2]; an amusing party; Lord P. looked very old and stiff and shaky. Didn't I remember my last party there, when we didn't see Fred for a long while, but at last he turned up and talked to me the rest of the evening!

LONDON, *May 28th*, 1865.—St. Martin's, where I had the pleasure of seeing 4 of our servants file into their pew.

[1] The original scheme of Proportional Representation.
[2] Lady Palmerston.

LONDON, *May* 29*th*, 1865.—Went to *Stafford House*, which has a corner of its own in my heart. We went to the very place where my Fred spoke to me; and I recalled it all vividly enough. What should happen this very night but a proposal! Lord Henry Scott [1] to Cissy Wortley. He has loved her for 10 years, but her ill-health led to the breaking-off of their engagement. Now it is happily *on* again.

LONDON, *May* 30*th*, 1865.—A great day! Dear, dear Eddy, after long having it in his heart, proposed to Emma Lascelles, and they are engaged and as happy, I do believe, as we were. It has been sad to see her, poor dear, for a long time past, looking thoroughly out of spirits, but behaving quite beautifully, under the doubt whether it was going to be; and now! Oh dear, I have an odd feeling like an echo of my golden spring! She looked so bright; and talked incoherently of being in a dream, etc., etc. As for dear Eddy, I kissed and hugged him with my whole heart. He would win anyone with his simple, truthful, humble goodness; and his nature which is as pure and sunny as Albert's. He squeezed my hands, and said, " Do you think (*fink*) I shall make a good husband? and that we shall be as happy as you are? " Lady Caroline's face did look good to see! I paid happy May a long visit: Di and Lucy came in, and we all jabbered in a mad way. Of course one is sorry for the 1st cousinship,[2] but nothing has been done to lead up to it; and what can one say in such a case of real, tried, and genuine affection, and when everyone has behaved rightly? Truly one may feel God's Providence over them. Meanwhile, what a moment he has chosen! His leave is up, his election coming on (the whole country is agog over the coming dissolution), Emma's waiting just over and she must have another! The poor Queen may have reason to complain and to wish the Lords Cavendish would not make a point of marrying her Maids! I suppose Cavendish will make choice of E.'s successor.

LONDON, *May* 31*st*, 1865.—We had a delightful

[1] Afterwards 1st Lord Montagu.
[2] Lady Caroline Lascelles was a sister of Lady Burlington, Lord Edward's mother.

LADY EDWARD CAVENDISH.

LORD EDWARD CAVENDISH.

I—266]

drive with Lou in the open carriage to Sydenham, to see Sir J. Paxton [1] (who is ill). How we did talk ! and how pleasant it was in the balmy summer beauty. Poor Sir Joseph shocked me terribly with his changed looks. He seemed very weak and low at first, but was brightened up a good deal by our visit. He by no means approved of Eddy's marriage ! His little house under the shadow of his great Palace was lovely with verandah and garden : and married daughters with him. Derby day, so the carriage was well yelled after by swarms of little ragamuffins.

LONDON, *June 1st,* 1865.—We spent most of the day in an expedition to Sheerness, to see the new Transatlantic telegraph : 1,800 *miles* of which are coiled up on board the *Great Eastern* ; there are 500 more miles not yet on board ; but before long she will set out on her mission of paying it out at the rate of 7 miles an hour. It is supposed it will take a fortnight. I have brought home a bit of the electric cord ; it is about the thickness of my middle finger, and consists of 7 copper wires enclosed in 5 layers of gutta-percha. This, in the cable as we saw it ready to be laid down, is surrounded by 10 steel wires, each wire cased in several strands of hemp, so that the whole looks like a hempen cable about the thickness of one's wrist. They are able to discover if the slightest puncture appears in the gutta-percha ! the whole cable being tested over and over again at all possible stages of its progress towards the paying out process. It seems a noble, gigantic work. The enormous ungainly ship took one's breath away by her size. . . .

Poor Morgan has lost an only brother.

CHATSWORTH, *June 2nd,* 1865.—I sent poor Morgan off to her sister-in-law, and got in the good old Grim One for stop-gap ! . . .

We went to Lady Caroline's and told Eddy and Emmy to come to luncheon with us. . . .

We shut them up together in the empty drawing-room, where I think they were tolerably happy. I saw M. At 6 we joined the D. and Lou and came here :

[1] Architect of the Crystal Palace ; originally superintendent of the gardens at Chatsworth.

even in the dark, how delicious the country is, with its deep stillness and fragrant smell !

CHATSWORTH, *June 3rd*, 1865.—This place in autumn, beautiful as I thought it in 3 successive Novembers, gave me no notion of what it would be in June. After breakfast I coaxed Fred out with me ; and we walked about the garden in a maze of loveliness ; rhododendrons and azaleas, in wonderful beauty ; the shrubs all crowned with their spring shoots, the young fern *in curl*, the hyacinths ! " It seemed the heavens upbreaking through the earth " : birds and bees filling the air with sweet sounds ; the distance soft blue, and all the intervening country varied green : *such* a walk it was ! Drove with Lou and the ponies Friar and Nun to the stand and the Warren. It all *was*.[1] Fiz delighted to see us. Gipsy and Moy in good health. We had tea with them in the Granville corner. Evening papers brought the good news of the Princess of Wales' 2nd baby[2] ; another little Prince ; born soon after 1 a.m. this morning after she had undergone a concert ! It is 6 weeks earlier than was expected ; curious, a 2nd premature baby. Willy has made a good, spirited modest speech at Chester : and is patted on the back by the *Spectator*. Uncle W. went there to back him.

CHATSWORTH, *June 6th*, 1865.—Eddy came, looking very bright and dear : says the Queen and Princess Helena have been very kind and cordial ; but the poor Queen says, as soon as anyone thoroughly suits and pleases her, she marries !

HAWARDEN, *June 8th*, 1865.—We left dear, beautiful Chatsworth about 10, and travelled here in much dust, dirt, and heat, arriving at the Rectory about 3. It is a year and a half since my last memorable visit here ; when the feeling which is now like my own life to me really began. There is a halo round the recollection, as round so many others ! I believe I haven't slept in this house since 1854, when I was 13 ; and everyone was full of the Crimean War. We find here Uncle Stephen, Auntie P., and Mazy[3] ; and after dinner

---

[1] Appendix A. [2] King George V.
[3] Mary Gladstone, afterwards Mrs. Drew.

Willy and Stephy turned up from Chester, where Willy has been hard at work canvassing. He seems thoroughly to have warmed up to the work ; and has made one speech which has gained him much applause for its good sense, manliness, and caution. We trolled electionums beyond ! The new curate and his wife, (Chamberlains), nice people, dined. O what a contrast to that 1st peaceful day of our pretty honeymoon ! But my Fred and I had a little honeymoon on the lawn here ; and I spouted to him my Hawarden bits of poetry.

LONDON, *June 12th*, 1865.—We picked a good load of daisies and clover for my poor old workhouse bodies ; and I bore off besides a lovely nosegay of other flowers.

LONDON, *June 13th*, 1865.—Hotter again. We saw field after field cleared of hay on our journey up. Lord Richard came to breakfast, and brought us lovely pinks and roses from Chislehurst. I took some, with my daisies and clover, to the workhouse : old folk charmed. Cut my way through my mountain of notes.

LONDON, *June 14th*, 1865.—Hot and fine. F. went off to Sussex before 8 a.m. and I had a solitary day. Made the best of it by hanging Lord Richard's beautiful engravings in the drawing-room (which also Lou and I decked out with wedding-presents), and the Smithian water-colours and " The Happy Valley " in the study, to surprise F. on his return. He *was* a little pleased ! Lou and Adéle d'Henin came to luncheon ; the Gladstone girls, Granny, Julia Robartes, and the Arthur Ellisons called, and all were great audience. I picked my Fred up about ½ past 4 ; but had to dine without him at Lady Rivers ', as he had a clashing engagement. Mr. Leveson took me in, and was pleasant. Met the Carmarthens,[1] and rather fell in love with her : two very pretty unmarried Pitts ; Hal with whom I had much confidential conversation.

LONDON, *June 15th*, 1865.—Went to All Saints' at the wrong hour for service, but remained there for quite 20 minutes, which was very nice.

---

[1] Afterwards 9th Duke and Duchess of Leeds. The Duchess was a daughter of 4th Lord Rivers : the Pitt ladies were, no doubt, her sisters.

LONDON, *June 16th*, 1865.—We drove together to get a wedding-present for dear Mr. Hugh Smith. At 6 we picked up Lou, and went off riding together. I was on Revolver, and the ill-behaved old fellow chose to come flop down on his knees at the end of a foolish gambol, rolled on his side, and deposited me on the ground. It is my 3rd tumble, and for the 3rd time I fell harmlessly on my side. I feel no worse result, thank God, than a bruised, aching leg. Lou fortunately was able to join on to the Lascelles, and F. and I rode sedately home at a foot's pace. We had one of our snug and rare tête-à-tête evenings, and sat in the drawing-room, which is too lovely lit up. Dear Lou came at 10 to see how I did, *and said the Duke was very near coming !*

CHISLEHURST, *June 17th*, 1865.—At ½ past 4 we set off for Chislehurst which it interests me to see. Lord Richard and his dog Maida (descended from Sir W. Scott's) received us very kindly. The pretty garden is full of roses.

CHISLEHURST, *June 18th*, 1865.—Grey and rather chilly all day. But we had a very pleasant, pretty afternoon walk to Lord · Sydney's fine park. The church close by Lord Richard's garden (N.B. I am to say *Uncle* Richard, says he !), pretty and carefully arranged. Singing very good and hearty. An excellent sermon from Mr. Murray on the apparent discrepancies between Scripture and Science. No after. sermon. We read Goulburn, and I some Th. à Kempis which Kitty Feilding has given me.

LONDON, *June 19th*, 1865.—Drove about getting mourning (4th since my marriage) for a great-uncle-in-law, Lord Charles Fitzroy.

LONDON, *June 20th*, 1865.—I fussed and fidgeted a good deal all day under the anticipation of our First Real Dinner Party ; arranged flowers, mused over the bill of fare, contemplated the table, displayed china, likewise did books which have hitherto proved fearfully high, received visits from Papa, Aunt Coque, and Albert who also dined with us and is very well ; we went to the Academy with F. which struck me less favourably than before. To dinner came M., John, and Edward, the Algys, Agnes, Albert, and Mr. E. Ashley. All went very well; but I began with a good fit of nervousness, which, however, I craftily concealed.

LONDON, *June 21st*, 1865.—We drove about paying some of the monster bills incident to setting up house. We much fear the total of the furnishing, including linen, crockery, and kitchen apparatus, will be quite £3,000. Dined at Lady de Grey's,[1] to meet the D. of Cambridge, and encountered great swells, viz. the Duke and Duchess [2] of Manchester, she looking brilliantly beautiful and attractive as usual; he certainly a foil! The Ailesburys (she has grand remains of beauty), the Skelmersdales, Lord Sefton, Sir R. and Lady Emily Peel, Mr. and Ly. Augusta Sturt, Ly. Molesworth, and one of the Ladies Cowper.

LONDON, *June 22nd*, 1865.—We went to one of Uncle William's man breakfasts, where we met the Duke and Duchess of Argyll, the Duke of Brabant, Mr. Goschen (a young M.P. whose abilities are much thought of), M. Van de Weyer, etc., and were reminded of certain last-year breakfasts of the sort, when somehow we did *not* sit at different tables, as to-day. It was sad and shocking to contrast with our bright associations the terrible news which came before we left the house. Lord Granville, who had been expected, wrote to say that he had that moment heard of the death of his niece Alice Arbuthnot—*killed by lightning*; at Interlachen, as they were coming home from their wedding tour. They were devotedly attached, and had been married barely 2 months. I did not know her, but remember her beautiful, gentle face. She was only 23. It is one of those things which make all earthly joys tremble under one; and when I think of our precious year of happiness I can hardly dare to look into the future, for how little do I deserve the sunshine which in the case of so many is eclipsed at its height. It is overwhelming to think of poor Lord and Lady Rivers, who have already had such sorrow in the death of their 3 sons. The Howards and Kitty Feilding with her

[1] Wife of Earl de Grey, afterwards the 1st Marquess of Ripon, the statesman.   [2] Afterwards Duchess of Devonshire.

sister Lady Adelaide Murray came to luncheon with us.
Lady Ade. was engaged to be married the same day as
the Arbuthnots. I went with M. and Mrs. Talbot and
Edward to Chiswick, which the Duchess of Sutherland
had lent for a P.M.W. fête. I went on the strength of
being Supplemental Lady to Limehouse, and saw its
2 mission women, Mrs. Bush and Sarah Darrington :
also Miss Lilley the Superintendent ; and heard a good
account of the mission. The poor bodies had a beautiful tea, with fruit and flowers ; and were immensely
pleased. M. and I went early on her baby's account ;
but we heard that they ended by singing, and made
Mrs. Talbot thank the Duchess for them. One woman
said it was like Paradise. The Duchess gave each a
rose to take away. I had a little walk by myself to
see certain dear spots in the garden, where we spent
" golden hours," also went into the house ; into the
drawing-room where we sat together on the sofa in the
deep summer stillness that June evening ; and all was
dreamlike to me, and fairyland. But to those who
knew and loved Alice Arbuthnot the place must be for
ever saddened, for the Rivers's used to live there.

LONDON, *June 23rd*, 1865.—To St. St., where Great-
Granny was entertaining with a picture-book little
George and Mary. Dined there, and *chaperoned* Aunt
C. afterwards to Ly. Windsor's.

LONDON, *June 24th*, 1865.—If only the time would
go quicker [1] ! but here is the 1st day only just over.
In some ways it was better than I expected, from
having plenty of things to do and people to see—much
better than in the country. I went to St. James',
thence to D. House and then home again, where I
found Mr. Thompson who awestruck me much by
deputing me to give F. his opinions on F.'s address,
which he sent him yesterday to criticize : also certain
remarks on other election topics. He especially flattered
me by strongly advising that I should go with my
Fred into the Division during the autumn that we might
be civil to the constituents. I wrote the necessary
troll to F. instantly ; and these different proceedings,

---

[1] Her husband was out with his Yeomanry.

with a little reading, filled up my morning. Had
luncheon at D. House, and told the Duke all about
Thompson : didn't find it blowing.[1]   Old M. is bereaved
like me, John having gone off high gee[1] a prospect of
getting in for Malmesbury.   She picked me up at 4
in her nice open carriage, and we dropped cards.   Mary
and Victoria Clive came to tea, M. to dinner, in the
middle of which turned up old Nevy, and was most
delightful all the evening.   His whole tone and turn
of mind does seem most sound, high-principled, manly,
and modest : just what one would wish and pray for
a young officer ; and one can't but rejoice in the hope
that he will have influence, and use it for good.

LONDON, *June 26th*, 1865.—*Two* letters from my Fred
gladdened my eyes, and brightened up the day.   He
wrote the 1st before 7½ on Saturday morning, hoping
it might reach me that evening ; O so dear of him.

LONDON, *June 28th*, 1865.—Ball at Auntie P.'s. to
meet the Prince of Wales.   I had to go, which I didn't
like without my Fred, but it was amusing.   Refused
stoutly to dance with Mr. Ashley !   Saw poor Aunt
Henrietta there :   one doesn't know how she has the
heart to go out ;   for Uncle Spencer has had one of his
turf smashes, and though kind, good Althorp has paid,
he is to go abroad for an indefinite time, partly to be
out of the way of (English) betting, partly with a
chance of finding something to do.   We much fear
that they have settled to live apart, she remaining in
England ; so terribly wrong.

LONDON, *June 29th*, 1865.—I at D. House, where I
had an agreeable dinner, sitting between old Panizzi
and Lord Houghton whose ungainly manners and vora-
cious appetite contrast curiously with the quick, deep,
poetical feeling which comes up in him now and then.
Gladstones were there ; really what with N.W. Riding,
E. Sussex, Oxford, Chester, and Malmesbury, I may
be said indeed to have the electionums.

LONDON, *June 30th*, 1865.—The happy day of my
Fred's return.   All sorts of vague fears have occurred

[1] Appendix A.

to me ; but he has come safe back to me, and everything looks different already ! Nevy, Aunt C., and I had the great treat of hearing the " Israel in Egypt " (that is, about ¾ths of it, being late) at the Crystal Palace. Much squash and crowd and rush and stoppage beset the journey to and fro ; not to speak of rain all day ; but the glorious things we heard made amends. Patti sang, but her voice isn't strong enough : it should have been Titiens. Mme Rudersdorf has immense power, but little sweetness ; and Mme Sainton Dolby ought to leave off as her voice is cracked ; but Sims Reeves and Schmidt were grand, and the choruses magnificent. I had to skurry into evening things after we had got home (taking a 3rd class carriage by storm), and dine at Aunt Wenlock's, and so was forced to miss my Fred's arrival ; but found him at home soon after 11.

LONDON, *July 1st*, 1865.—I came back at 5½ to say good-bye to Nevy, who went to Hagley. He has been most delightful and companionable, what with his fun, his cleverness, his pleasant, *good* tone, and his love of music, which has resulted in the mansion echoing with all sorts, parts, and fragments of song and anthem.

LONDON, *July 2nd*, 1865.—All Saints, where I sat by a poor woman, who said she was a Roman Catholic, and that " you Puseyites are almost the same as Catholics " ; to which I demurred. She joined in much of the Service when I gave her my book, and sung both the beautiful hymns very much out of tune, with great fervour.

LONDON, *July 4th*, 1865.—Lou picked me up at 2, and we went (with 40 or 50 other folk) to St. George's Hill,[1] a lovely heathy place, all fragrant with bracken and honeysuckle and firs, where Ly. Blanche Egerton and her brothers picnicked us. Old Ly. Ellesmere also was there ; and young Ld. Ellesmere ; and a very pretty, noble-looking, open-faced fair boy of 16. I saw much of Tallee, and had a little bit of capping with her. Also saw dear Miss Dennett, now a little old lady, with traces in her worn face of the wretched life

[1] St. George's Hill, near Weybridge, later Lady Louisa's own home, after her marriage.

she must have had, striving to make peace between the poor Duke of Newcastle in his fatal anger and mismanagement, and his miserable daughter, when her whole self-will was set upon that tragical marriage. Lovely little Lady Dalkeith [1] and certain pretty unmarried sisters of hers— etc., etc., were there.

LONDON, *July 5th*, 1865.—Had the accountums in the morning; find we have spent £121 (inclusive of a good many small extras) on housekeeping since we set up. This I *must* cut down! We dined at D. House, where was a family dinner, with a *tail*, in honour of Eddy and Emma; as last year of us, when I remember undergoing much in the way of introductions. Hideous reports are about that the Conservatives are getting up a contest for us, but first catch your hare—they can't find anybody to undertake the inevitable beating! Oxford, Chester, and Malmesbury are all frightfully doubtful: I had *all but* rather Fred was beaten than Uncle W.; he will feel it deeply, and so will she.

LONDON, *July 7th*, 1865.—Cavendish dined, to my great satisfaction; Auntie P. and Mary came in afterwards. There has been an exceedingly good drawing in *Punch* of " Mamma Russell and Mamma Gladstone " (the states*men*, in bonnets) teaching their respective babies to walk, alluding to Lord Amberley and Willy standing for Leeds and Chester.

BOLTON, *July 9th*, 1865.—We sat much in the dear little stone court before the house; also on the terrace; and walked to the Strid. Very honeylunar! Read Goulburn, Keble, Thomas à Kempis; all 3 with my Fred.

BOLTON, *July 12th*, 1865.—F. is over the moon at divers Liberals having been returned in London; especially Mill the philosopher and Hughes the author of " Tom Brown." Mill's return notable from his having refused either to solicit votes or to spend a farthing *himself*. . . .

After luncheon, up we went to dear Glorious Hazlewood; the view clearer than I ever remember seeing

[1] Daughter of the 1st Duke of Abercorn and wife of the 6th Duke of Buccleuch.

it, and my familiarity with it all, as is always the case
with " things of beauty," making it strike and delight
me more than ever.   As in old music,

Ever in its melodious store
Finding a spell unheard before.

We had one delightful sit on the heather, which is
beginning to blossom, when I lay back looking straight
up into the lovely sky, conscious of the breezy, undulat-
ing expanse all round, and of my own happiness, so
that my heart rather overflowed !

HEADINGLEY, *July 13th,* 1865.—A contrast ! Here
we are up to the ears in electionums.   Arrived in
Leeds which we found inundated by triumphant Blues,
the Conservative candidate Beecroft having come in
at the head of the poll ; Baines (proposer of a £6
franchise) next, and poor Lord Amberley being beaten
rather hollow.   Said Lord A. and his wife are staying
here ;   and take their defeat with admirable good
temper and philosophy.   We did not leave Bolton
till 3.   Walked before luncheon in pretty Wood, and
back by the Terrace.   Alas ! alas ! poor old John is
beaten hollow at Malmesbury.   Willy has come in for
Chester, which I *am* glad of.

HEADINGLEY, *July 14th,* 1865.—The Oxford polling
has begun ; Uncle W. a little below Hardy, but only a
few hundred votes are yet polled.   It is frightfully
close.   My poor Fred had the speechums a little.

HEADINGLEY, *July 15th,* 1865.—An exciting and
wonderful day !   First, my Fred's election (unopposed)
as one of the members for the new N. division of the
W. Riding together with Sir F. Crossley.   Fred spoke
on the hustings for about ½ an hour, and was cheered
immensely, and altogether most delightfully received.
All he said was full of energy and *conviction,* and proved
to one (what I knew already) the strength and depth
and enthusiasm of his faith in the people, and of his
love of truth and liberty.   Perhaps he won't turn out
eloquent : his style is too stern, and his voice, especially
his curious " th " and " r," against him ; he expresses
himself sometimes abruptly, and sometimes his ideas

come too fast for his words and make him confused;
but at all events he is original, and eager, and to the
point; and by every tone and word shows that he
means and feels what he says. Never have I gone
through such excitement, or felt so proud! The climax
was dear old Mr. Thompson proposing 3 cheers for me,
whereat I was ready to burst! Old Fred brought
pretty strongly before them his Liberalism! but he
has caution and humility and toleration as checks.

But all this is eclipsed by the news that greeted us
here. Captain Egerton [1] has written to the Duke asking
to be allowed to ask Lou to marry him; and darling
Lou is as happy as happy can be.

He cannot be good enough for her! but I do hope
and believe will make her *very* happy; and it is nice
to find I am really most beautifully unselfish, for in
spite of what the loss of her will be to me, I know too
well the blessedness of the joy not to rejoice for her
with all my heart. And I am too pompée [2] to say
anything more.

CHATSWORTH, *July 16th*, 1865.—I came down first
to breakfast, and, the Duke arriving next, I had the
courage to speak of the great news, and to say something
of what the loss to him must be. Indeed that is a
thought I can't bear to face; but one trusts it will
be smoothed down to us all somehow! and he is happy
in her happiness, as who could help being? The Duke
wrote to the Captain recommending him to come here;
so we may expect a very interesting week. One can't
manage aft. church, it being at the cruel hour of $2\frac{1}{2}$,
and the walk a $\frac{1}{2}$ hour's one. Psalms and Lessons with
my Fred. St. Thomas à Kempis.

CHATSWORTH, *July 17th*, 1865.—Grey and ugly all
day, which was unpoetical, as the romance came to
an upshot, Captain Egerton turning up this afternoon
and spending an incomprehensibly long time with Lou
in the stately garden. Oh, dear me! I could fancy
the statues looking out of spirits at the sight of this
horrible interloper! but it is all right and good and

[1] The Hon. Francis Egerton, son of the 1st Earl of Ellesmere; afterwards an admiral and M.P.   [2] Appendix A.

happy. May and I watched the fly drive up, and the Captain puzzled us by marching to the Porter's lodge, collecting his thoughts maybe, or perhaps in search of the Duke. With whom by and bye he appeared in front of the perron. Duke, May, and I disappeared, and left the two with nobody but Fiz *en tiers*, at the Granville Corner. And so it is all settled, and I have had a cry, and mean to be—*am*—very happy at it. We talked electionums between acts, as F. and I used to talk Garibaldiums! Sat very tight all the evening for news of Eddy and Sussex, but none came. And now in about 2 hours I am hoping and longing to see Fred, who didn't think Capt. Egerton could have turned up to-day, and to whom I trust I shall have the telling of the news.

CHATSWORTH, *July 18th*, 1865.—This naval person has brought rain and clouds in his train; nevertheless he and Lou managed to find the weather fine enough for divers tête-à-têtes in the garden. We thought the less of them to-day from the election news being exciting. Eddy has won by nearly 200, therefore the 3 brethren are now all county M.P.s, and will all 3 distinguish themselves I trust. I build Castles in the air of Uncle W. Prime Minister, with Cavendish Secretary of War, Freddy Chancellor of the Exchequer, and Eddy Home Secretary;[1] or, further on still, Cavendish Prime Minister. But to descend to earth meanwhile, the unworthy University has driven out Uncle William by 186 votes, after his 18 years' representation of it; revealing that it is not worthy of the greatest statesman in England. Oh, it is disgraceful and pitiable! Gathorne Hardy, a good, respectable, slow-coach Conservative, comes in with Sir W. Heathcote, who heads the poll by a great deal.

CHATSWORTH, *July 19th*, 1865.—We three drove to Eyam, tucking a big R.N. Captain into the little dicky of the p. carriage beside Lou; the said man and I are already on terms of great intimacy and mutual quizzing.

---

[1] This bold prophecy was nearly fulfilled. Gladstone became Prime Minister in 1868, Hartington Secretary of War in 1866, and Gladstone more than once said that if Frederick Cavendish had been alive in 1886 he would have offered him the Exchequer. And Hartington was offered the Prime Ministership in 1887.

I wrote to Granny fishing for an invitation to Hagley for him next week! My Fred spouted to me a grand speech Uncle W. has made at a Liverpool meeting; having gone to stand for S. Lancashire. He is late in the field; but the enthusiasm was glorious.

CHATSWORTH, *July 20th*, 1865.—The Royal Navy went away, Lou driving him to the station; a very improper proceeding. Late in the evening came Cavendish, with hopeful accounts of U. Wm.'s S. Lancashire prospects. I walked about the kitchen-garden with the Duke, Fred, and the scientific Mr. Taplin; and ate a good deal of fruit. The *Guardian* almost speechless with rage at the Oxford election. There is much fear that ridiculous old Locock (I only quiz him on this occasion: we owe him a great deal) will beat Sir John Simeon in the Isle of Wight; folk have the No-poperyums to such a degree.

CHATSWORTH, *July 22nd*, 1865.—Drove one of a new pair of ponies, to be dubbed Sussex and Success in honour of Eddy; Miss Success went very well. We drove over a poor little *swallow* (of all wonderful things to do!) which was lying, hurt I suppose, in the middle of the road. Constance Kent has pled Guilty, and been condemned to death, but will, I believe, certainly not be hung.

CHATSWORTH, *July 23rd*, 1865.—I made Sir James [1] read us the " Cinque Maggio," which he did very finely; but it was difficult to follow.

HAGLEY, *July 27th*, 1865.—The Duke, Lou, and *Frank* arrived by the same train as we did. Oh, how entirely mad and inside-out I felt! half receiving them at Hagley, and half being a guest like them: so much a bit of Hagley still, that I am always saying " we " do this and that here, and yet in another point of view more belonging to them than to it.

HAGLEY, *July 28th*, 1865.—This glorious summer has seldom failed to bring us bright days whenever we most wanted them: the morning was perfect, and

---

[1] Sir James Lacaita who was Librarian at Chatsworth. The " Cinque Maggio " is, of course, the famous poem of Manzoni on the death of Napoleon.

the view *was*.[1] After church, soon after 12, we all
went up the dear obelisk hill; and in the afternoon,
Clent Hill. The view rather hazed over after 3, but it
was very nice. A good deal cooler. I am very happy
in the thought of Lou associating Hagley with all her
own deep happiness now; and have a feeling the old
place, which has seen such a long sunny day of married
blessedness in the past, must shed brightness over
them. For the same reason I love to think of our own
beautiful Whitsuntide here. The spire—O to think I
haven't mentioned it!—is finished up to the golden
cock at top, and one longs to tear down the scaffolding,
which remains up for some last touches. From all
sorts of points of view, it comes in beautifully (the spire,
not the scaffolding!), and what a thing it is to see the
dear church complete! Very idle but moving thoughts
cross one from time to time, of how it would please
and interest darling Mamma to come down to us again
for a little while, just to see the changes; which, thank
God, have been mostly such happy ones. How she
would have loved Meriel's little children! and the sight
of her own boys growing up into such comforts to Papa
—his great joy and pride. But such thoughts must
not dwell with one, remembering how her own deep
earthly affections, though not weakened or changed,
were absorbed in the hope of what we now trust is her
Everlasting Joy: the Presence of our Lord.

LONDON, *August 2nd*, 1865.—Went to bed pretty tired,
with the happy expectation of seeing my Fred turn up
about 4 a.m.

LONDON, *August 3rd*, 1865.—Which he did. Dear
Eddy and Emma's wedding-day; reminding me much
of mine, especially as I wore for the 1st time *since*,
the lovely gown and cloak I went away in! It was
at St. Michael's, Chester Square. A little faint sunshine struggled out just at the right time; but most
of the day was dark and pouring. Emma looked nicer
than I have ever seen her. There was very little
crying, and all went well but the weather; I feel for
them arriving at Chiswick (whither they drove, as we
did) without being able to plunge into the glorious

[1] Appendix A.

summer brightness and peace which greeted us. Oh, how I hope and pray for them that they may be as happy as we are !

HOLKER, *August 8th*, 1865.—Arrived after sunset, a lovely evening, about 8½. I little thought last August 8th of arriving here that day year with Eddy married and Lou engaged ! Certainly it is better than if I was only just launched ; I think the Duke is a little fond of me now, and at all events I have ceased to be terrified at him! I am sure it is a break to him when F. and I turn up.

HOLKER, *August 10th*, 1865.—Heavy rain a great part of the day. F. and the Duke off again, upon Haematite steel business in which big sums are being invested. Would that I could see any prospect of mastering either railwayums or Haematiteums enough to be properly interested !

BOLTON, *August 15th*, 1865.—Rained with little cessation till past four : no shooting. F. and I had some tiny honeymoon sits and a walk to the Terrace. I have begun Fawcett a 2nd time, meaning really to give my mind to as much as it is up to of Political Economy. Also we read together Palgrave's " Arabia." Womankind drove in 2 vehicles, and walked, to the Strid, the Valley of Desolation, and round by Barden. The waterfall was at its best, foaming and leaping down : the *bottled-porter* colour exactly !

BOLTON, *August 16th*, 1865.—Lou and I did not go up to the moors, but paid visits to 10 cottages : the folk at Halton most pleasant, attractive people, their nice unpolished ways a good deal more to my taste than Worcestersh. propriety and semi-gentility. One poor old, old man cannot at all get over the death of his wife in the spring, and sobbed piteously at the sight of Lou who took me to see them both last August. They had been married above 50 years.

BOLTON, *August 19th*, 1865.—At last, a lovely serene day without a drop of rain. Very fortunate, for the great Crook Rise day. They set off at 9½ ; we drove to Thorpe Fell and came in for the last drive before luncheon, which did not come off till 3. We saw 3 drives afterwards. The sport was glorious, and the total the biggest ever known here : viz. 250½ brace. Fred's was the 3rd best bag : 37½ brace. We did not dine till 9.

BOLTON, *August 20th*, 1865.—Drove to call on Mrs. Holmes and Mrs. Benson, the latter of whom treated us to gooseberry wine and sponge cake. We disposed of most of the cake into our pockets surreptitiously.

BOLTON, *August 25th*, 1865.—It was Crook Rise again to-day, and still more birds were killed : about 508. F. the 2nd biggest bag : 68.

BOLTON, *August 28th*, 1865.—The Duke had to go to a Skipton meeting, with a view to taking steps about the frightful new cattle epidemic which is spreading over the country. (À propos of that, there is also much fear of cholera, which has been making one of its marches over Europe ; and the harvest is in danger from the late rain, so there are breakers ahead ; and the prayer against plague, pestilence, and famine has terrible meaning.)

The other gentlemen shot about Aigill, and got nearly 100 brace ; F. much the best : 27½ brace. I have a heart-pinch this evening, thinking of Nevy's first night at sea. It will possibly be 4 years before we see him again, and what may they not bring forth !

BOLTON, *August 30th*, 1865.—There have been fearful cholera ravages at Constantinople. Constance Kent has made a detailed confession of her cool, well-planned, and most devilish murder of her baby-brother ; hideous enough ; the genuine repentance of such a nature is little short of a miracle, and will make a lasting impression, one may well hope, after the silly panic about popery, sisterhoods, and confessionals has died out. There have been other murders, too heart-sickening to comment on : a woman called Windsor convicted, who made a trade of killing babies for a few pounds, when wretched mothers wished to get rid of them ; another woman murdered her infant by breaking one of its bones daily ; a man has killed his wife and child and his three illegitimate children, with the barest shadow of motive.

BOLTON, *September 3rd*, 1865.—Some of the Eastern Church have lately admitted English Churchmen to Communion : a blessed thing. No Holy Communion here to-day, alas !

BOLTON, *September 4th*, 1865.—Shooting not out of the common : Charles did well at Nelly Park, killing right and left, twice running. Total bag, 120 brace. Have I ever mentioned what was amiss with the Atlantic cable ? It broke in mid-Atlantic, from fraying against a part of the machinery, while being hauled in to mend a fault ; again and again they grappled for it, and dropped it after dragging it up a great distance, the hauling ropes breaking, till all the rope was exhausted. And now we are to try again next spring, and, failing the present one, to buy another. All went well but for certain defects in the hauling-in machinery. Two defects in the cable itself had been set right.

BOLTON, *September 5th*, 1865.—My old birthday, making me 24. I am not quite ½way to 30 from 20, which proves that I am not so old as might be. And being married has in some ways made me feel younger —partly from the long holyday so much of my new life has been, partly from being the youngest of my new nears and dears (in both which respects things make a great contrast with my Hagley life), but perhaps mostly from the blessed satisfied sense of dependence on one who is as my own self to me, and without whom I should feel lost. Ah ! how difficult it is to keep this great blessedness subordinate to the feeling akin to it, but higher and more divine !—*the* Love which leads to the Peace that passeth understanding, and for which, over and above all this wealth of human love, one's inner soul is for ever hungering and thirsting.

HOLKER, *September 7th*, 1865.—I poked up Cavendish, and we took him to see our dear little room after tea ; he had not seen it before. Was struck. We had a pleasant *brotherly* little dinner.

HOLKER, *September 8th*, 1865.—We heard of a very interesting marriage : Lord Granville to a pretty Scotch Miss Campbell, only 17 and just out. 33 years between

them ! rather awful.   Lou put out her wedding presents ;
the upper servants have given her a pretty silver inkstand, the under ones here a charming wooden blotting-
book cornered with silver.

HOLKER, *September 9th,* 1865.—I meditated over
money matters, for once, with agreeable results. . . .

There is some dismay over Lord Granville's marriage :
such frightful disparity of years : the poor little body
will be in all human probability a widow before she is
40 ; they say she is full of fun and high spirits.

HOLKER, *September 12th,* 1865.—We had 2 pulls at
discarded Lord Russell [1] who is rather a bore.

HOLKER, *September 19th,* 1865.—Folk drove, couples
coupled.   We had a delightful series of scampers on
a fine long strip of sand near Park Head : Kinataloon
gave Lou's horse a slight kick, but no harm came of
it.   Palgrave and dear Paradise Lost. . . .

Lou's trousseau has arrived, and causes great excitement : she showed off to us a specially charming *plush*
gown, in colour very like a mouse-coloured Scotch
bullock.   It is curious how quietly and *humdrummily*
we manage to slip on from day to day.

HOLKER, *September 23rd,* 1865.—Arrived the two
Ladies Ellesmere, Lord Ellesmere, Ly. Blanche, the
Enfields, and Uncle Richard ; and we are 27 in the
house.   Presents of the kind that sink deepest into
one's heart came in : a beautiful quaint little gold
tea-service and a silver tray from Keighley and other
places, an ivory Prayer Book from the Flookburgh
school, and a diamond and ruby necklace from Chatsworth !   We all dawdled rather : sat outside, entertained arrivals, etc.   Fawcett,[2] however !   The table
at dinner had to be put with one end in the bow-window.

HOLKER, *September 24th,* 1865.—Our big numbers
divided themselves between Cartmel and Flookburgh :
I walked to Cartmel.   Escorted old Lady Ellesmere
to Flookb., in the afternoon ; was a little afraid of
her, but found her a kind, decided, pretty old lady.
Lou paid me a little visit in my room.   We were a

---

[1] That is, a book of his.   [2] I.e. his " Political Economy."

vast army streaming in to prayers from 2 ends of the passage. These days are rather dreadful and bewildering, and I shan't dislike finding myself in next week. Read some "Pensées de Pascal," with which I was much delighted.

HOLKER, *September 25th*, 1865.—Emma and I appeared in all our diamonds, to show the Duke, and to do honour to this grim last evening.

HOLKER, *September 26th*, 1865.—Frank and Lou were married in Cartmel Church, and, O dear, I am almost too tired and pompée [1] to say anything about it. But must. The weather quite perfect; warm and serene and sunny, and with breeze enough to wave the flags with which house, church, and villages were adorned. Nothing could have been nicer than the feeling shown by all the people : it went through and through one. The day, of course, managed to be endless ; every hour taking 2 hours to pass ; owing to the big intervals between acts. The church was carpeted with red-cloth and looked its best. I did not expect to be upset by the service which is a calming thing, I think ; but when dear Lou came up the choir with the poor Duke, to the sound of a beautiful wedding-hymn, and one looked at her dear, tall, bending figure standing by her father, to whom she has been all the world !—Cavendish's face, too, struck me and moved me exceedingly—full of deep feeling which I had never seen called forth in him before. My poor Fred's love for her I knew all about, and pretty well Eddy's too ; so that I did not wonder at their regularly crying— and could only be a little glad that they have wives to comfort them ! I can't go into all the details of the cheers, the crowds, and the triumphant arches : everything meant the same : true, loving enthusiasm. It was a pretty compliment to Frank, the sticking up in the arches divers little ships, full rig—but he was rather distressed at one being a *merchantman*. When we got home, following immediately after the Duke (who drove back with Cavendish and Eddy—without *her*, O dear !), and I came upon him standing alone in

[1] Appendix A.

the corridor, if you had shot me I couldn't have helped it, I went up and kissed him and squeezed his hand. It was the very spot where he kissed me so kindly when Freddy first brought me to Holker, and ever since Lou has been a sister to me. Then I made Frank kiss me, which he did very warmly. She kept herself composed with some difficulty, and broke down more than once in private ; especially when Cavendish went to her room before, and was much overcome himself. Most of us went to the tenants' dinner which I would not have missed for anything. The Duke could not trust himself to go, so Cavendish returned thanks for him, his voice trembling, and his face quite white. What he said was *perfect*, in its simplicity and depth of feeling : it gives me a new affection for him, showing me how tender his heart is. Freddy and Eddy each had to say a word or two of thanks for their healths being drunk. Fred spoke very well. At last came the going away, and I realized *fully* for the first time how terribly we shall all miss her, and Freddy and I went upstairs and cried frightfully. The three kept much with their father, and it was very comforting to see them with him, and to know that they are *almost* like daughters to him.

For about 24 hours, I should say, judging by the exhaustion that followed, we stood on a bench against the garden wall, being great audience [1] to games ; and finally the evening blew up in fireworks, and that's all I can put down about it. P.S.—Lord Granville was married to his 18-year-old bride to-day : and they *telegraphed* congratulations, which were returned.

HOLKER, *September 28th*, 1865.—I had a great treat of a nice, dear, warm letter from Frank, in answer to a bit to Lou that I went and wrote as soon as her back was turned. He said she was so overtired and excited as to be almost hysterical yesterday, poor dear ; but he had made her lie down on the sofa, where she had gone sound asleep. His letter was full of tenderness for her, and of happiness. F. made me take it to the Duke in his room : the 1st time I have gone to him there ! but despair and bewilderment of

[1] Appendix A.

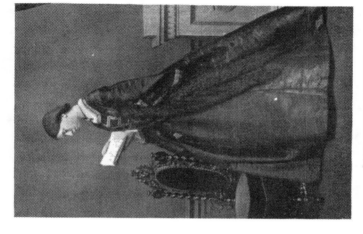

LADY LOUISA EGERTON.

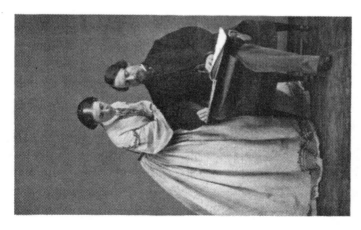

LORD AND LADY FREDERICK CAVENDISH.

[1—286]

soul made me desperate ! and I marched in. The letter quite overcame him. He gave me a dear one from Lou to him to read, which was full of happiness (" I am very, very happy "), but also full of loving sorrow at leaving her father. Now one may think of her calmed down and resting in the wonderful joy that is like no other.

HOLKER, *Michaelmas Day*, 1865.—Rather raw and nasty. Eddy and Emma, Freddy and I, May, Walter, Lord Richard, and Mr. Grey went to Barrow and saw the new Bessemer process of making steel out of Haematite iron ore : too interesting and wonderful, especially the great blast of air by which the carbon is driven out of the ore : the contact of the two gases making the most tremendous white-hot fire. The hammering delightful too. The town is spreading out and springing up vigorously, and gathers population tolerably fast. The great docks making strides.

HOLKER, *October 2nd*, 1865.—I went with Mr. Rigg to about 16 Flookburghers ; liked many of them. Old Geoffrey Thompson, who is over 90, said he could remember the time of Sir William Lowther, but I fear it is a delusion, as he died more than 100 years ago. " Lords ? " he said : " I remember 5 lords at Holker."

I saw a terrible sight : a child of 12 or 13, who has been wasting away for nearly a year : does not look more than 6, and her poor little arms and legs were like claws : *no* flesh whatever : the large joints and the bones barely covered with skin : I could not have believed thinness could be so fearful to look at.

HARDWICK, *October 6th*, 1865.—We came to Hardwick, in the same regal style as last year : special train, swarms of horses, dogs, carriages, and servants, and barouche and four to meet us at Chesterfield.

HARDWICK, *October 8th*, 1865.—A prayer was used by authority, for deliverance from the cattle-plague, and from the threatened cholera. God grant it !

HARDWICK, *October 9th*, 1865.—A little before 6 took place the exciting arrival of Frank and Lou from

Chatsworth.   Two little arches greeted them, and they were dragged up to the house door, and famously cheered.   Nothing could look happier and brighter than dear Lou, and it is too nice and refreshing to see her just like herself and falling back into her old ways, with only the difference of so much new happiness. Blessings and sunshine are outpoured upon us all round !

HARDWICK, *October 12th*, 1865.—Palgrave, Milton. I am reading with immense interest a book by Dr. Pusey, just out, written to Keble in answer to an attack of Manning's on the English Church, and called " The Truth and Office of the Eng. Ch. : an Eirenicon."

HARDWICK, *October 15th*, 1865.—Afternoon sermon on the godly helped in temptations.   They sang a wedding hymn and rang a peal in honour of Lou.   A yellow dog appeared in the pew, and *would* make himself agreeable, the more he was requested to withdraw.

CASTLE HOWARD, *October 16th*, 1865.—Came to Castle Howard of which I have heard so much since our marriage, especially from the Lascelles since Lord Carlisle's death,[1] that it saddens me to have no old memories of my own clinging to it.   His life seems to have been one of those that gilds all the lives among which it is cast, as Mamma's and Aunt Lavinia's did.

CASTLE HOWARD, *October 17th*, 1865.—Rained most of the day.   Nevertheless I could take in a good deal of the beauty of the place, as the Admiral,[2] Fred, and I walked about the gardens in the afternoon.   The inside of the house disappointed me, as the hall and gallery seem to be the only fine rooms ; but the pictures are *something*.   The outside I thought very handsome, and more graceful and ornamental than Chatsworth.   We went over the house in the morning ; F. has not been here since just after the late Duke's death, when his grandmother Carlisle was still alive, in '58.   I was introduced to Rosalind's baby,[3] a nice, fat, thriving thing, with a promise of pretty eyes, but otherwise not lovely ;

[1] The 7th Earl, twice Lord-Lieutenant of Ireland.
[2] The Hon. Edward Howard, son of the 6th and father of the 9th Earl of Carlisle, afterwards Lord Lanerton.
[3] Now Lady Mary Murray.

very forward and lively, and delighted with her tub.
Rosalind is only 20 : she is an original little person, and
half attracts and half repels one with her ways and
words ; she dresses madly in odd-coloured gowns with
long trains, which cling around her *unbecrinolined.*

CASTLE HOWARD, *October* 19*th*, 1865.—Lord Palmerston died yesterday morning. He would have been 81
to-morrow ; and it is wonderful to think of a man's
dying in office who was born before the fall of the old
French monarchy, and was in office before Uncle
William was born. He caught cold out driving, being
already ill with disease of the bladder. It is piteous to
think of poor old Lady Palmerston. She wished him
to give up office in the summer. It is hoped that the
Queen will send for Lord Russell ; but there is no one
now to advise her, and how terribly she must want the
Prince ! . . .

The *Guardian* gave an awful account of the state of
religion in Italy : Mariolatry more and more absorbing
all the devotion of the people.

CASTLE   HOWARD,   *October*   21*st*,   1865.—Directly
after luncheon I went to the station on the car, and
brought back my Fred, and my sunshine of sunshine
with him. We had a little walk to the pheasantry.
Miss Kinnaird is here, a pleasant, agreeable old lady,
of an old-fashioned depth of Low-Churchism which
amuses me.

CASTLE HOWARD, *October* 22*nd*, 1865.—We went in
the morning to an awful little apartment which calls
itself Coneysthorpe Chapel, and which certainly adds
another to my list of unsatisfactory church arrangements at great places. However, the place does not
belong to Lord Carlisle. I felt as if I must have got
into a meeting-house ! . . .

I walked with F. to see the mausoleum, a terribly
grim building, without anything about it to remind
one of Christianity or of the Resurrection, unless it
might be the lovely view from it.

FRYSTON, *October* 23*rd*, 1865.—We left beautiful
Castle Howard, and came here, to Lord Houghton's,

in time for luncheon. Drove with Ly. H. afterwards :
the country flat, but with one pleasant wide view.
I made great friends of the 3 children, Anicia, Florence,
and Robin.[1] Three nice old moths [2] are here, aunts of
Lord H. The Queen has appointed Ld. Russell to
form a ministry, to the violent rage of the *Times*.
Letters : to and from Papa and Lou.

FRYSTON, *October 24th*, 1865.—Mild pleasant day. I
looked through the newspaper accounts of the Duke of
Wellington's funeral, which Lord Houghton has kept.
I am so glad I can so clearly remember Papa looking
into the old school-room out of his old little study to
tell us of the Duke's death, and Mamma writing to us
about the funeral which I longed to see. This death
of Lord Palmerston's makes nothing like the same
impression that *that* did, or the Prince's.

CHATSWORTH, *October 31st*, 1865.—My Fred went
with the others to shoot, and then to Leeds, where
he was to hold forth on Schools of Art ; and be back
to-night at one. The Cawdors and two daughters,
Aunt Fanny, husband and daughters, and Mr. Philips
came. Lord Cawdor, his daughters told me, is so colour-
blind that they have to hide the red sealing-wax when
they are in mourning for fear of his using it ; and he
sees no difference between people's ordinary complexion
and that which snap-dragon and salt gives them ! We
walked about the garden. I finished Pusey, and feel
perhaps more dismayed than ever at the terrible state
of the Roman Church, and yet somehow more hopeful
of reunion following upon its reformation : the loving-
hearted, earnest, sanguine character of Dr. Pusey
shines through the whole book, the more striking combined as it is with such theological learning and research
—and it kindles one into hope.

CHATSWORTH, *November 10th*, 1865.—Poor Lord Boyle [3]
poured out to me some of his terrible trials, and made
my heart ache. His home miserable, from the un-
kindness and extravagance of his parents—himself
with no occupation, and with the light of his eyes

---

[1] Now Marquess of Crewe.   [2] Appendix A.
[3] Afterwards 5th Earl of Shannon. He had lately lost his wife, who
had been Lady Blanche Lascelles, daughter of the 3rd Earl of Harewood.

gone.   His children, poor little fellows, seem to be more
anxiety than pleasure to him now that they are motherless, as is very natural.   It is most piteous.

CHATSWORTH, *November 15th,* 1865.—I finished Mr.
Trevelyan's book, " Cawnpore," which is fearfully
graphic and said to be entirely accurate.   I can remember, even in the midst of our own great grief in
the autumn of 1857, the frightful heart-rending news
from India, and specially the massacre of women and
children : the outcries for vengeance, and the day of
humiliation.   It has left a horror and shudder at India
in my heart which I can never get rid of.

CHATSWORTH, *November 16th,* 1865.—Dear old Meriel
and John came.   She looks very well, though, alas !
No. 5 hopes to arrive next June.   It is a sad trial to
the poor old thing, who would stop *very* willingly at 4 ;
and would have been satisfied to have no children at
all, which is all but inconceivable to me.

CHATSWORTH, *November 22nd,* 1865.—Yesterday Lord
Dudley married Miss Georgina Moncrieffe, a beautiful
girl under 20.   Charles was best man ! but must have
looked more like the bridegroom.

CHATSWORTH, *November 25th,* 1865.—Evening whist,
with the Houghtons and Mr. Howard, while the rest
of the world, except the Duke, Ly. Newburgh, Aunt
Fanny, and old slowcoach Fred, played billiard-battle :
even Lord Stanley.[1]   Freddy Howard has much touched
my heart by an outpour of his fervent attachment to a
Miss Horrocks whom he met abroad.   It seems he was
a little snubbed by authorities, which he thought
hard " when people come to a *certain age.*"   He is
barely 19 ! and the damsel 20.   I gave him my wisest
advice : specially to wait till he was two-and-twenty
before considering himself of a certain age.

CHATSWORTH, *November 27th,* 1865.—Lord Houghton
spouted 2 of his bits of poetry, but ill.   " Long ago "
is lovely.

CHATSWORTH, *November 28th,* 1865.—Sir James

---

[1] The statesman ; afterwards 15th Earl of Derby : not a person
much given to the lighter side of life.

Lacaita delighted many of us with a spout of Tasso, but especially with the glorious " Cinque Maggio."

CHATSWORTH, *November* 30*th*, 1865.—My darling Fred 29 to-day : it seems a little old to me, alack ! I gave him a pair of muffatees, which have cost me gigantic efforts ! God grant us our *heart's desire*, if it is His Will, to make a new sunshine over Fred's next birthday.

CHATSWORTH, *December* 2*nd*, 1865.—I went with Claud and Fr. Howd. to see the cover shooting which was too much of a massacre to be quite pleasing.

CHATSWORTH, *December* 3*rd*, 1865.—A dear happy day, full of help and blessing. My Sundays have not the delight they used to have in beautiful services, but this makes me the more appreciate the feeling of refreshment and renewal, when it comes ; for it must be straight from Heaven, I hope. We read Vaughan and " Xtian Year."

CHATSWORTH, *December* 4*th*, 1865.—Poodle Byng is 81 to-day : we drank his health at dinner, and he made a good little speech, returning thanks. He remembers dancing at Devonshire House 72 years ago, when the late Duke was 3 or 4 years old. He was born long before the great Fr. Revolution was even thought of. To-day he walked up to the Stand, and a good deal besides, but he seems altered and rather stiffened. Lou, Emma, and I presented him with a photograph stand containing our 3 selves.

ESHOLT, *December* 7*th*, 1865.—Good-bye to Chatsworth and our smartest month of the year. I am in love with Ly. Dalkeith, and bewitched with Ly. Dufferin. We came here (the Fairbairns) for a Mechanics' Institute meeting at Idle—a big, overgrown, manufacturing village, with 9,000 people in it, but no particular streets. I was much delighted with the warmth and heartiness of the audience, all apparently working folk. My Fred spoke well. One old gentleman, in broad Yorkshire, got into such cloudland about Freddy's future among Cabinets and Councils that I feared he would come down with a bump ; but it rather thrilled me !

HAWARDEN, *December 9th*, 1865.—The Jamaica massacre, in which it seems 2,000 blacks have been killed to revenge the deaths of 18 whites, was much talked of.

HAWARDEN, *December 15th*, 1865.—The King of the Belgians is dead, and there is a general mourning for 10 days. The Queen will nevertheless appear at the opening of Parliament, but will not read the Speech, or wear the robes (which are to be laid on the throne !). A great thing it is, however.

We turned a " little dancing " into a mad and scampering little ball, which ended with an uproarious country dance, a final waltz, and " God save the Queen."

HAGLEY, *December 19th*, 1865. . . . Later arrived the 3 little boys, escorted by Newmany, looking famously well ; Bob with a good conduct prize, Edward with one for classics : jolly little Alfred with nothing but his own charms.

HOLKER, *December 29th*, 1865.—I took Lou's place in giving away Xmas charities of sheeting, blankets, flannel, etc., to divers poor folk, under the excellent Mrs. Birkett's eye. Got into the p. carriage in an interval of fine weather with Lord Rd. and drove to call on Mrs. Hubberty, but we were well wetted with driving rain. The poor little skeleton child is dead. Palgrave, Milton, letter-sorting. We had a snug little tea in our room, and entertained Cavendish, to my pride.

HOLKER, *December 31st*, 1865.—I had a class (before morning church) at the school, of nice little boys, 2 or 3 very intelligent.

HOLKER, *New Year's Day*, 1866.—God grant us another year of peaceful happiness, if it be His Will, and the one thing wanting to us. Emma has that precious hope for which I long sadly.

HOLKER, *January 2nd*, 1866.—It is wrong to set out on the New Year without thinking of *the* great event of 1865 : the American war ending with the downfall of Slavery. It is nothing short of a fulfilment of the words : " With men it is impossible : but with God all things are possible."

Of course there is awful perplexity and misery connected with the coloured people ; but one may trust that God, Who has worked one miracle for them, will make a way for bringing good and blessing upon their future. The worst fear at present seems to be of their dying out in the mysterious way uncivilized nations have before, when attempts have been made to make them live on equal terms with civilized men.

HOLKER, *January 4th*, 1866.—Fearful accounts in the *Times* of the state of London houses for the poor. If something is not done, the country will deserve to be destroyed.

HOLKER, *January 5th*, 1866.—I began dear " Kenilworth " for the 2nd time, the 1st being at St. Leonard's in the happy spring of 1856.

HOLKER, *January 6th*, 1866.—The cattle-plague is fearful, more than 7,600 attacked a week, by the last return. We tremble for the beautiful herd of shorthorn cows and bulls here ; but it is not in the near neighbourhood. Worcestershire has been wonderfully free ; but it is bad on one of the Hawarden farms. Many places are forbidding all transfer of cattle. There is a notion that it is small-pox.

HOLKER, *January 11th*, 1866.—There is good deal of talk about Mr. Goschen being made something of the Duchy of Lancaster, unbeknown to Lord Russell's colleagues, and not having had time to do much to deserve it. Sir R. Peel over the moon at having been made K.C.B.

HOLKER, *January 12th*, 1866.—Yesterday I finished " Kenilworth," which excited and interested me fully as much as when I was 14 ; perhaps more, as it has haunted me at night.

HOLKER, *January 13th*, 1866.—Eddy and Emma came from London, having done a good spell of Sussex civilities. Emma very well and prosperous. Her baby is expected early in August. Oh, how I hope it may be a good omen for Lou and me !

HOLKEB, *January 14th*, 1866.—I verily believe I have never mentioned F.'s having got the oppressive honour of moving the Address before him ! My day much overclouded by a tiff with Morgan, serious enough to entail upon her a talking-to from Fred and a threat of giving her warning ; but the sky is all clear again this evening ; and possibly all the clearer !

HOLKER, *January 17th*, 1866.—Ld. Stanhope, who flatters me with his attentions, sent me some letters that passed between certain French big-wigs and the then Ld. Stanhope in 1792, of which he has just had 50 copies printed ; they have not much in them, but I feel much grattered and flattified. Ly. Henry Scott, Ly. Granville, and Ly. Dudley are all said to be expecting babies. Ah, dear me !

HOLKER, *January 25th*, 1866.—The never-ending, still-beginning shooting, which becomes a serious tax to pay for the necessity of ducal preserves. Uncle Rd. and I walked by the park and fields to Flookburgh, where I hooked on to Lou, and we did a selection of poor folk ; viz. Mesdames Ellen Rose, Betty Turman, Cornthwaite, Bradley, Cooperthwaite, and wonderful old Geoffrey, who *will* stick to his assertion that he came to Flookburgh in Sir Something Lowther's time.

HOLKER, *January 26th*, 1866.—After luncheon, Flookburgh remains, viz. dear doting Betty Moore, late washerwoman, and dreadfully dirty Agnes Haddath, bedridden.

HOLKER, *January 27th*, 1866.—Grey and Scotch-misty all day. Shooting as before. Palgrave, *Comus*, Hume ; began " The Heart of Midlothian " to the girls. Had a charming ride on Punchy with Lavinia on Empress and Georgina on Ossa, by Mt. Barnett and Hill Mill to Speel Bank.

HOLKER, *January 29th*, 1866.—A most merry, successful servants' ball came off in the corridor downstairs, reminding me of old Hagley doings. Dear me ! my last was at the coming of age ! For the 1st time in my life, indulged in polkas and other whisks, with Frank and Eddy, and enjoyed them hugely. Little Mary Cavendish [1] danced delightfully.

[1] Daughter of the 2nd Lord Chesham and, later, wife of Lady Frederick's eldest brother, Lord Cobham.

LONDON, *February 1st*, 1866.—We went across the way, and F. had a sit with Uncle Wm. who gave him the heads of the Queen's Speech ; which are ticklish enough to handle, what with Fenianism, Jamaica, Cattle-plague, and Reform Bill. Would it were all triumphantly over ! Fenianism, though apparently aimless and frantic as to organisation and object, is a terrible symptom of the miserable cankers of Ireland. The hope about vaccination is pretty nearly at an end. More than 10,000 beasts were attacked by the last week's return. Farmers and even gentry are ruined or ½ ruined. Cheshire is the worst county. Joints of beef are 1*s.* a lb., which is a cheat just now, as the market is full of meat ; but by and bye higher prices are inevitable.

F. went to a meeting about improving poor people's houses in Westminster, and to the House for the 1st time as M.P. to help re-elect the Speaker. I drove with Auntie P. and Mary (the great man with us part of the way, in high force) in the well-known old park, with a handful of riders adorning it already.

LONDON, *February 5th*, 1866.—We went to luncheon at Aunt Caroline's. They are all uneasy about the Dow. Duchess of Sutherland's [1] health. Instead of the unwieldy title I might perhaps adopt Freddy's " Arnt Suverland." But I have always held her in awe, in spite of, or because of, her gentle, Royal sort of kindness.

LONDON, *February 6th*, 1866.—A notable red-letter day. The dear Queen opened Parliament in person for the first time since her widowhood ; going in great state, drawn by 8 cream-colours, all her other carriages with 6 horses ; a large escort attending her. I went to the terrace of No. 11 and saw famously. She looked out, and bowed incessantly—her own gracious bow ; the enthusiasm was great among the big crowd ; and she had " Queen's weather." Arthur, to his great delight, was in waiting, and arrayed himself here, which gave much enjoyment to our household ! According to *his* report, the Queen wore pale lilac (qu. grey ?) silk, but according to Papa, it was black, and according to others it was to have been purple velvet ; so my

---

[1] Wife of the 2nd Duke : sister of Lord Frederick's mother.

ideas are not very clear on the subject. As she seated herself on the Throne it appears that she wrapped herself in the state mantle which was laid ready for her. She did not read the Speech herself : it was uncommonly long. My great excitement of hearing F. move the Address came off about 5. He was nervous, but got through it very well ; his voice much better and clearer than I expected, and plenty *in* his speech, which has received enough compliments to turn my head : " full of thought "—" the stuff to make a good speaker " —" the best mover and seconder speeches in somebody's recollection." Mr. Graham, the seconder, was very successful, and a good deal the most fluent. The funny thing was that old Yankee Freddy entirely forgot to allude to the American peace and the abolition of slavery ! after carefully preparing his say on that point. But he spoke nearly ½ an hour, which was long enough. Great is my repose and relief to-night, and I am proud of my Fred. He went off to the House after dinner, a fate which must inevitably befall me very often, and I sat solitary.

LONDON, *February 7th*, 1866.—Cavendish got a mysterious scrap from Ld. Granville yesterday or the day before, containing the words : " Of course I congratulate you." Not being aware that he was going to be married, the Markiss was puzzled ; but lo and behold ! the cat is out and he succeeds Ld. De Grey in the War Office, to the satisfaction of all parties, which is a fine thing for a man of 32. He has gained a well-deserved character for hard work and knowledge of his business as Under Secretary. Lord Dufferin succeeds him. The Duke dined with us, and looked over the moon and very proud ; also Uncle G. and Eddy dined, and we were very snug.

LONDON, *February 10th*, 1866.—Wonderfully warm : the poor silly buds are on the burst. We chose a pretty quaint bit of old china for a tardy wedding-present to Lady Granville. F. dined in full figg at the Speaker's. I sponged a dinner at the G.'s, where were Glynne uncles ; the Rev. one high gee [1] Convocation, as is his

---

[1] Appendix A.

wont ! I can't but be sorry (daresay I'm wrong) at
Convocation snubbing down all and any " conscience "
clause by a great majority. The plain justice of giving
dissenters (whose tax-paying goes to support the
school) the *option* of withdrawing their children from
the *religious* instruction of a Church school, while they
profit by the secular, in the few cases where it is impossible for them to have a school of their own, seems
undeniable. The mass of the clergy *will* stop their
ears to the whole thing. If they won't propose or admit
any right " conscience " clause like what I have described, they will have some horrid religion-that-will-
suit-all-creeds one forced upon them willy-nilly.[1]

LONDON, *February 12th,* 1866.—We had luncheon
at the Speaker's, meeting the Adams (American Minister) and Dr. Vaughan. Mrs. Adams tickled me by
saying " vāgăries " and dĕcŏrous." . . . Workhouse.
Went to the House to hear Cattle-plague debate. We
dined snug together, then F. to the House again, and I
to Dudley House ball with the Gladstones, which felt
rather mad. Ly. Dudley too lovely.

LONDON, *February 13th,* 1866.—I crammed my day
pretty full. First did books ; then went to Mrs.
Humphrey's who took me to see their capital schools ;
mem. especially, a little school held in the roof of a
mission-chapel lately built in a squalid street, where
they get hold of wretched neglected children. At 12
I found myself with the Mesd. Talbot in their delightful
soup-kitchen, which they have set up in Westminster.
Poor people (not beggars) are given tickets, on showing
which and paying a sum not exceeding 2*d.* they get good
meat, soup, beef-tea, or pudding of at least twice the
value of what they pay. Fred is going to be treasurer.
Got home to luncheon, where we entertained Mr. St.
Aubyn who is going to be married. May Lascelles
came to see me about 4, after which I smiled for a few
minutes upon a little tea-business at Auntie P.'s, and
then drove off to S. Ann's National Schools, Limehouse,
where a most charming, successful " mission tea-party "
was held, under the auspices of my dear Miss Lilley,

[1] " Came too true " (added later).

and the other good folk. Was glad to see Sarah Dorrington the 2nd mission woman looking busy and bright, but, alas! not well. There were 210 women and 49 babies! I poured out for one table. Had to go off directly after tea, hearing only one chorus, to my grief: but as it was, in spite of getting home by superhuman exertions in 35 minutes, I arrived after 8, with His Grace the Duke of Devonshire, the Secretary of War, the Lord-Lieutenant of Worcestershire, and Mr. Charles Howard, M.P., to entertain at dinner. I was a little jeered. But would not have missed the tea-party.

LONDON, *February 16th*, 1866.—Cattle-plague rages in the House: a very stringent Bill is being passed, forbidding *all* movement of cattle along railways, and ordering the immediate slaughter of all diseased beasts. It is poor, science having entirely failed to find a remedy. There is rather a plausible one up just now, discovered by a Mr. Worms; a mixture of onions and asafœtida (nice it must be!), but people don't trust it. We dined at home, then F. to the House till 1.

LONDON, *February 18th*, 1866.—Bright pleasant frost: a real enjoyment it was. Mazy and I fired away a class at one of the S. Martin's schools; I was a good deal taken off my legs by the coolness and talkativeness of my pale-faced cockney damsels who were very ready to put me in the right way. The row was great, and my numbers unmanageable, so I did not make a satisfactory start. S. Martin's in the morning (as it always is, unless I say to the contrary); Mr. Helps called, and made us late for 3 o'clock Abbey; so we poked in upon M. and then pounded off to S. Paul's, where was a big congregation. Two pretty baptisms which brought tears to my eyes, so foolishly did I long to see a baby of our own christened.

LONDON, *February 22nd*, 1866.—I got smuggled into the House, and heard Uncle Wm. speak upon the Queen's messages about granting money to Princess Helena on her marriage, and to Prince Alfred on his coming-of-age. He did it well, speaking of what Princess Helena had been to the Queen, which I know something of. She is to have £6,000 a year, and £30,000

down, which is rather stingy, considering how poor
her marriage is : Prince Alfred £15,000 a year. Then
Uncle Wm. delivered " a fine panegyric " on Lord
Palmerston, proposing a monument to him in the
Abbey. He did it very well. Then came Jamaica
and Cattle-plague; dull enough. We dined quite
promiscuous at Ly. James' ; as did the Gladstones, and
I enjoyed hearing and seeing something of Uncle Wm.
again. He is certainly not yet overdone by the Leadership ! but in great force.

LONDON, *February 26th*, 1866.—London House. I
have undertaken to go once a fortnight to St. George's-
in-the-East workhouse.

LONDON, *February 27th*, 1866.—I drove with Auntie
P. and a Miss Smith in an excellent Greek Madame
Ralli's carriage, she coming too. We went 1st to the
London Hospital, where we talked and read to divers
poor men and some poor little children ; then to the
workhouse, a paradise of freshness, good order, and
comfort compared with S. Martin's. I am to have a
ward of decrepit old men, who enjoyed some peppermints I brought. There are 850 in the House. The
chaplain showed me the oakum-picking room, crowded
with women, some looking horrid enough, poor souls !

We dined at D. House : I hope it is not wrongly
selfish to feel refreshed by one's comforts and pleasant
refined things after going a little into the depths. One
knows the poor people do not crave for *these* things,
and one has been trying to cheer them ; still, it feels
selfish.

LONDON, *March 2nd*, 1866.—Many calls in the afternoon ; last but not least, upon George, Mary, Agnes,
and Bertram Talbot ; who were all at home and delighted to see me and a picture-book I brought. They
were sitting like olive-branches round about the table,
at tea : all blooming, merry, and rosy. O such con-
trasts to a poor tiny whose mother came this morning
for a beef-tea ticket ; and whose little year of life
seemed to have been all suffering and cold and starvation. I have been thinking of it revived by the good
beef-tea ; but it is terrible to know that I only see

glimpses of the deep, wide misery all round us, and can hardly do any good.

LONDON, *March 3rd*, 1866.—Had to go, as an inevitable civility, to a party at Lady De Grey's as we had refused 3 other invitations of hers. I had the Lentums, and didn't like it at all ! Dinners feel *much* less frivolous to me : connected quiet talk, saving of trouble (and expense !) at home, and early getting away, and no squash or roar, or crowd of footmen, linkmen, and unwashed, gaping and shouting outside. I am glad to say we saved Sunday by ½ a minute.

LONDON, *March 6th*, 1866.—We dined at Ld. Granville's ; his little wife is a most winsome, pretty creature, with a bright sunshiny manner, and I should think plenty of character. It isn't proper for a bride to have the measles, and a bridegroom the gout ! but it has been their case. We met clever young Mr. Trevelyan (I should like to know once for all how to spell his name !).

LONDON, *March 7th*, 1866.—We dined at Mr. Bob Lowe's, which was very pleasant. He is immensely clever, agreeable, and humorous, but rubbed me up the wrong way with his bitter, low view of people and politics. Afterwards for a little while to Ly. Russell's drum, against my grain ; but it was a necessary civility. Was introduced to Carlyle who launched into a broad Scotch troll on Reform to F. An odd, shrewd, rough, weatherbeaten face, and an astonishing choker ! . . .

We dined at Ly. Cowper's, meeting her sons and daughters, Lord Houghton, Mr. Trevelyan, Mr. Barrett Browning, Mr. Stanhope, and Froude the historian who looks very clever and great, and is young and handsome, which I shouldn't have expected. F. to the perpetual House after dinner : I stayed on into a small party that dropped in, and talked to Mr. Cowper, Froude himself, and a Yankee called Lockwood, of agreeable manners.

LONDON, *March 13th*, 1866.—F. shirked Marlborough House ball in the coolest way, not to miss the debate ; but I went, and curtseyed to the Princess of Wales and

Princess Helena : the latter looks as happy as a queen.

LONDON, *March 15th*, 1866.—Had luncheon with M. at Ly. Augusta Stanley's. I should think no couple in the world were so unlike as Dean Stanley and his wife. She, big, vigorous-looking, very dark and ugly and coarse-featured (but with a nice good face all the same) ; he, wonderfully shrunk, small and squinny, with little sharply-cut features and light complexion. They are devoted to each other. We had luncheon in the very room where I sat waiting in my veil on my marriage-day, with my Fred beside me, and every-body else looking like a dream.

LONDON, *March 19th*, 1866.—Auntie P. popped in before dinner, with the news that the House had actually divided upon Uncle Wm.'s motion that the committee and petition business should be put off till 2 to-morrow, viewing [1] it is the fast-day for the cattle-plague in this diocese. So it is to be ; but it was rather disgraceful that it was not an unanimous opinion.

LONDON, *March 20th*, 1866.—I did St. Martin's work-house in the morning, S. George's with Mrs. Spiers in the afternoon. Read 2 P.M.[2] stories to some women at work with great success. Distributed peppermints.

HOLKER, *Lady Day and Palm Sunday*, 1866.—A heavenly early-spring day : much warmer out than in. The very walk to the poor little hideous chapel along the muddy road was pleasant ! How much more Middle Bigland Scarr, Hobarrow and Ellerside. To Morgan, began the dear old " Warnings of the Holy Week."

HOLKER, *March 26th*, 1866.—I have not spent such a lonely day for a long while. F. went off at 8¼ to Leeds, high gee [1] a meeting precursory of a big Reform meeting, and was only back for 8½ dinner. I went through breakfast and luncheon tête-à-tête with my Papa-in-law in a state of great trepidation ; and feel sure he wished me at the bottom of the Baltic.

HOLKER, *March 27th*, 1866.—Went to see Mrs.

---

[1] Appendix A.   [2] I.e. Parochial Mission.

Pollard, also Mrs. Mackreth the woodman's wife, and Mrs. Telfer the huntsman's; Aggy Hastings, Hannah Hewitson, John Brookes, and Mrs. Wilson in the cottages near Mr. Drewry's; and Jenny Wilman at the lodge. All very cordial and nice to me.

HOLKER, *April 2nd*, 1866.—My Fred away all day, doing a monster Reform Meeting at Leeds, where he moved the 1st resolution in a 25-minutes speech. I *should* like to have heard him! Got very successfully through my tête-à-tête meals with my Papa-in-law, which I dreaded considerably.

HOLKER, *April 6th,* 1866.—Finished "Sylvia's Lovers" in floods of tears! and think it one of the best novels I ever read; but a *cruel* one; a thing it is really bad for one to have a heartache over.

LONDON, *April 9th*, 1866.—Lovely radiant morning; the hills all sorts of violet shades. After packing, letters, etc., I went out at 12, picked daisies in the garden, and a lot more primroses in Watham: Fred rode on the sands, where he said it was beautiful. Left dear Holker, which made me sad at heart, at 2. Got home about 10½.

LONDON, *April 12th*, 1866.—I spent a good deal of time at the House, where Uncle W. moved the 2nd reading of the Bill, in a spirited, eloquent speech. Lord Grosvenor moved his amendment (that the Bill was incomplete without redistribution being considered at the same time), and was seconded by Lord Stanley. I could hear little of either as Ld. G.'s voice is weak and low, and Lord S. tumbles over his tongue in an odd way; but I believe Lord S.'s speech was very effective. Cavendish spoke after dinner: his 1st speech *not* upon Armyums: he hesitated a good deal, and seemed nervous: no wonder, for the Opposition chose to hoot and howl and roar with laughter in a way rather peculiar to after-dinner occasions and thoroughly disgraceful. There was stuff in his speech.

LONDON, *April 13th*, 1866.—This is my *never-to-be-forgotten day*. Auntie P. and I did St. G. in the E.,

taking flowers there. I read to a roomful of oakum-
picking women. We went to the House afterwards,
quite on the chance; and had the immense luck of
hearing the famous Mr. J. S. Mill make a most perfect
speech in favour of the Franchise Bill. In spite of the
cry-down humour the Tories are in, it was striking to
have this small-voiced philosopher listened to with the
greatest possible attention and respect; and indeed
the speech was irresistibly fair, profound, and trenchant.
Three or 4 times he made a dead pause of more than a
minute, but only to produce some new, cogent argument
armed at all points and perfectly expressed; though
he was keenly satirical once or twice, the whole tone
of his speech was gentle and temperate to a degree.
The Opposition held their tongues as if bewitched! He
followed Sir Bulwer Lytton, who made a slashing,
clever speech. I found myself a good deal struck and
moved, coming straight out of one of the depths of
misery and pauperism, to hear the claims of the people
so grandly brought forward : those " dumb " thousands,
as Bright called them, among whom there must be so
many feeling, as none of us can feel, for all this degrada-
tion; and voiceless in the nation whom they might
help to rouse to the most noble of battles.

LONDON, *April* 14*th*, 1866.—I drove with the Talbots
to the Crystal Palace; that is, alone with M. there, and
with all coming home. It was very nice. We squabbled
over politics a little.

LONDON, *April* 16*th*, 1866.—Having been poked up
by a sneering article in the *Spectator* upon the " Xtian
Year," I wrote a little rejoinder; but F. and the Mesds.
Talbot, tho' they think it rather good, think I had better
not send it! Drove with the ladies shopping. The
Government prospects are very doubtful, owing to
deserters among the slow-coach Whigs, against whom
my Fred indulges in violent language. I went in lonely
dignity to Ly. Taunton's ball; Sir Walter Farquhar
poured terrified Toryism into my ear.

LONDON, *April* 17*th*, 1866.—Charles dined with us;
he is immensely interested in the political crisis, and

seems to weigh all sides ; but I fear he is a horrid old Tory still : he don't commit himself much.

LONDON, *April 18th*, 1866.—We had luncheon at Devonshire House where Ld. Richard had turned up. Who should come to luncheon but Ld. Grosvenor [1] ? He told us his boy Belgrave (14 or 15 years old) asked him, " Do Whigs and Tories ever inter-marry ? "

LONDON, *April 19th*, 1866.—I drove with old M. to Campden Hill, and to call on the Longleys [2] at glorious old Lambeth which I never saw before. It seemed to take one " above the smoke and stir of this dim spot," which indeed *is* in a stir just now.

LONDON, *April 28th*, 1866.—Fred came to bed at ¼ to 5 in the morning, announcing a majority of 5 for the 2nd reading. One didn't expect more. It is impossible, I suppose, for the poor Bill to survive Committee and pass the Lords. Dizzy spoke for near 3 hours, and was dull, they say, wishing to exhaust the House ! as he well might, the atmosphere being frightful in the heat of the weather. Uncle W. got up at one, and spoke for 2 hours, magnificently, so as to poke up great enthusiasm even at that time of night, and after the endless debates. He was dead tired all day. F. had tea at No. 11, and said he seemed strung up and excited, and indignant with Dizzy, who had sent Uncle W. word he meant to speak 1 hour and then spoke 3. Uncle W. said (N.B. *not* in the House !) that Dizzy had generosity and temper, but was hopelessly *false.*

H.M.S. VICTORY, *May 12th*, 1866.—We had the fun of coming with the D. to see Lou and Frank on board their harbour ship—the old original *Victory*, with the brass plate marking where Nelson fell ; but not much of the actual old ship left. She has never made a voyage since Trafalgar. Lou has made her fine big cabin look charming with wedding presents and Hatchford flowers ;

---

[1] Afterwards the 1st Duke of Westminster. He was active at this time among the Whigs who were opposing the Government Reform Bill.

[2] The Archbishop of Canterbury was then Archbishop Longley (1862–8).

and we are delightfully lodged in a ridiculous little corner where F. marches about ducking like a goose under a barn door. Certain naval and marine persons dined. There is a mysterious little urn on the dining-room chimney piece, which I suggest contains Nelson's ashes.

END OF VOL. I